# ASK THE RIGHT QUESTIONS

# Creating the Answers That Work

By

**Gerald Nadler**
**&**
**William J. Chandon**
with
**Thomas A. Dworetzky**

The Center for Breakthrough Thinking Press
Los Angeles
2003

ISBN: 1-4107-1107-2 (e-book)
ISBN: 1-4107-1108-0 (Paperback)
ISBN: 1-4107-1109-9 (Dust Jacket)

Library of Congress Control Number: 2003090388


This book is printed on acid free paper.


Printed in the United States of America
Bloomington, IN

The Center for Breakthrough Thinking Press
P.O. Box 18A12
Los Angeles CA 90018
Tel.: 213 740 6415 Fax : 213 740 1120


Question Forward, Software for the Mind, Full Spectrum Creativity, and Breakthrough Thinking are registered trademarks or service marks of The Center for Breakthrough Thinking, Inc.


1stBooks - rev. 5/8/03

# ACKNOWLEDGMENTS

A book that presents a synthesis of a lot of research and practice has an extremely large number of people, from producing grand content ideas to editing and formatting for consistent reading, and organizations to thank. It would take many pages to list all of them, so we won't because you would probably not read all the pages, and we are almost certain to omit several important names. To every one of you, as well as the authors of other articles and books we read and often quoted, we offer sincere appreciation for your help.

We do want to acknowledge the major influence Thomas A. Dworetzky had on preparing an engaging manuscript, contributing to several content ideas, and arranging for very competent copyediting and formatting. We know you will enjoy reading the material he shaped for easing the path to your enlightenment about the new thinking of Question Forward.

We dedicate this book to our wives, Elaine and Bridget, who supported us throughout our writing, and, often enough, helped us by reading sections of the manuscript.

GN and BC

# TABLE OF CONTENTS

People are taught a certain mental model to plan, design, develop, improve, and create systems and solutions, a model that leads to certain kinds of questions. The over forty years of research that form the basis for this book show that the leading architects, engineers, managers, consultants, lawyers, and so on—only eight percent of the population—intuitively ask a different set of questions. How they think about and do their work produced the questions we present. A Question Forward Framework presents their questions—foundation, action, and organization. Question Forward is "software for the mind" that lets you ask the right questions in the right way in the right order at the right time in developing creative and usable living solutions.

The three foundation questions in the three chapters of this section are followed by and used in four chapters on action questions in Section II and two chapters on organizational questions in Section III. The three **foundation questions** about uniqueness, purposeful information, and systems are compared to the "questions backward" that stem from the typical, mental frameworks now used by most people. The chapters in this section will demonstrate that there is no such thing as *the* right questions; rather there are "more right" questions that are much better than the sample old questions. The words "right" and "backward" in all the chapters of this book are to be read with our recognition of this interpretation.

## Chapter 1. UNIQUENESS 3

**The Uniqueness Question Forward: How can we initially consider every problem, situation, and issue as unique?**

Current pitfalls in solution creation and problem-solving efforts come from common false assumptions about the transferability of solutions from specific past situations and from other organizations. Some of these hidden assumptions include using either/or dichotomies; words have objective meanings; categorizations are always inclusive; metaphors justify actions; management fads are good; ignoring people differences from one location to another; and predictions and statistics are good as stated.

## Chapter 2. PURPOSEFUL INFORMATION 29

**The Purposeful Information Question Forward: How can we identify and collect only purposeful information?**

The traditional "research approach" can lead to a bottomless hole of information gathering—and then bury you in data that is of no use and will confuse the picture. A brief history of information provides an understanding of a most difficult and sophisticated subtlety: that information is only a description of how we see reality, not the reality itself. Information can never be complete, accurate or precise. There is no way to get all the facts. Purposeful information determines what types and how much to get to lead to the needed decisions.

Information is described as a human construct, coming from all the senses, increasing exponentially, something that has a time value—and a larger quantity of information does not ensure quality or reduce uncertainty. There are different types: raw data, real information, knowledge, understanding, and wisdom.

## Chapter 3. SYSTEMS 49

**The Systems Question Forward: What are all the elements and dimensions that need to be considered to develop a creative, workable, and integrated living solution?**

No human is an island, so to speak. Every solution is really a system. And every system is part of larger systems and contains smaller systems, so they all have to fit together and work together.

A system is a matrix (checkerboard of element rows and dimension columns) of elements and their dimensions. The elements are: purposes, inputs, outputs, process, environment, human agents, physical catalysts, and information aids. Each of these has the following dimensions: fundamental characteristics, values, measures of performance, controls, interfaces with other systems, and future changes or needs. The system matrix generates a way to ask the "right" questions ensuring that all key and unique issues are raised, only purposeful information is obtained, and technology is pulled in as really needed

## SECTION II.

## ACTION QUESTIONS 87

The four **action questions** are abbreviated as the PPTR (people, purposes, target, results) process, which are the titles of the chapters in this section. PPTR provides the basis for asking the right questions in the *right* order in the *right* way at the *right* time, as well as an iterative framework. Each action Question Forward is accomplished with the following sub-questions:

1. **List** alternatives—What are many ideas and options to consider?
2. **Build** details for several of the most promising list items— How can we develop a major grouping of list ideas for greater consideration?

3. **Select** the option that most creatively and effectively meets the purposes of the action Question Forward—How can we evaluate the major build groupings to choose the most promising one?

## Chapter 4. PEOPLE INVOLVEMENT 93

**The People Involvement Question Forward: How can we give people who will be affected by, or are possible contributors to, the solution many opportunities to take part in the solution creating process?**

Getting people (external as well as internal to the organization) involved in the issue area is necessary for each PPTR question in creating a solution. Breakthrough solutions begin and end with these people, what they know and what they need. Implementation of the eventually developed living solution begins with People Involvement questions.

This action Question Forward uses a Question Forward Process Worksheet to raise the right questions for selecting the appropriate people to involve in developing and enacting a plan of action. Various techniques are presented as possible assistance in using the list, build, and select questions for the Question Forward Process Worksheet.

Because there would be no problems if humans did not exist, determining the particular, applicable aspects of the uniqueness of each individual (Chapter 1), the infinity of information (Chapter 2), and the whole system framework (Chapter 3) are used in putting together the team to tackle the problem at hand.

## Chapter 5. PURPOSES 119

**The Purposes Question Forward: How can we consider and exp    and a number of possible purposes and choose those that provide the largest feasible "creative thinking space"?**

This action Question Forward tackles one of the thorniest areas in any solution-developing process—avoid the pitfalls of working on the wrong problem. These questions show how to develop a focus purpose(s) that is a "real" end to achieve, the real problem opportunity to address. The "focus purpose(s)" is the phrase we use to identify this end or opportunity—always within the context of its larger purposes.

Techniques for each of the list-build-select questions are both structured and free form. They aid in expanding purposes to both address the necessary purposes and have room to grow, and arealso effective in asking any of the questions in PPTR. They also are used to determine the factors to be measured that will indicate successful accomplishment of the focus purpose(s), sometimes called the key success factors.

## Chapter 6 TARGET 151

**The Target Question Forward: How can we develop a target solution for the future that will guide what changes or designs to adopt today to achieve our focus and larger purposes?**

There is always more than one way to achieve focus and larger purposes, and listing as many ideal and "technology-fiction" possibilities now opens the door to considering what the future might be. Building major alternatives from the listed solution ideas leads to selecting both the most promising future ideal solution target (FIST) and some areas of research and development you need to sponsor or keep apprised of that will be needed to move today's solution closer to the target. The Question Forward Decision Worksheet is presented as an aid to selecting the FIST.

## Chapter 7. RESULTS 173

**The Results Question Forward: How can we develop a living solution(s) and implementation plans that work within their surrounding environments and systems for achieving the focus and larger purposes and also stay as close as possible to the target?**

Listing alternatives close to the target leads to building solution options for now. The systems matrix identifies the questions to ask that weigh and measure all possible specifications of the alternatives to ensure measurable change that is workable, correctable, manageable—and integrated with all other systems within which their solution will operate. The Question Forward Decision Worksheet is again a guide in asking the Select questions. The PPTR process is used for all installation activities (e.g., equipment purchase, phase-in, training, normalizing operations) as part of measuring-and-getting results.

## SECTION III.

## ORGANIZATION QUESTIONS 199

It is one thing to ask Questions Forward by yourself to develop solutions for yourself. But what happens when you need to develop solutions in a group or organizational setting? Organizational dynamics come into play. We address these dynamics in this section. The dynamics make it easier to see and face the whole spectrum of workplace interests, challenges and needs, whether in an organization or as a home business free agent, and do better in achieving all the good values sought in society by integrating them into a holistic process of thinking, feeling, and action. Learning from our lives as creators of solutions and reflection about thinking are the core themes in this section on three **organizational questions**, leading in Chapter 8 to how we can create a "Question Forward Organization" (QFO). A QFO lives with the advantages of change-enabling questions and the organizational dynamics of using language powerfully, a wholeness perceptiveness, and "real" empowerment in order to thrive in the fast-paced and changing global world. A QFO provides a stimulating environment that unleashes the "free" creativity inherent in each person.

Similarly, Question Forward lets you and your fellow citizens do better in promoting superior results in professional and societal activities outside of organizations. Chapter 9 deals with how Question Forward and its organization dynamics and questions can improve many specific disciplines and common areas of societal concerns, each of which will be the subject of follow-up books with the subtitle of Ask the Right Questions.

## Chapter 8. BECOMING A
## QUESTION FORWARD ORGANIZATION 201

This chapter acknowledges and describes briefly the characteristics of what many researchers, executives, and employees consider a modern, global, innovative, and responsive organization of excellence to be. This poses a basic issue of this book –*how* does an organization turn these very good ideas into practice, *how* does it create and manage its conditions in a complex world to lead to breakthroughs in thought and action, in effect, *how* does it become a Question Forward Organization (QFO)? *How* can we extend the intuitive Question Forward creativity of some individuals to bring forth the "free creativity" of everyone in the whole organization?

Our living answer is described by three organizational questions of the QFO adaptability culture that builds on the Question Forward foundation and action questions:

- **The Language Question Forward:** What language of innovation can bring a sense of meaning to and enroll others in bringing solutions to life?
- **The Perceptiveness Question Forward:** How can we develop perceptiveness of systems for individuals, customers, suppliers, and society?

- **The Empowerment Question Forward:** How can we empower people in all functions to be leaders and think of what is currently not possible?

A Question Forward Organization can develop, in minimal time and with minimal use of resources, creative and effective living solutions that have a high likelihood of being implemented, as well as the ability to reinvent itself and fundamentally shift directions.

## Chapter 9. QUESTION FORWARD: A DISCIPLINED APPROACH 223

This chapter illustrates how Question Forward concepts have been applied in several broad societal and policy arenas and could significantly increase the likelihood of creative and effective living solutions in some current issue areas. How professionals in many disciplines could significantly enhance their results will be the subject of books that will follow this one. Some of these books are already in the planning stage, such as *Conflict Management: Ask the Right Questions; Strategic Planning: Ask the Right Questions; Management Consulting: Ask the Right Questions; Project Management: Ask the Right Questions;* and *Negotiations: Ask the Right Questions.*

# PREFACE

The year was 1948. A moment of great optimism nestled between two wars. The country and the world were in the throes of a surge of growth and rebuilding. Industrial systems and theories were being used to build vast suburbs, cars and consumer products, and transportation and communication infrastructure at a dizzying pace.

Along with this came the application of the burgeoning field of industrial engineering. So it was no surprise that Gerry Nadler, then a young industrial engineer and a graduate student working at a food processing plant in Wisconsin, was given his first problem to solve as a professional.

The president of the company called Nadler into his office. He explained that a logjam on the loading docks was killing them. Freshness is critical when processing foods. Every second of delay from the fields to the cans or to freezing created costly waste and hurt quality.

"Gerry, what is the problem in our field-to-warehouse process?" asked the president. "After you find out, give me a one-page report on what I should do."

All the academic techniques the young engineer had learned would work beautifully to address this problem. He rushed off to prepare flowcharts, statistical analysis, measurements of work and productivity. This report would be a masterpiece. He flawlessly applied many techniques he had learned and, to be sure not to miss anything, performed exhaustive analysis and put it all together into his first professional report. A page? He'd do even better. He wanted to impress his first boss with his first project so he crammed everything—data, recommendations, the works—into a ten-page report and eagerly turned it in.

The president called him into his office. "Gerry," he said, "you know what I think of this report?" The president took the report gingerly in his hands as if he was weighing it. Then he tore it in half and pitched it into the wastebasket by the desk. "If you were in my shoes how would you solve the problem? That is what I really need to know."

After the shock wore off, the young engineer cut the report down to one page of recommendations and their justifications, as ordered. The recommendations were adopted and worked.

But more important, the seeds of Asking the Right Questions were planted. "I'd done exactly what my professors had taught me to do in answering the question, what is the problem," Nadler recalls. He'd analyzed the problem thoroughly, applied various techniques skillfully, like he'd been taught. Yet that wasn't the intent of the assignment. He had not "heard" the what-should-I-do part and had blithely gone on to focus on the what-is-the-problem question as he had been taught to do.

This lesson stuck. Over the next forty years he informally observed those managers, engineers, and others whom he thought the most creative and effective. He wanted to find out what they did differently than the rest of the people. He fortunately found others from diverse fields (anthropology, management, philosophy, and sociology in the initial research) who suspected that the way leading people convert knowledge into creative and award-winning practice was indeed different than the way we are taught.

What he and the others discovered was that the most effective solution developers threw out almost everything they had learned about how to plan, design, develop, improve, and create solutions! From that point, they proceeded with an intuitively structured set of thinking assumptions and way of asking questions. Over the course of the next decades, Nadler and others continued this research, and from it came in the early 1990s the principles, theories, and practices collectively referred to as Breakthrough Thinking. This book adds the latest research and practice and changes the format of the concepts to become Question Forward.

*"The primary skills [of education] should be*
*[to] know how to frame a question."*
Leon Botstein

There have been many books by Nadler and others since then that have explained and developed the basic concepts and the modes of applying them. They have been used by professionals in many walks of life and industry, and by individuals in family, community and societal situations with great success.

But until now there has not been one that addresses what might be called the first insight. Namely, what the young engineer learned on his first assignment: How to find the right questions. You've heard it many times: "Be sure to ask the right questions." Peter Drucker, the major management guru, says that, regardless of their individual styles, leaders ask the right questions. Jacques Nasser, the president of Ford Motor Co, told Congress in the 2000 hearings about the problems of Firestone tires on Ford Explorers that he wished he had asked the right questions sooner.

The phrase is a dictum handed down from above that no one doubts—and no one goes to the next step of finding out what the questions are. That is our mission—what *are* the right questions?

So get ready to throw out your own personal ten-page reports! The journey to the right questions begins with unloading all our excess mental baggage, which is the only way any of us ever get the most creative and effective answers.

*"The ancestor of every action is a thought."* Emerson

*"You need to* think *about thinking while you're thinking*
*in order to maintain the quality of that process."*[1]

# INTRODUCTION

Before you jump into giving our approach a try we have to warn you: This approach is a double-edged sword. It will really work and may both solve your problem and cost you your business-as-usual approach to a job.

So if you aren't ready to deal with the answers that come from asking the right questions, just quietly put this book back on the shelf and pick one of the many other best-sellers that will let you reinforce the failed approaches you've used in the past.

We are not kidding. The core of how to ask the right questions will change things in your life or work forever. If you aren't ready to change as well, this approach could lead to more trouble than you already have.

To illustrate the power of the questioning concepts of this book, here's an example of what happens with Question Forward.

### A so-called no-brainer decision

Paul, vice president for general operations of a very large national semi-perishable product company, gave a report from the director of distribution to Cliff, his staff assistant. "Look this over and let me know in about a week if I should approve it."

At first glance, the proposal looked good.

It solved the problem (as defined) of high costs, excessive overtime, poor delivery record, and diminished product quality at a loading dock in one of twenty-four national warehouses, proposing an automated loading dock (costing $60,000 with a payback period of eight months). Its justification was good, too. The report had flow charts, statistical analyses of time delays, accounting evaluation of excessive costs and overtime, studies of the damage to the quality of the product due to overcrowding on the loading dock, and so forth.

But Cliff had another idea—he'd been using a different approach in his own work for the last year. He talked a few colleagues, Bob, Terry and George, into helping with his assignment.

Cliff began the group's first meeting by proposing the following: "Let's start by asking about the purposes of the loading dock, the place where the initial problem was identified. I'll record your statements on the easel."

They put their random statements on some chart paper: to fill orders, to supply dealers, to load trucks, to have customers use our products, to consolidate shipments to dealers, to make company products available for sale, to deliver products to dealers, to transport products to dealers, to provide service about our products, to sell company products.

Cliff: "Now, let's organize these and other purposes we think of from small to large scope. We can start by asking about what the smallest scope purpose is. Then we will continue to ask 'what's the purpose of that purpose' for each of the successively larger purposes until we have included the purposes of our customers and our customers' customers."

The smallest purpose the group selected was—to load trucks.

Cliff: "Now what's the purpose of loading trucks?"

Terry: "What about 'to deliver products?'"

George: "But it seems there is a more direct yet larger purpose of loading trucks. What about 'to consolidate shipments?'"

Such probing led to the rest of the expanded purposes: to consolidate shipments to dealers, to transport products to dealers, to distribute company products to dealers, to make company products available for sale, to sell company products, to put company products in possession of customers, and to provide customers with service of company products.

Cliff: "Now we need to start with our biggest purpose and ask if we should try to develop a solution to achieve it or move to the next smaller one to determine if it should be our focus."

The group, asking this question over and over at each step, then decided that the larger purpose "to distribute company products to dealers" was what really needed to be accomplished (they were determining the right problem to work on).

Cliff: "Given this focus purpose, let's develop what measures we should use to determine how well it is accomplished. They will almost certainly be different than those used for evaluating loading dock solutions."

Bob: "Speed of delivery to dealer."

George: "Cost of whole distribution system. Dealer satisfaction."

They developed several "ideal" options:
1. move mini-manufacturing facilities to sites of big customers
2. produce all products at each factory to eliminate consolidation need
3. ship directly from factory to customer based on electronic ordering from customer, etc.

This let them, based on getting the information they knew they now needed, develop a future solution that would serve as a guide for developing the actual recommendation. Their future solution: Sell the twenty-four warehouses that are not needed because of the new way of distributing company products (option 3 above)!

Terry: "The VP may really toss you out if you tell him that! We better go over that system to make sure it can work and that huge savings and much better customer service will occur."

Cliff: "That leads to the next question. How can we 'see' the whole picture to determine what modifications, if any, would make the system workable and yet stay as close as possible to the ideal?"

The group used primarily a systems-based method (which we will explain later) for working out the details of the solution. They wound up proposing that twenty of the warehouses be sold. The four warehouses that remained consolidated small orders of products being shipped primarily to low-volume customers. The group sketched out the recommendation and included such factors as training current employees for new positions; arranging for possible early retirements; developing the details of interrelationships with the remaining four warehouses, all the factories, and shippers; and prepared for the re-assignment of personnel. They also suggested steps the company might take in the future to move the distribution system toward their ideal future solution.

The results were spectacular even when compared with the outstanding eight-month payback (a "creative" and workable solution for the wrong problem). In addition, an operational issue at the start became a competitive strategic change. (And Cliff never did check the validity of the information in the report!)

Now, compare what you thought were the questions to ask and what Cliff did. (It's OK to be honest—we won't grade what you write even if you send it to us.) We believe this will help you grasp the following dissection of what happens when you ask the old questions and what will happen when you ask the Question Forward ones.

You saw in Cliff's project just how powerful this right-questioning approach can be. It also showed you that you don't have to be top dog to make a radical difference at home or in the workplace. With right-questioning, it *is* possible to make a real difference, a truly valuable contribution.

*Revolutions in thinking (in contrast with politics and science) are the most influential and far-reaching. They affect our actions and sense of the possible, of the potentials of humans.*

Let's dig into another real-life example from one authors' experience as a change-management professional.

It was at the height of the Total Quality movement in the late 1980s when young Bill Chandon decided that he could make more of a contribution and help people better by going into business. He left the Jesuit seminary where he had studied philosophy for a couple of years and took his first position as a consultant with an organization that specialized in change management.

Things were not going well at all. "I had a desire to do well, had a great sense and passion that if we could improve our thinking, the results would be there…it would be different, but I became frustrated when I saw the best thinking that people were doing, including me, wasn't getting results….It was like story of Moses and the promised land, where he journeys for forty years to go to this great place. He gets to a big hill looking out at it…but Moses never gets to go there.

"I could see what needed to happen, but didn't know the path to get there. It was disillusioning in some sense but lit a fire in me….I could see that the better way to make breakthroughs in business was a different kind of thinking."

But what that type of thinking was, Bill's years of studying philosophy and reading the change management literature had not revealed to him.

In his consultant work, he was first assigned to be a facilitator in a group at a high-tech firm trying to deal with a problem that threatened the very life of the company. Rapid expansion was forcing the company to continuously move people to different facilities, and the telecom, networking and desktop computer teams were having a hard time getting things to work right. In fact, complaints from users had reached a point where it was looking more like they couldn't get anything to work at all. Every problem fixed seemed to create a host of others.

So the conventional problem-oriented approach was put in place. A team of the leaders of all three groups was formed, and they tried to get at the root problems. The assumption was that if they could find and fix those, then the other problems would go away.

Unfortunately, the people in the group didn't want to see that each of their problems was part of a larger problem. Each person focused only on the area that he or she were responsible for. The desktop department would make up their list of things to deal with and the network people did the same and the telecom folks did likewise.

The real problems came, naturally, in the interaction among the three. But for the users, the effect of all this was the same. Minor improvements did take place but it was still impossible to get a problem with your computer resolved in less than days.

The solutions were of the order of more handholding of users and faster replacement of desktop machines (which usually left the problem intact and forced users to start all over modifying their machines to be the way they had them before). There was more e-mail feedback put in place, more meetings held, more reports were issued—none of it actually making the situation better for the end user. A newsletter was even created, which just made people even more aware of how bad the situation really was!

Still the leaders involved refused to see that their individual problems were part of bigger issues. The real issue was that they weren't working together. And the real purpose of all the team members was to look good to their bosses so that they would keep their jobs. And the real reason for that was that each leader in the team wanted to make sure that he or she would look good to his or her boss. So they each developed problems within their own areas that they could address and/or solve. That way they could say that they were doing their jobs, addressing the issue. And so could their bosses.

Bill tried every imaginable technique to break through the logjam. But he failed. Finally, realizing that he could do nothing more with this team, he left it. The team continued and the problems remained until, eventually, this way of doing business damaged the company so badly that it lost business and was finally sold.

The key purpose wasn't found because the team was not asking the right questions. The right questions were: who needs to be involved, what are the purposes, what is the future solution going to be, and what information do we need to address that?

The wrong question was what led to all the problems in individual functional areas. This got them off track, led to more bad questions and a series of bad or irrelevant solutions.

Bill became driven to find a better way to deal with these issues on his next assignment. He scoured the literature and finally came across Gerry's earlier work, *Breakthrough Thinking*. "It was an "A-ha! moment," he recalls. It created the path he was looking for to that "promised land."

Ironically, he was assigned to a firm with the same problem about a year later. This time he swore to himself that he wouldn't make the same mistake twice.

And he didn't. This time he began by getting everyone to buy into the plan of action. He explained the different questioning methods to them, and they came up with a simple, elegant solution that involved a card that the technicians would leave on the desks of end users when they had fixed a machine. The card let the firm get feedback on each technician and also let end users know when a technician had done something to his or her machine. The simple card provided the measurement of success that the firm needed. This measurement had never been managed at the first firm.

One of the things the card approach revealed was that the technicians being supplied by the vendor weren't advanced enough to handle all the problems that were coming up. As a result of this ability to accurately measure results, the vendor, who had been part of the original group that developed the card solution, lost the account within a year to one that supplied better technicians because the vendor wouldn't make the changes needed to improve their technician's skills.

*The questions you ask determine the answers.*

Hence the warning at the beginning of this book. This is a powerful approach. Once you begin to use Question Forward, the name for the new insights from additional research and practice this book describes, to help ask the right questions, you better learn how to make your own changes. Each worker must take responsibility for improving himself or herself and getting the job done better for all to survive. Modern problem-solving and solution creation efforts have to be about serving all your customers, inside or outside the company (or family, community, social club), better, smarter, and faster. Question Forward helps create a path that shows you what needs to be delivered, how to do it, and if you've succeeded or not.

There are very few places left to hide unproductively in today's modern organizations. You either kill your problems and move on, or they kill you. Here's how we would put it on a T-shirt: "No matter how many alligators you kill, if they're not the problem, you'll still be in a swamp!"

**Here then are the most important messages we have gleaned from almost forty years of rigorous research into the way leading people and companies find solutions in the real world in the most successful companies and individuals.**

**MOST IMPORTANT MESSAGE #1:**

**The rush to resolve a problem into its smaller manageable parts actually makes the *real* problems, the ones under the surface of the symptom-problems, a whole lot worse.**

This kind of thinking is known as "reductionism," and was the cornerstone of the Renaissance. It was what spawned the scientific revolution, and its basic methodology carried over to the Industrial Revolution. Reductionism for planning, designing, developing, improving, and creating solutions represents a 200-year-old approach that no longer works in the modern world, although it is still quite useful, mostly for scientific problems and finding causes of, say, accidents. Reductionism for creating solutions solves only the problems we recognize, not the ones we really have. Unfortunately it's the way all of us have been taught. This old-fashioned approach focuses on the problems at hand and the past that led to them—not on the purposes of solving these problems or of creating solutions for the issue the problem is about. Where are you going? After this problem, situation, or need, what's the next one? And the next? If you don't Question Forward, by the time you see the problem or need, you'll have already missed many opportunities at dealing with it.

Furthermore, knowledge work and technology are causing a shift in our organizations. They are becoming more complex, requiring more intellectual horsepower to be effective. In addition, organizations are becoming more connected and networked, less like hierarchies or pyramids and more like spider webs. These changing organizations are requiring knowledge, work and technology to develop new capabilities in how the organizations operate. We call these capabilities an adaptability culture, and the organization questions present the need for a powerful language of change, to continually raise their level of perceptiveness, and to continually to elevate the level of empowerment or ability to take meaningful action in the organization.

By now, you're probably asking yourself, "Why do people continue to think and ask questions in the same way and then expect different outcomes? And for that matter, why do I? And why is the same approach still being taught?"

# MOST IMPORTANT MESSAGE #2

**Knowledge about how to approach the whole issue of *asking* the right questions is the key to solving problems and changing your life.**

Creating solutions is a part of human existence and progress. The outlook for the future of each individual and for societies depends to a great extent on how well we create solutions—how well we plan, design, improve, develop, and implement.

In the course of our research we have studied many different types of problem situations. Many of these arose in the *Fortune* 500 companies that asked us to come in to help them solve their problems, especially those involved in managing change.

**Our bottom line:** We drew the questions and the concepts in this book from our many studies done over the years. In short, what all these studies showed us was that only about 8 percent of the population, the leading solution creators, intuitively discarded classical Reductionist methods. (A recent study a colleague conducted with third graders showed that around 6 percent of them followed a solution-development approach that differed from what they had been taught, and that they used the basic approach of right-questioning as employed by this small minority of "gifted" adult creators of solutions.)

Here then is the simple, while-standing-on-one-foot outline of what questions these very special thinkers/solvers ask (review the no-brainer case to see how someone who learned the concepts later in his life used them). They ask the following kinds of questions:

- How can I initially consider this problem or situation as unique?

- How can I identify and collect only purposeful information?

- How can I use a systems framework or holistic approach to integrate any solution into the other existing surrounding systems in the real world?

- Who are the stakeholders to involve from the beginning, for what purposes, and how?

- What language can I use to most effectively involve the people in the whole solution creation process?

- How can I use and enlarge people's perceptiveness of the "whole" world in developing and using a living solution?

- How can I empower those involved throughout the process and in the whole organization for meaningful and creative action?

- What is the purpose of the issue area? What are its larger purposes?

- What purpose ought to be the focus?

- What are the various ideal ways to accomplish this and larger purposes?

- How close can we come today to the target?

- What is the plan of action to keep changing what we do today, so we keep moving in the future toward creating a new target again every couple of years?

*It's better to know some of the questions than all of the answers.*
James Thurber

Consider the impact on people and groups when they are asked these kinds of questions.

They:

- see an opportunity to contribute

- find a sense of meaning in what they do

- are challenged to release their "free" creativity

- are willing to implement the solutions they develop

- understand that change is always going to occur (we use *living solution* as the code words for a *change of today that has built-in seeds of continuing change*)

- are motivated

- develop trust in the process and with others

- can see the whole picture

- find a way to communicate easily with others

The thinking wisdom of the leading solution creators in positively affecting individual, organizational, and societal actions and performances is what we want to address. Their concepts can transform these levels of action, transitioning them and the individuals involved to higher levels of solution creating performances. Their thinking and the questions they ask now provide a way for everyone to expect significantly higher quality and a higher quantity of creative and practical solutions. Their and our techniques for doing these things are critical parts of the chapters in this book.

We would never knock learning, of course, but remember the rope that can pull you ahead can also hold you back. So before racing into a problem-solving frenzy, eager to put to use all that hard-won knowledge, first pause and ask yourself, "Is this really the question I should be asking right now?"

We present Question Forward as three basic questions: foundation questions, action questions, and organization questions. Figure Intro-1 summarizes the Question Forward framework of asking the right questions. Listed on the side are foundation and organization questions that are integrated into all the action questions—uniqueness questions, information questions, and systems questions (Chapters 1 through 3); and language, perception, and empowerment questions (Chapters 8 and 9). Across the top are the action questions to follow from start to finish—People Involvement questions, Purposes questions, Target questions, and Results questions (Chapters 4 through 7).

**Figure Intro – 1**

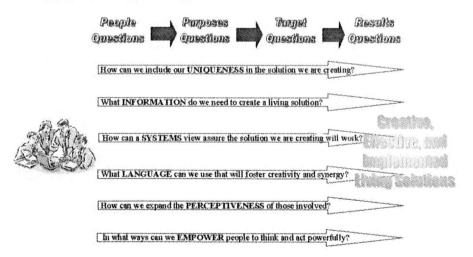

# QUESTION FORWARD Framework

People Questions → Purposes Questions → Target Questions → Results Questions

How can we include our UNIQUENESS in the solution we are creating?

What INFORMATION do we need to create a living solution?

How can a SYSTEMS view assure the solution we are creating will work?

What LANGUAGE can we use that will foster creativity and synergy?

How can we expand the PERCEPTIVENESS of those involved?

In what ways can we EMPOWER people to think and act powerfully?

Many questions are presented throughout the book to increase your understanding and scope of thinking about the concepts, but it will become apparent to you that identifying which of the questions you ought to use in a particular situation is still a critical decision. We summarize here the criteria you can use to make the decision:

- Does it align with foundation, action, and organization Question Forward questions?
- Does it open and expand look-to-the-future responses and possibilities?
- Does it create new Question Forward-type metaphors?
- Does it feel like an interesting or important Question Forward?
- Does it spark creative responses (many options, other Question Forward-type questions)?
- Is it likely to bring people together enthusiastically and with commitment to focus on building a desired future and getting results?

*"The manner in which a thing is done
has more influence than is commonly imagined."*
Alexander Hamilton

**Question Forward is Software for the Mind to let a person ask the right questions in the right way in the right order at the right time in developing creative and usable living solutions.**

**Note to readers:**

The cases and examples used in the rest of the book using the word "I" will refer to one or the other of us or both of us.

In order to avoid confusion, all cases and examples will refer to using Question Forward rather than Breakthrough Thinking, Planning and Design Approach, PTR Approach, or any other names used for earlier versions of Question Forward. The other names would be found in the references provided throughout this book.

Our use of the words "right questions" is to be interpreted as meaning significantly "more right questions" than conventional, or what we call "backward," questions. The chapters in Section I, Foundation Questions, will clearly demonstrate that there is no such thing as *the* right questions.

# SECTION I. FOUNDATION QUESTIONS

Everything in life comes down to asking the right questions.

For example, Einstein asked why space and time were separate "things" and changed the way we think about the universe. It turned out that just because there were two separate words for them didn't mean they were two different things. You couldn't define one without the other; that is, they were related to each other (hence the term *relativity theory*). He made up a new word—spacetime—to describe that relationship, and suddenly all the strange mathematical problems that had plagued astronomers for a millennium could be explained (well, not all, but this isn't a book about astronomy).

What Einstein did was change the underlying mental picture, or model. This model lay at the heart of the way physicists thought. That's what is so powerful about good questions. They challenge us to examine assumptions and consider the previously unexamined and, therefore, unthinkable. Further, good questions are always actionable. They immediately get us into meaningful dialogue with one another considering possibilities about "why not" rather than simply "why."

Hidden assumptions cause us to ask the wrong questions and miss the right solutions, creating stagnation and sometimes chaos and conflict. But there is a way to manage the chaos of the daily interaction between all of us. It is based on accepting that we all have mental models or assumptions about ourselves and our world that will remain unconscious unless we stop to look at them.

Unless we take these assumptions into account we are doomed to getting the same kind of limited results, and sense of dissatisfaction, every time. And not just our assumptions, but also those of the people involved with us in our activities. This is true whether the situation involves coworkers or neighbors or family members.

So if you want to change your world, or what we "experts" call paradigm (or model) shifting or transformation, you've got to be ready to bring those fundamental assumptions to the surface. You have to be ready to challenge some commonly accepted ideas and practices. That is why the three questions in this section are called Foundation Questions.

The first three chapters present the beginning steps of our journey:

Chapter 1 poses: How can we initially consider every problem or situation as **unique**?

Chapter 2 asks: How can we identify and collect only **purposeful information**?

Chapter 3 inquires: How can we use a **systems** framework (a matrix of elements and dimensions) to ensure development of creative, workable, and integrated living solutions?

# Chapter 1

# UNIQUENESS

*QB (Question Backward): Why reinvent the wheel?*

Ever notice how often someone says this, or something like it, at a meeting?

It's a classic "bad" question. Here's why.

First, look around. Notice how many "wheels" there are out there in the real world? Fancy chrome ones, plain ones on your spare in the trunk, wooden ones, big ones, little ones. Face it, there are tons of wheels out there. If one wheel solved every problem and met every need in this heavily trafficked world of ours, then one size and type would fit all. The wheel store would have only the one type of wheel for sale.

You know that isn't the case. But when someone suggests using a solution to a problem you have at work by "doing it like they do it" at some other place that is kind of like yours, people leap at the chance, presumably to save time, money, effort and, above all, to avoid thinking about the unique situation at hand. They may even conclude by congratulating themselves, saying, in effect, "Good idea, after all, why reinvent the wheel?"

The short answer is that sometimes you need a different type of wheel. Sometimes, in fact, you don't need a wheel at all. You need something completely different.

For example, once I consulted for a hospital that wanted to improve its medical record-keeping system. About a year before, another hospital had brought me in to consult on a similar issue and that team put together a very successful high-tech solution. It was so good that it won awards.

One of the main reasons the second hospital's CEO brought me in on the project was because he had heard about the first success and didn't want "to reinvent the wheel."

It turned out, however, that by resisting the urge to treat both situations as the same, the team at the second hospital discovered a cheaper, lower-tech solution that worked better for the institution. It was a solution that the personnel could use and would be committed to making work. The more sophisticated technologic approach wouldn't have worked because this staff was not "in the same place" technologically as the staff at the other hospital. It was also overkill; that much technology wasn't needed to address the real needs, which were different than at the first hospital.

Importing solutions almost never works because people often don't understand all aspects of the solution and it may be more than is needed and too complicated for anyone to use. Or the employees invoke the "not invented here" symptoms of resisting the change. Even in different divisions of the same organization, what is a "best practice" in one cannot be perfectly copied in another. Even "standardized" systems – fast food restaurants, grocery markets, gas stations, auditing processes—have dozens of differences. Initially considering each situation as unique saves a lot of time and effort in the long run, compared to trying to force the situation into a "standard" solution from somewhere else—no matter how meticulous your attention to each detail.

If you manage people you know that if they can't or won't play along, then any solution will fail. Trying to get people to do something they don't want to do is like trying to push cooked spaghetti uphill. If you work for someone, you know how hopeless it is to try to do what your boss wants when it doesn't correspond to the reality of your actual situation.

There are a number of strategies you can use to get things done at work. Ordering the troops around from on high is one. Endless rounds of group-think retreats is another.

No matter how you approach it, however, the bottom line is that questions must be asked and answered. When the hospital CEO changed his question from, basically, "What system can we borrow from somewhere else?" to "What system do we need here?" the possibility for a good solution to his actual problems appeared, in large part because the people there "invented" it.

That's the thing about questions. Whether it's done in a spirit of dictatorship or democracy, if these questions are poorly constructed, they will lead to answers that are either of no use, or worse, lead you in the wrong direction.

There are a number of reasons questions are incorrectly framed. If you follow along, we hope to clarify the key culprits so that you can begin to recognize good from bad questions.

**QF (Question Forward): How can we find out if we need a wheel?**

**The Uniqueness Question Forward: How Can We Initially Consider Every Problem, Situation, and Issue as Unique?**

*QB: Why should we consider that our situation is different?*

After over forty years of research examining the reasoning processes of people in decision-making situations, we found that only about 8 percent of all people are clearly the best at creating solutions, and their Number One assumption or rule is that every situation is initially unique! Not that they would avoid seeing parallels in situations for the whole length of the process leading to a solution, of course, but they always assume this uniqueness at the outset.

There are several reasons that this is the most critical of your new assumptions:

- The people in every seemingly identical situation or system are *always* different,
- The purposes to be accomplished in every seemingly identical situation are very likely to be different,

- The technology available today is likely to be more advanced than that used yesterday in a seemingly similar situation.

Make these three ideas a mantra you repeat to yourself every time you find yourself having to deal with a new problem at work, at home, or in any situation. Write them on a scrap of paper and carry it in your wallet. Teach them to your kids.

But maybe you think people are all the same, or that they don't change. Consider this.

What are the odds that any two people are the same? That is, that they have the biological makeup or genetics, mental model, family experiences, life experiences or memories (which change daily), larger community cultural mindset or zeitgeist (as sociologists like to say), and so on?

The odds are basically zero, regardless of the recent findings that the human genome is a shared inheritance of all of us. Most brothers don't think the same; most sisters don't think the same—and that's about as close to identical in genetics and environment as people are going to get! Furthermore, studies of identical twins show that many, if not most, of their characteristics are not the same even with identical genes.

**QF: How can we include consideration of our uniqueness in the process for creating and, as needed, in our solution?**

Now consider any two situations (that is, any two systems, needs, issues, problems, etc.). Unless you are meditating solo on a mountaintop, these will always involve a group of people, who we now realize are not going to be the same as any other group of people.

Talking about these odds is important because so many management approaches use a lot of math to try to calculate the likelihood of success. It comforts us to look at those graphs of productivity increases and comparisons between time-to-market, and so forth.

Unfortunately, the graphs can look great but they don't mean a thing if your basic assumption is that two sets of people or two problems are identical, because they "ain't." Your initial consideration in solving a problem has to be to embrace the uniqueness of each situation. Otherwise, you'll wind up picking the same wrong solution, and make your tried-and-true mistakes, proceeding logically from your same old mental model, all over again.

In other words, there is no general "right" solution in any absolute sense; the solution is always relative or, in our words, "unique."

*"Remember you are unique, just like everybody else."* Bumper sticker

**QF: What is unique about this problem or situation?**

**Assumptions Hidden in Language And Logic**

*QB: What's the single best solution that will make our problem go away?*

Since questions are made up of words and the assumptions contained in them, that's where we have to begin.

We wish, for example, that everyone used another simple word or short phrase instead of "solution," which has the ring of claiming to be *the* answer. For that reason, our definition of the word solution everywhere in this book is *"a change for today that has built-in seeds of continuing change."* We will use *"living solution"* as the code words for this definition.

This mistake about the nature of a solution, amusingly, has its root in the precise grammatical nature of the word solution itself. Put simply, it is a noun.

By definition a noun is a thing. A thing is something that has no action to it ("cat"); it is linked to an action by a verb ("chases birds"). Verbs, on the other hand, have no "thingness" to them; they are about action.

This gets us down to the nub of some of our most profound hidden assumptions. That is, that we depend on words and grammar, usually in an unconscious way, to structure our so-called logical thinking.

That's why Einstein's creation of a new word—spacetime—was such a big deal; he broke the grammatical bonds of the two nouns space and time that had shackled physicists into thinking about them as two different things, when they are really one thing.

There have been volumes written about this "deep-structure" of languages, and this is not going to be one of them, so we'll keep it brief by getting back to the word solution.

Solution is a noun, but there is also a verb lurking out there that has a lot in common with it. The verb is "to solve." Solve is not a thing, it is an act; a process, to be precise. But there is a funny form of a verb in the English language called a participle. A participle is the "-ing" version of a verb, which in the case of "solve" is "solving."

This funny little grammatical cousin can be used as a noun, that is, you can talk about "a solving," and people will get what you mean. Just like when you talk about a meeting, the participle of the verb "to meet."

Participles can turn an action into a thing. That is, you can use one grammatically any place you can use a noun. It still isn't a thing, but rather a process or action that is put in the general case.

For example, in the general case of "meeting," we mean any meeting and we don't know about what. If we did we would express it by saying, for example, "let's meet for dinner" or "let's discuss it at a dinner meeting."

8

The neat thing about "solving" is that it still contains the seeds of change, of action, within it. It doesn't become static—which actually makes it closer to the truth about the way "solutions" really are. They are solvings that keep changing.

*"[What are] the shades of gray inherent in a situation[?]"[2]*

**QF: Since there is always more than one way to solve a problem (think gray), what are the alternatives we should consider before selecting one of them?**

## Either/or and other dichotomies

*QB: Is that a technology or a people problem?*

This search for dichotomies where none exist may be a basic part of human nature. It's the most basic setup of most arguments ("there are always two sides to every question") because each side tends to maintain an absolute and irreconcilable position. Many times the best solutions, and the right questions to ask, are somewhere in the middle.

The French philosopher Rene Descartes (1596-1650) introduced the idea that things either were of the mind or of the body (the either/or dichotomy) over 350 years ago, smack at the beginning of the scientific revolution known as the Renaissance.

Unfortunately, his ambitious effort has logical problems. It's a nice theory, but not all that practical in real life.

The concept didn't die because it is useful as the basis of the research approach used by "hard" scientists and lawyers, both of which have enjoyed a real growth spurt since the Renaissance.

In these arenas of thought, there are valid practical either/ors—the electricity is either flowing in this line or it is not, the automobile hit the wall or it did not, the house grant deed is officially recorded or it is not.

Unfortunately, people also seek either/or distinctions for many life activities where things almost always are not that simple – he is either good or evil, she is either a feminist or a traditionalist, they are either a hard-working or lazy group, the politician is either liberal or conservative, the company is either a community asset or an environmental disaster.

The failure of the either/or approach lies in what Aristotle called the "law of the excluded middle." In many real-world situations, things are just not black and white.

Simple example. How many hairs on your head make you hairy versus bald? One? No, that's bald. Two? No. 300? No. 15,000? Well, maybe. But where is the hard line? What number is the dividing line between bald and hairy? In reality, the line is fuzzy and so are most lines in nature, once you look at them closely. So this either/or thing is still approximate, or fuzzy. It just seems to give you absolute answers.

It turns out that once you get used to taking a less black-and-white approach, you can comfortably manage to keep all sides of a problem in focus at the same time. This mental flexibility is the secret to asking the right questions. If you can resist framing your questions as either/or, you can find whole new ways of approaching your problem and find new solutions that you would've missed otherwise.

General Motors thought in the 1980s that its factories had to automate and use robots, like the Japanese companies did, or it would be outclassed in the highly competitive market. It spent around $40 billion to do this, and then found in a couple of years that it had to abandon almost all of the equipment and investment. That fiasco, caused by trying to impose a solution from elsewhere and thinking in either/or terms, created an extra $600-800 cost per vehicle produced for most of the 1990s. The resulting decline in market share reflects the consequences of asking the wrong (conventional) questions.

**QF: What are all the "language" elements and dimensions of possible solutions?[3]**

## The subjective, variable meanings of words and phrases

*QB: Is that a solution that satisfies everyone?*

You look up "satisfies" in a dictionary and there is its meaning in black and white. What could be clearer or more absolute?

It turns out words have no absolute meanings. They have only meanings from the way they are used by people. And how people figure out what a word means depends on many subjective aspects: how the word was used in their homes when they were first learning to talk; their culture, neighborhood, education.

Take "satisfies." For the CFO it might mean that it makes sense to the bottom line. To the COO it might mean that there are no complaints from workers and timetables are met—regardless of what it costs. To the workers it might mean their jobs are easier or the opportunity for personal fulfillment is greater—without regard to either costs or timetables.

In other words, what a word really means depends on whom you ask. Most of the time such subtle differences in meaning are hidden, and most management approaches do little or nothing to bring such distinctions to the surface. Because no one asks the right questions about the meanings of such critical words, there is a communication breakdown—the whole group never actually understands what "satisfies" or other key words mean in the context of the unique situation or problem they are in the midst of "solving."

And words change their meanings over time. Good means good, but these days some people say "bad" when they want to say how good something is, for example, "That is a really bad car you are driving."

*The bride's father in Babylon 4,000 years ago supplied his son-in-law with all the mead (honey beer) he could drink for a month. This period was called the honey month, and, since the lunar calendar was used, has become known today as the honeymoon.*

11

Try an experiment and you will quickly see how unclear words really are. Ask four friends what is meant by these common words or phrases: physical abuse, democracy, strategic planning, the color red, family values, total quality management, light traffic, pinch of salt, or beautiful. What is the likelihood all four will agree on the meaning? Pretty slim, we propose.

Or consider the manager who set a one-month deadline for her team to present a recommendation. After almost three and a half weeks, the team asked for more time "because we hadn't collected all the data." The manager exploded! "Didn't you guys recognize that the deadline was critical?" How is the urgency of a "deadline" understood by different people?

All this shows that words (and knowledge, too) cannot be viewed as entities separated from their context. They have unique shades of meanings in particular contexts. Words, then, are essentially subjective, not objective (Chapter 2 explains more of this). They are embedded in a particular frame of reference, and always relative and open to reinterpretation.[4] That's why polls so often come up with conflicting results. People's answers depend on how the questions were asked, the exact words used. If I asked you, "If someone is bright" or "Are they intellectual," you would quite possibly give different answers. (Pollsters know this and use it to the advantage of their clients with regularity, which is why you should always be very wary of such "data.")

As another illustration, even the supposed objectivity of science and its language are not value-neutral. Studies have shown that different scientists, especially from different cultures and speaking different languages, wind up structuring so-called objective experiments differently and also interpret the results differently. And male and female scientists may also perceive differently many aspects of at least the questions they pose as well as the meaning of many phrases.

And since even scientific experiments involve people to the extent that people think up the experimental models, observe the results and do the analysis; that means that almost every problem you can imagine must be approached with the idea of its uniqueness firmly in mind.

**QF: What implied and assumed categories should the people involved in this particular situation consider in selecting a recommended solution?**

## Categorization

*QB: How will our typical worker deal with our proposed solution?*

The short answer is that there is no such thing as typical. It's a classification, or category that is based on arbitrary techniques to divide and stereotype people.

Categorizing, stereotyping, and labeling individuals, situations, beliefs, and organizations are companions to either/or thinking. "Girls can't do math." "White men can't jump." "Ditzy blondes." "Forgetful seniors." They have a terrible effect—the people or situations categorized lose all semblance of their individuality or uniqueness.

Take personality, skill, and intelligence tests, for example. These masquerade as objective, but in fact label people arbitrarily and inaccurately in the guise of determining where a person might be aided by further education or what job a person might do best in a company.

These tests may have some modest use, but their widespread application has great dangers. What they do, in almost all cases, is apply to people the categories that are the result of the values and experiences of the "cultural elite."

This "elite" is actually just a certain group of people whose background has prepared them to prepare these tests, to offer up the "preferred" answers. But in no way do such tests truly measure the total abilities of the unique individual. More often than not these answers reflect the use of language among a small subset of the entire population. For example, users of proper English, rather than a dialect of the language will regularly do better. But all this measures is skill with the proper dialect; it doesn't measure how smart a person is.

Veterans, baby-boomers, generation Xers, and "Gen-nexers" are recent age-based categories of the generations now living in the United States. These labels arise primarily because someone is looking for one and accepts any "unusual" characteristic that appears among the more vocal or noticeable of the age category. As cultural markers, they are still as dangerous to apply to a specific individual in the group as is using the various either/or societal culture descriptors when dealing with a person or organization in another country. We are, in other words, all unique individuals.

This categorization syndrome relates in a direct way to the focus of this book—asking the right questions in order to create solutions that accomplish our purposes.

The case at the beginning of this chapter illustrates the point about categorization. The CEO of the second hospital assumed that all members of the category of medical records systems were the same—a medical records system is a medical records system is a medical records system. And the CEO was wrong.

Another type of categorization is equally misleading and harmful.

Too often a person or organization will try to select, in advance of trying to create a solution, the level or category of change desired. They try to decide beforehand what they expect the solution should be, from minimum to maximum change: do things right, do things better, do the right things, get rid of things, copy what others do, do things differently than others, or do things that are "impossible."

The president of a 600-employee manufacturing company and several executives were concerned about the late delivery of almost all of the company's products. They met for nearly eight months to find a solution that would "do things better." They decided to build a new facility that would double capacity. The president called me to help them design a state-of-the-art factory. After spending an afternoon in the current facility, I requested a project team to do the planning with Question Forward. By expanding the purposes for the project, the team decided that it should focus as well on how to "get rid of things." This effort produced a living solution that could be accomplished within the current facility, and a new one was never built. A great factory *could* have been built if the initial categorization had been followed, but it would have wasted good money for a "thing" that shouldn't exist at all.

By determining the criteria and techniques that will be used to measure the problem arbitrarily before even looking at it, people can easily wind up focusing on just one of these aspects at the expense of the others. This categorization often leads to solutions that solve one thing but make other things worse.

Even worse, many times the actual problem was the wrong one to focus on anyway. The better solution would have been to fix something else in the organization that never came to light because people were using the measurement or other categories to focus on finding the best solution for the problem at hand.

A third problem is that categorization leads people to focus on elements rather than the whole when trying to solve a problem. Such categorization stems from what behavioral economists call representation thinking—the present is representative of the future. Breaking down a problem too soon into elements or sub-problems is putting the cart before the horse. It almost always causes people to insist that those elements will be present in the future. This leap to break it down invariably leads to partial solutions. You may solve one sub-problem but in a way that makes it impossible to solve another part.

**QF: What benefits, if any, do we get by using that categorization in trying to create a living solution instead of considering the uniqueness of the situation?**

*Gerald Nadler and William J. Chandon*

# Metaphors

*QB: Will this solution be a home run for us?*

Simple truth about baseball. Those who hit home runs also strike out the most because they swing for the fences every time. Is that the type of solution you are really looking for? Or do you just want to get a man on base (another metaphor) and drive in runs with singles and doubles? It makes a big difference to the type of solutions you will consider. Maybe hitting home runs is not really an apt metaphor with which to characterize your desired strategy. After all, you will fail more often than you will succeed with such an all-or-nothing approach.

People use metaphors, similes, plays-on-words, aphorisms, and allegories (and, too often, jargon) to explain a goal or situation in terms of some other evocative ideal or well-known thing.

We often resort to proverbs used as metaphors to justify an action—the early bird gets the worm; a penny saved is a penny earned; early to bed, early to rise, makes a man healthy, wealthy and wise; time is like a river; don't kill the goose that lays the golden eggs; haste makes waste.

*Dilbert's boss to Dilbert: You need to socialize your idea with the rest of the department.*
*Dilbert: Socialize? Is that the same as buy-in?*
*DB: It's one step below buy-in. It's more like dialoging for feedback.*
*D: Wait. I thought building a consensus was one step below buy-in.*
*DB: Just run it up a flagpole and see who salutes.*
*D: Wouldn't it be better to do a temperature check using a straw man?*
*DB: Maybe, but is that going to inoculate the stakeholders?*
*Last panel: Dear reader, if you or anyone you love understands the preceding conversation, you have my deepest sympathy. SA*

Scott Adams, Dilbert cartoon, Sunday, May 5, 2002.

Similar to our compulsion for either/or distinctions is the human need for metaphors. These are forms of storytelling that help us interpret what is happening and decide what to do. They subtly permeate our minds, determining how we think and understand our world.

But they can be dangerous. They don't always help us understand—and often lead to unintended and undesirable results. They are words with all the lack of consistent meaning noted before.

Although metaphors and aphorisms can be empowering (and thought-provoking in the solution creation process described in Section II), they are not proof of anything. That's why they are dangerous—you can lead people to take the wrong actions with a metaphor.

Metaphors, which we will always have to use, should be picked with care. They are limiting, and produce questions and actions that stultify the creativity and big-picture thinking of people. "Time is money" can make people ignore consideration of many factors important to the solution because of the perceived "extra" time involved.

It's better to rephrase many of these timeworn metaphors, if you want them to work for you. "Time, purposeful thinking, and workability are money," will lead people to different outcomes than merely telling them to move quickly because it's expensive to pause and try to think of something better.

Telling the story in ordinary words is difficult enough without the confusion of even the best metaphors. For example, if you are talking to someone in English and that is not their first language, you are well advised to avoid metaphors and analogies. They are idiosyncratic and often don't translate meaningfully.

Metaphors get our attention because they often contain a lot of meaning for some groups. But they require careful use. If you speak in metaphors, try ones that enable yourself and others to see new aspects of a particular phenomenon and then also look at the ways in which the metaphor does not apply to the uniqueness of a particular situation.

### QF: How can we "play" the whole game most creatively and effectively?

## Assumptions Embedded in Culture and Society

*QB: Can we find a solution that furthers and rewards outstanding individual effort?*

In America this might be a fine idea. We have a noble tradition of rugged individualism borne of our frontier beginnings. But in Japan, for example, efforts to foster such individualism run counter to deeply held cultural attitudes.

To illustrate, the Japanese have a saying, "The tall nail gets hammered down." It speaks to a very different tradition, one in which "standing out" is not a good thing, but a bad one. In Japan being a humble member of a successful team is preferable than being known for individual achievement.

Never forget that a culture is really a collection of hidden assumptions, many of which even natives can't tell you about. Even the idea of who your parents are can be different between cultures. (In some, for example, you might refer to your uncles and aunts as "parents.") And that culture is a label or categorization that is not monolithic; people in every culture do not all subscribe to, believe in, or practice what the culture supposedly claims is appropriate.

Even countries that are close culturally have subtle differences. Canada is culturally close to the United States in some regards, but quite unique nonetheless. But how irate do you become (assuming you are an American) over the issue of mandatory bilingual signs in French and English?

This uniqueness of cultures should make you extremely wary of any attempt to impose a successful approach from somewhere else. And subtle cultural differences are not just found between countries; regions and cities within a country also have distinctly different cultures.

For example, the advent of the "silicon valley" phenomenon has produced many copycat technological initiatives in countries (even in different regions in the United States).[5] Considering how different countries' cultures are makes this type of effort even more risky and less likely to succeed.

Many of these efforts have failed because they failed to take into account certain unique characteristics of the initial "silicon valley." Even though information technology has made location and distance a seemingly inconsequential factor in the global economy, the chief advantages it had were traditional ones. It succeeded because of proximity—to higher education and research resources, an influential market, competing and ancillary firms, venture capital, and new technologies and ideas.[6]

**QF: How might the cultural norms be integrated (or modified) into the range of potential solutions we are considering?**

## Analogies

*QB: How can our organization be designed like a living organism?*

Analogies, "why reinvent the wheel," and sometimes metaphors hold out the promise of an easy route to developing a solution for a problem. "Can't we make our accounts receivable system like supplier XYZ?" The words "like," "such as," and "similar to" are the frequent fingerprints of an analogy. An analogy is often a sudden thought that occurs when trying to explain something to someone else or to develop a solution for something. An analogy seldom becomes a fixture of language or a part of the vernacular as does a metaphor.

19

An analogy has the characteristic of presenting a model of something else you could use in developing a solution or system. An analogy plays on the mind as a framework for your solution. And this is its most powerful use—when brought to bear at the right time in the right way in the solution creation process.

In the meantime, it should be clear by now that uniqueness completely overrides the mapping of a solution or system you want to develop an analogy presumably is meant to provide.

**QF: What ideas might we get for our organization structure if we think about it as a living organism, or a network of information links, or an ant colony, or a pancake, or ….?**

## Management Fads

*QB: How can we put quality circles into our organization structure?*

The rage or craze to adopt and use the latest program or management approach happens in all types of organizations. Sometimes people just want to be "in" with the latest jargon, or are afraid they will be blamed for being out-of-date if something goes wrong and they haven't been using the latest theory-du-jour (also known as CYA). Sometimes they just hope that if they use the right words, then they will wind up with the right solutions automatically.

The usual scenario is that a company rushes to adopt a program and impose the structures defined by its promoters, and then, out of frustration, seeks out the next program because the earlier one did not produce anywhere near the promised results. Management often believes each program it adopts as the final stage of development— "the solution," even though there is a "life cycle of management fads: discovery, wild acceptance, digestion, disillusionment, and, for a rare few, hard core use."[7]

These buzz-word programs come in many cultish flavors, including quality circles, automation, total quality management, process reengineering, management by objectives, Six Sigma management, the learning organization, excellence, culture change, and knowledge management.

Beware of such "magical" thinking.

> *"Buzzwords are the problem, not the solution.*
> *Hot techniques dazzle us and then fizzle."*
> Henry Mintzberg

Why call such cultish management techniques "magical" thinking? Mostly because they suggest that if you just use their general program, use their words, and follow their generic "recipes," you will solve any unique problem you're facing.

This type of "magical" thinking is really a very ancient approach to management of real-world events. Its basic assumption is that spells or other forms of magic words, incantations or prayers have a direct connection to and can affect the outcome of events in the real world. (We are using the world "magical" here in a technical, non-judgmental sense, like "ethical" thinking.)

In all fairness, such divine interventions are a distinct possibility. Most religions believe in this link and the history of all peoples contains many stories of such powers. That said, the profound aspects of "magical" thinking are far beyond the subject of this book!

We would like to suggest, however, that this natural human urge to put faith in powers-greater-than-our-own is also pretty far beyond what you need to solve your everyday work problems.

At the very least, use "magical" thinking with some discretion. Praying for peace is an appropriate invocation of such divine connections between the spiritual and the mundane worlds.

But it is inexcusably lazy, for example, to resort to magic mutterings about total quality management, "personal empowerment," or generic management-speak from the HR manual when trying to find a better way to handle violence in your workplace. It's irresponsible leadership when you don't look at these situations and deal with them as unique problems. If you deal with a troubled employee in such an automatic fashion ("It says here in the HR bible...bla-bla-bla"), there is a chance that people will get hurt—maybe even killed.

Yet that is just what many managers do. They put faith in the "power" of the latest management jargon or techniques as if just using the jargon will automatically solve problems. This sort of thinking leads to the unfortunate outcome in which "Just saying it don't make it so." (Like saying an approach is a solution, when it doesn't solve anything, or calling any random group of workers a "quality circle" when they aren't.)

Why do managers mostly rush to adopt fads? Fads of any type—systems, ideas, products, language, behaviors—obviously start slowly because someone, the first adopters, have to wax enthusiastically about how great their results are. One concept about the use of fads is that they then spread leisurely until they explode into an epidemic, similar to viruses.[8] Another explanation claims that competitive pressures and global markets reduce the time available to consider options for creating solutions, so "let's do what the Joneses do" seems attractive.

Once such fad jargon is used, managers can prattle off these empty words while abdicating their accountability. Most of the standard assumptions about how their specific organization really works are never challenged. The program exudes the hidden "magical" assumption that its use will automatically produce the one right solution. For example, benchmarking what the best are doing regarding a particular activity (order processing, customer service, layout of kitchens) to determine what you should do makes for interesting reading but most likely provides you with a solution that doesn't fit your organization (people, purposes, technological level).

Such reasoning fails to take uniqueness into account—and fails in general to achieve positive results. "The success rate of any of these [fad programs] is pretty low" appeared in a *Wall Street Journal* front-page article. "Employees, as well as customers, rate the effectiveness of these management fads at between just 10% to 20%…"[9]

Or as the National Research Council reported concerning management fads: They "have emerged so quickly [they] spotlight a growing willingness among managers to embrace [them] in the absence of solid evidence of their effectiveness."[10] In addition, "management fashions introduced in recent years have shorter life spans than their earlier counterparts….[F]ashions that are difficult to implement take a toll on the labor force…."[11]

Beyond that, the idea of best process and system practices borrowed from elsewhere also fails to account for uniqueness. Wherever such advice or best practices were developed, that was someplace else, a unique situation. That's why best practices can have as much trouble traveling across town as they do across continents.[12] And even if a fad program would be useful in an organization, the culture of the organization, just as the cultures of countries and societies, is unique and the program needs to be "designed" with the process presented in Section II to achieve that organization's purposes with its people.

Chapter 9 will extend this discussion of fads to the larger setting of societal and political realms.

> **QF: Can the concepts of this program (e.g., quality circles) add anything to any of our possible living solutions?"**

## Predictions

*QB: What are the odds that the predicted demographics will affect how each of our proposed solutions will work?*

It's been said there are "lies, damned lies and statistics." The uniqueness principle offers insight into why the use of statistics to make predictions is such a big problem.

It turns out most of our assumptions are not based on some ultimate truth; they are our best guess, based on past experience. They are a statistical approach that is based on what has happened in the past.

Unfortunately, this statistical approach turns out to be the first underlying assumption for almost everyone—and it's a killer. Many creative and successful living solutions (like the Walkman, airplane, or personal computer, to name just a few) would never have occurred if technological, demographic, economic, and many other predictions had not been ignored.

To be precise, statistics only tell you what has happened in the past. They never actually tell you with certainty what will happen next. For example, if I know that when I flip a nickel there is a 50-50 chance it will land heads or tails (because it has two sides with an equal chance of showing), that doesn't ever tell me which way it will land the next time I flip it. The odds aren't changed no matter how many heads-in-a-row or tails-in-a-row I have already flipped.

The reason for this is the Uniqueness Question Forward. To wit: No matter how many times you think you have been in the exact same situation before, the situation you are now in is unique. Sounds strangely obvious, but the fact is, the flip you are about to make has never happened before!

In other words, once you flip that coin and it lands heads up, then the chances that it would land heads up on that flip were 100 percent. Unfortunately, that tells you nothing about the next time you flip it. The odds don't change, or mature. They remain exactly the same as before, 50-50.

If you think we are talking through our hats, feel free to visit any casino. There you will see an opulent world paid for by millions of people who thought that they could use statistics based on past experience to predict the future.

All people are interested in getting predictions in almost any form (consider, for example, the stock market frenzy of the 1990s). But the

Uniqueness Question Forward emphasizes how important it is to carefully consider the largely unstated factors that surround each situation before making any effort to "predict" anything about it and before taking the necessarily risky action based on such predictions.

**QF: What are the possible impacts of the whole range of conditions from which a prediction of a future situation is drawn?**

## The Uniqueness Paradox

*QB: Is every situation really unique?*

Is taking a shower tomorrow morning or brushing your teeth tonight going to be a unique situation for you every single time you do it?

On a microscopic level, yes, because statistical theory shows you will not do these routine tasks in exactly the same way every time. On a realistic level, no.

We all need certain things to be routine…on autopilot. There just isn't enough time in the day to approach each moment uniquely. Likewise, certain procedures in business also are and should be routine. For instance, controlling a nuclear power plant, inspecting an airplane before loading passengers, and driving a bus are all good spots for having set routines in place! You want people in these jobs to do each routine task the "same" way every time.

But you also want them to treat the overriding big-picture purpose of these tasks, to run the thing safely, to be the place where they apply the uniqueness idea. They must always view these routines with an eye toward unique signs that an emergency is developing.

That's the paradox: Perform routines the same each time while also viewing each of them with the uniqueness perspective in mind— as if you were doing it for the first time. That way, you eventually may be develop a major breakthrough for doing what others consider routine.

Thus, always starting from the premise of uniqueness is a powerful force in getting each of us to transcend habitual thinking traps that come from being socialized into systems of thought and practice. It moves us to another level of consciousness. At the same time, paradoxically, we also have to understand that many of our routines, while microscopically unique, do exist as established processes.

To sum up the paradox and put into useful terms: A good minimum threshold to set for invoking uniqueness questions is that every interaction with others should be viewed as unique.

**QF: What potential buy-ins for my "great idea" can I obtain by considering initially every situation as unique?**

## Watch Out for Your Own Hidden Agenda
## When Asking Questions

*"You talking to me?"*

If you remember this line from the film *Taxi Driver*, then you recall that the character had an agenda when he asked the question. He was picking a fight.

The question you have got to ask yourself is, "What is the agenda hidden behind my question(s)?"

You've read all this and probably now you think you're pretty clever. You are going to go in to work tomorrow and ask questions that show them the way.

If you do this, your agenda is to lead with questions. A typical leading question is of the form, "Doesn't it seem like the only reasonable approach is to (fill in your great idea here)?"

This is very dangerous and not in the spirit of asking the right questions. Plus, you will probably be stunned by the rejection your questions generate.

"Why can't they see that the answer is bla-bla-bla?" you will think to yourself.

Then you will probably try to tell them what the answer should be. This is also not in the spirit of asking the right questions.

The only agenda behind Question Forward is to try to frame questions along the lines of the Uniqueness Question Forward and others that we are going to explain in the following chapters.

## RECAP

Let the idea of uniqueness guide you whenever you face a problem, opportunity, or issue. When you ask those questions about what to do and will this approach work here, remember that you have to keep foremost in your mind that other solutions from other times and places can only serve at best as a rough possibility.

Let uniqueness underscore the importance of variety and differences. This way you won't fall into the trap of mistakenly seeking premature solutions. The human desire to find what is common between things, to use metaphors, categorization, and either/or dualisms has to be fought, if you hope to find a new, unique and successful answer to your questions and problems.

Starting the process by stressing uniqueness also makes dealing with change a transformational, rather than destructive, opportunity. New metaphors emphasizing the uniqueness of the situation, for example, can be used as a lens to explore dimensions of interpretations and meanings.

Even though this effort to focus on the uniqueness of the situation may produce a fair amount of mental strain, it's worth it. It lets you reach a new depth, to dive past the rote answers and pat solutions that will not work so that you can reach something new. It can let you

*Gerald Nadler and William J. Chandon*

embrace the richness of life's variety and open yourself to possibilities and learning. Starting with uniqueness is a way of getting "unstuck."

## The Uniqueness Question Forward : How Can We Initially Consider Every Problem, Situation, and Issue as Unique?

## Reflective question

In what ways are you (or your family) unique—what is it that you (or the family) bring to the world that no one else does?

# Chapter 2

# PURPOSEFUL INFORMATION

Every question generates information in the form of answers. Ask me for the facts and I will give them to you. At least I will give you what I see as the facts.

**The questions you ask determine the answers.**

*Ask me for the time it takes to move a specific item from the factory floor to the loading dock and I will give you that information. You may need to know that to solve your problem, or you may not need to know it and it may mislead you.*

The movement of that specific item may be irrelevant to the real hidden problem and the time it takes may just be a symptom. How can you tell what information is purposeful versus that which isn't purposeful? The short answer is that you have to figure out the purposes of solving the problem first and then start to consider possible solutions. This will begin to help sort out what information is purposeful and what isn't. Information that pertains to developing and implementing solutions is more likely to be relevant than information that pertains to problems or analyzing the "current state." This will become clearer in Chapters 4-7 where you will see how we use a systems matrix for information gathering purposes; but for now, suffice it to say, that as you become clearer about possible solutions, you will become clearer about what information is likely to be relevant.

**The Purposeful Information Question Forward: How Can We Identify and Collect Only Purposeful Information?**

*QB (Question Backward): Why don't you collect all the information so we can make this decision?*

You've seen it many times already if you work at a company that has meetings. People show up with gobs of data, PowerPoint presentations, charts, and graphs, but how do you know what you need? Usually the kind of information that people typically collect is about the problem or the current state. This plunges people even further into a cycle of confusion and cynicism.

The only way to cut through the morass of meaningless information is the recognition that information, facts, and data are all very subjective, non-absolute "things." They are shaped by the questions we ask, to which they are, at best, a partial answer. You will see that the questions we ask in Question Forward about information are more about the purposes and solutions than they are about the problem or the current state.

**QF: What information will help us begin
to think about creating a solution?**

## A BRIEF HISTORY OF THE NATURE OF INFORMATION

**QF: What information is needed to stimulate creativity
in developing and specifying our living solution?**

In order to help answer the question about what information is useful or relevant, we need to first say some things about "information."

Some say we are in the Information Age, when our progress is defined by our ability to use, transport, and manipulate information.

They suggest that it's much like the Industrial Age, which was defined by our ability to use, transport, and manipulate raw materials and the available information about them in newly devised and massively more efficient ways. Humans had used iron and fire and steam before. But it was the first time we had organized the activity of manufacturing on such a massive scale.

For better and for worse, by the way.

30

This massive organization made more stuff available and improved the lot of consumers everywhere. It brought lifesaving engineering feats, like vast public sewer and transportation systems that together made starvation and diseases like the plague a thing of the past in the industrial nations.

The Industrial Age was first a machine age, when we first started making things like interchangeable parts and machines to automatically do repetitive tasks, including making other machines. This developed into the full-blown industrial age of manufacturing beginning around 1900. The information about this age glowed with the optimism about what benefits industrialization would bring to people. But did the information include all the facts about the reality of the industrial age? For example, did it describe how it broke up families by moving the center of work from the home into factories and offices?

The daily family-based lifestyle or "very local" group style served the species well during man's earliest nomadic tribal days and through the Neolithic (when people first settled down to herd and farm). This lifestyle stayed in vogue until the dawn of the Industrial Age in the late 1800s.

At no moment did the developers of interchangeable parts and assembly lines include in their solutions information about the impact on the reality of parenting, or family or "me."

And viola! Here we are.

Our newly dawning Information Age doubtlessly also creates a huge lack of information about the age's "reality." We've already got an epidemic of carpel tunnel from too much clicking on badly built keyboards. The isolation from hours spent on the machine and the disembodied online experience have led to a like rise in mental disorders—and given greater leverage and capabilities to the deranged among us.

Have your ever asked yourself, "Do we have information about how instant access for everyone, including criminals and children, to all forms of good and bad information will affect parenting or family or me, the individual?" Wouldn't we all have preferred it if people developing stuff on the Net had given more weight to getting information about that and many other questions concerning the reality a wee bit earlier on? (Chapter 3 on systems will show how such unintended consequences might be ameliorated given the circumstances that any information about any reality is always incomplete.)

## INORMATION ONLY REPRESENTS REALITY

*"Mysticism is not how the world is, but that it is."*
Ludwig Wittgenstein

*Once upon a time three blind men came upon an elephant. Elephants did not live in their country, so they had never encountered one before and had no idea what sort of beast it might be. Each ran his hands over a different part of the animal's body. The one who felt the elephant's hind leg said, "This animal is stout and shaped like a tree."*

*The second blind man ran his hands over the elephant's tail and said, "This animal is slim and moves quickly, like a snake."*

*The third blind man handled the tip of the elephant's snout and the very tip of his trunk. He said, "No, you are both wrong. This animal has a delicate hand-like appendage at the end of a massive arm. He is doubtless built like we are, with arms and hands."*

*None of them could gather the information they needed to describe the elephant.*

The real nature of anything is an approximation, because our information or knowledge of it is always incomplete. Information is always distinguishable from its physical entity or social reality. But technological seers continue to make estimates, for example, of how much information is contained in a person's lifetime of experiences (inputs to the brain) and when sufficient computer memory will be available to store the, say, $2.2 \times 10^{17}$ bits. Or when a person's individuality (estimated at $10^{27}$ bits) can be stored. Are these seers asking the right questions? Not if they understood the nature and representational character of information. Even if enough computer memory were available, would the computer memory be a brain that many of them claim it would be? Of course not, because it is only a representation of the experiences or individuality, not the experiences and individuality themselves nor the ability to get more experiences. Plus, the brain is also much more for tomorrow's life—motor control, emotions, sense mechanisms, and so on. At best, all that information may provide some tentative conclusions about the reality of the brain, just as the "conclusions" provided before the $17^{th}$ century were that the sun moved around the earth.

If you don't ask the right question, you still get an answer, but not necessarily the right one. That is, the information it contains won't include any data about whatever you did not ask—and the missing information might be crucial to understanding the thing that you are trying to get an idea of. We use this partial information, combined with both explicit and hidden assumptions to draw our conclusions about any situation or "real" thing (or elephant) in this world. And we assume that what we didn't ask about, the information we didn't gather, is not important in creating our pictures of reality or making our decisions

*"Nature will always exceed our perceptions and our language."*[13]

Here are some premises to keep in mind when trying to figure out what is *really* going on:

- Information is a human construct.
- Information comes from all the senses.
- Information is never complete.
- Information is inaccurate and imprecise.
- The amount of information available increases exponentially. Huge amounts of quickly available

Information do not ensure quality or reduction of uncertainty.

- Information has a time value.

**QF: Does this information make sense to you?**

- **Information is a human construct.**

*"The ends of information, after all, are human ends.... For all information's independence and extent, it is people, in their communities, organizations, and institutions, who ultimately decide what it all means and why it matters."[14]*

People communicate with people and observe reality. Animals before humans did the same things with grunts, motions, bodily agitation, and stares. People bring to both these activities a raft of values and preconceptions that appear in language (a type of information). Every work problem is like a crime in a police drama. The eyewitnesses will each describe the event differently, even though they all "saw" the same thing. Here are some things that can make information unreliable.

There are so many languages, not to mention each of our own verbal mannerisms, each describing the same thing differently. Eskimos have five words for snow that subtly describe different types of snow. In English we have just the word for snow. Hidden in the word(s) are vastly different cultural values.

When you talk about information or data or facts, you are talking about a representation of some situation. What you state is not the actual situation itself. This means that you have translated whatever it is that is really there into some language that represents it. The language can be math or English or French—or bar charts.

**QF: What are you trying to convey
by the information you present?**

*QB: Is all the information in this report from measurements you made at the scene?*

- **Information comes from all the senses.**

Your eyes can fool you…and so can any other sense you care to name, including common sense. And let's not forget intuition, sometimes called a sixth sense, whatever it really is.

All six of these senses (and even more based on modern understanding—balance, pain, heat, hunger, thirst, etc.) can be wrong at point-blank range. A poignant op-ed article in the *New York Times*, "I Was Certain, but I Was Wrong," makes this clear. It told of a victim who testified at several trials that some man was her attacker, only later to be proven wrong by a DNA test. During her ordeal, she had even made heroic efforts to memorize her attacker's characteristics so she could identify him with absolute certainty, if she ever had the chance.

**QF: Did you get any other impressions about the scene that would add to the measurements?**

*QB: Did you get all the facts?*

- **Information is never complete.**

How much information do you estimate it would take to describe the reality of the book that you are holding? You can start with the blurb on the cover and end up with a mathematical description of a quark. Along the way you would need to describe the ink used and its composition, the chemistry of the paper, the glue used to hold the cover on, and the color spectrum used on the book jacket as well as the content.

The amount of information to gather about any reality to no particular purpose is infinite. So all those fancy models (be they mathematical, graphical, physical, or pictorial), and however useful they may be, are by definition incomplete representations of the actual reality.

**QF: What other perspectives about the situation should we consider beyond the information we have?**

*QB: Is this information accurate?*

- **Information is inaccurate and imprecise.**

Perfect information is not attainable simply because information is always incomplete. There are no such things as "hard" facts or perfect information, regardless of how often people, managers in companies especially, insist on getting them and even with the most advanced statistical techniques that verify the inaccuracies. Personal, group, community, client, and cultural biases lead to inescapable "errors."

These most important aspects of any situation are usually impossible to measure clearly or put a figure to. Many organizations today, for instance, realize that real financial (today's most revered measurement) success is based primarily on attitudinal and behavioral relations its employees have with all stakeholders—not just on price-to-earnings ratios and the like. All measurements have some dysfunction, regardless of how much anyone proclaims they have *accurate* measures of the *right* things. And measures hardly make a dent in describing a reality. However much the measure of gross domestic product, as an illustration, is changed to make it more "realistic," it never represents the whole reality of the economy. What index of well-being, costs of health care, beauty of writing, safety of our communities, strength of our compassion, or early death from pollution are included in the GDP?

*"[Gross domestic product] measures everything...except that which makes life worth living, and it can tell us everything about our country except those things which make us proud to be part of it."*
Robert Kennedy

Yet the glamor of the Information Age continues to lead technologists to proclaim that the day of complete accuracy will be with us soon. Measurement thinking is the language of American public life. The infinite amount of information about any reality, be it physical, social, or organizational, means that the finite amount we do collect, however large it may be, will always be inaccurate.

**QF: With how much inaccurate and imprecise information are we willing to make a decision about this situation?**

*QB: How much information is available about this situation?*

- **The amount of information available increases exponentially.**

The lack of completeness, accuracy, and precision and the availability of ever-faster computers combined with our interest in new abstractions and representations of reality increase the rate of information overload and, at worst, create disinformation. Information garbage (or data smog) is already overwhelming people. Even filtering software to identify information you want based on your current pattern of use depends on the unreasonable assumption, in our dynamic times, that our information needs of yesterday reflect our needs of tomorrow. Nor does the software promote the brain's amazing ability to find novel connections between seemingly disparate types of information.

The conventional approach that requires the collection of a lot of data often so overwhelms a group or individual that it's known as 'analysis-paralysis' in the change management field. A frequent question in almost any business is, "How do we stay afloat on the oceans of data?"

**QF: How long might we have to wait until more reasonable information will be available?**

*QB: Shouldn't we wait until new information increases the quality of what we have?*

- **Huge amounts of quickly available information do not ensure quality or reduction of uncertainty.**

*Gerald Nadler and William J. Chandon*

Asking endless questions so that you get an overwhelming amount of information can bury what's useful to create a solution.

Decreasing quality and increasing uncertainty are illustrated by distortions that take place now that we have more "news" than ever, thanks to the Internet. News providers can now spread unfounded rumors and gossip, passing as information. As the inaccurate information spreads, it becomes considered more authoritative, more accurate, of higher quality, and less uncertain. It is not; it is disinformation.

**QF: What is the reliability of the sources of this huge amount of information?**

*QB: How can the information about this type of situation that we collected three years ago help us now?*

- **Information has a time value.**

The more time that has elapsed between the gathering of data and creation of information, the more likely it is to be wrong. A decade-old biology textbook contains a bunch of bad information. Your data collected to solve a problem will most likely become increasingly wrong the further away in time it is from the implementation of your solution.

**QF: What factors about this type of situation have changed in three years that might make the information from then less valuable?**

## ALL INFORMATION IS NOT EQUAL

Saying something is "information" is like calling anything that flies a bird. Not everything that zooms through the air is of avian nature. Clouds, rocks, planes, rockets, soccer balls all fly, too. That's why it is important to recognize that calling something information doesn't make it the same thing as some other type of information. And doesn't make it right, either.

Some information just looks like information; it's really just garbage that describes nothing, like circumstantial evidence, which is not real evidence at all. Beyond that, even if it is information, not all information is the same.

## LEVELS OF INFORMATION

*"Where is the wisdom we have lost in chaos and complexity?*
*"Where is the knowledge we corrupted in 'Knowledge is Power'?*
*"Where is the information we have lost in information overload?*
*"Where is the data we have lost in answering*
*the wrong questions?"[15]*

In order to squeeze a useful truth from information, you have to ask yourself, "What can I make of this information?" A better question might be, "What kind of information is this?" (There are no fine dividing lines between any of the following levels of information. The levels are only meant to be descriptors of many of the words associated and loosely used interchangeably with the word "information.")

## RAW DATA

*QB: Is this all the data about what happened here?*

It's like you're a cop arriving at the scene. You collect the initial "raw" observations using your senses and the help of experts (like the coroner) and various technologies (like DNA matching). In more everyday situations, these might be outputs of a manufacturing line, level of accomplishment of a seventh grade class, responses on a survey questionnaire, acres flooded by a river, testimony of a trial witness.

Trying to completely abstract or represent any reality with raw data, however, is not possible.

The ultimate validity of all such raw data depends on the way in which it was gathered and the context associated with it. If you measure room temperature by a heating vent, you will not get the average room temperature. If you assume that your temperature readings are the same throughout the room, you will be very cold or hot indeed.

If you measure your productivity by the number of items you ship, without regard for the number returned because they are defective, you will not get a very good idea of it. If you ask your workers how morale is you will probably get different "raw data" than you'll get from asking management the same question.

In other words, both human observation and physical measurement criteria play a role in whether or not your "raw data" is data that informs, or garbage that confuses.[16]

This sounds pretty obvious. But today the first question most people ask when faced with a problem is "Can you get me the data?" Because data is so easily transmitted anywhere in the world with modern technology, this question leads to the flood that overcomes almost everyone.

Instead, they should be asking, "What is the criteria that will allow us to collect the data that will actually inform us so that we can create a real solution to the actual problem?" Mere volumes of useless or irrelevant data do not add anything to creating solutions that work.

The questions that are posed before the data-gathering process is set up are far more important to a successful outcome than the volume of raw data collected. If you rush in with the wrong question, that is ask for action before determining what the purpose of collecting the data is, you will drown in pointless non-information.

**QF: What are pertinent types of data to gather and how do we minimize messing it up?**

## "REAL" INFORMATION

*QB: What really happened here?*

Putting raw data together is like making a house out of cards or a word out of letters. It gives you the next level of representation, or "real information." That the cards are making a house or the letters a word are the assumption you make, to make sense of the cards, letters—or data. What's right depends on them. Like a good detective, you should always ask yourself, "Are the assumptions I used when gathering the data appropriate for coming up with solutions to the problem at hand?"

There are many techniques for putting data together in a way that helps you see "the forest" and not just the "trees." The most popular ones are statistics, charts, and graphs (models that could range from descriptive to mathematical) that can also be transmitted quickly around the world because of modern technology. These do help. But this manipulation of raw data has to be done carefully, with ever-present attention to the underlying assumptions with which you collected the data in the first place as well as those assumptions that underlie statistical manipulation. Otherwise you may corrupt your raw data's value by ignoring the limitations of such manipulation imposed by such hidden assumptions. Almost all models, especially forecasting, omit almost everything of interest: national politics, technological change, greed, fear, ambition, and even the weather.

For example, if you collected temperature data in a room during the summer months, you can't assume that it will be the same during winter. If the room was empty of computers and people (both give off considerable heat), you can't assume that the average temperature in the room will be the same when filled with your gear and staff as when it was empty.

Raw data is always about the past, too. If El Nino strikes, your temperature measurement may be way off. So you must always use care when drawing conclusions about what will be from what has been.

We tend to worship information, and worse, to worship anything that is in the form of information. Remember that there is no actual truth in information, that it is not necessarily or objectively connected to the reality of your problem. You made certain assumptions when you were gathering it and manipulating it that, if true, made the representation as information of the underlying problem appropriate and helpful. But if you ignore or distort these assumptions, then whatever information you come up with will be wrong.

**QF: What possible scenarios could explain the set of data?**

## KNOWLEDGE

*QB: How can these charts and statistics support my theory?*

Once you are informed by information, you are at the gateway to knowledge. In other words, being informed about current events doesn't mean that you know what happened. Only after digesting and putting together all the real, relevant information yourself do you know what happened. Knowledge is complex and interactive. It has meaning to you. You can do something with it. You can make decisions, take action, or decide not to take action.

Knowledge is the next level of representation. To know implies that you have "triangulated" on your purpose. You have been able to validate information from multiple sources or perspectives. You have been able to ask questions and get answers that provide real information that has been weighed, like evidence. Now you are putting together all those answers and real information to see the big picture.

By combining different types of real information, knowledge adds interpretation, experience, history, and additional context to your representation of the issue. Standardized test scores, for example, are combined and manipulated in many ways with other information (such as essays and grade-point averages) and individual perceptions by teachers to figure out what pupils know.

Another thing about knowledge that makes it different from information is that it is not separate from the person who knows it. You can ask, "Where is the information?" But "Where is the knowledge?" sounds wrong somehow, unless you mean it in the sense of "Who knows it?" Even the most advanced technology cannot transmit knowledge embedded in the brain of an individual. People, not machines, have knowledge.

According to John Seely Brown, director of the Xerox Palo Alto Research Center, and Paul Duguid, social and cultural studies research specialist at the University of California at Berkeley, there are three generally accepted distinctions between knowledge and information.

"1. Knowledge usually entails a knower.

"2. Given this personal attachment, knowledge appears harder to detach than information. Someone can send you the information they have, but not the knowledge.

"3. Knowledge seems to require more by way of assimilation. A person can have conflicting information, but not have conflicting knowledge."

In other words, while real information can exist on its own, knowledge does not exist outside the minds of people. Thus, although technology is assumed to mean some modification of nature to meet human needs, it also includes the knowledge about processes that create and operate the products and services as well as the infrastructure required to design, make, and repair them.

*What does it mean when we say we know something in a world governed by chance?*

A note of warning about the misuse of the word knowledge

"Knowledge management" is a current phrase that has all the markings of a fad (as in the fads described in Chapter 1). The distinctions among the levels of information noted here would indicate clearly that almost all efforts at knowledge management are really information management at best. Knowledge management is, among other things, an attempt to make explicit what is tacit—knowledge about content, culture, process, and infrastructure—among members of the group, trying to make collective what is now individual knowledge.

I had the opportunity to review a CD from a very large company that was labeled knowledge management for its marketing research activities. The compilation of reports was extensive, but reading quite a few of them showed clearly that they were compilations of data and information. Any knowledge that might be ascribed to them would have to be imposed by the reader.

> *"Real knowledge is to know the extent of one's ignorance."*
> Confucius

Databases of "best practices," another current phrase describing others' solutions either for benchmarking what you might be doing or for outright adoption (or imposition), do not and cannot incorporate some of the most important and elusive aspects of successful solution creation. This includes various types of knowledge such as expertise, personal contacts and relationships. These cannot be described accurately in databases because there is no clear and standardized way to collect such intuitive and subtle information other than asking a knowledgeable person what they think of the raw and real information you've gathered.

**QF: What does your background in this field
indicate these data and charts mean regarding our situation?**

## UNDERSTANDING

*QB: Who do I believe did it?*

Knowledge is not understanding. To understand means that you not only know the real story told by your digested information, but that you know what it means and how it fits in the big picture. You have gained broad insight about the area of concern or reality including its stories, morals, values, beliefs, implications, explanations, methods, and history. This lets you judge (like a jury and judge during the first part of a trial) guilt or innocence based on the case put forward by the knowledgeable prosecutor.

Another popular word to describe this level of representation is "intelligence." Many companies use this term when assessing their industry and competitors or in the military to provide a "picture" of the enemy. This is the level where you start asking, "How would a CEO, or the guy on the loading dock, or the competition down the street interpret these data, information, and knowledge?"

Integration of many types of knowledge, information, and data, one of the most complex of mental tasks, is the basis of this representation called understanding. Besides the usual patents and trademarks, "intellectual capital" is used as a phrase to denote the hidden value that employees and managers have of customer or client relationships, experiences, competencies, corporate culture and morale, and know-how, in effect, understanding the organization.

Understanding provides some overall logic or reasoning about what is known about the reality and the forming of possible mental models and conceptual frameworks about it. Knowing the relative worth of different types of knowledge about any given problem is the essence of your understanding of it.

### QF: Which scenario makes the more compelling explanation of the evidence?

## WISDOM

*QB: What does the law say to do (Free the innocent or what sentence do I give the guilty party)?*

Wisdom is the ability to put your understanding to use. Wisdom is the transformation of understanding into concrete action. It's like being the judge in the second half of a criminal trial when you decide what sentence fits the particular crime.

**QF: What purposes are we seeking to achieve in the solution creation process with these questions leading to information collection (the wisdom of deciding what's relevant)?**

Wisdom is pragmatic—the prisoner goes to jail or goes free. It applies a sense of values and beliefs—like justice and compassion—to knowledge and understanding in particular circumstances to come up with desirable results. How long should the guilty man serve? It's the insight into what is called for by the absorption of the raw data, information, knowledge, and understanding.

*"Experts often possess more data than judgment."[17]*

Everyone possesses some amount of wisdom just to survive, that is, they cope with daily life based on their ability to integrate and use the understanding of the reality in which they exist. The wiser you are, the better your ability to cope with and handle unusual local, community, societal, and international circumstances.

*For a biblical example, consider the famous tale of Solomon. Who is the mother of the child? The one who says no to the king's decision to cut the infant in two and give half to each petitioner.*

**QF: How do I act fairly and with compassion in this matter?**

## RECAP

*All information is wrong, but some is useful.*
Adapted from George Box.

Information only represents reality. There's an infinite amount of information, and you need to determine which data are useful to creating solutions and which will confuse the issue.

Information is also not absolute. It comes from your senses and measuring instruments that are fallible, so it's distorted by a number of factors. Thus, it is not accurate nor is it precise. It also ages; the longer the time between gathering information and the implementation of a solution, the more likely it is that your information will no longer represent the situation on the ground.

Beyond that, there are five different levels of information; that is, all information is not of the same type. There is raw data; "real" information that is synthesized from this raw data; knowledge that expresses your picture of the information; understanding that comes from putting your knowledge into a larger context of other types of knowledge that you have of the world; and wisdom that comes from applying your knowledge to come up with a practical, creative living solution.

**The Purposeful Information Question Forward: How can we identify and collect only purposeful information?**

**Reflective Question**

What do you think are all the types of data and information that could possibly describe any object or situation (e.g., pen, auto, couch, layout of your living room, an event many people attended)? Ask three to five colleagues if your list is complete.

*Gerald Nadler and William J. Chandon*

# Chapter 3

# SYSTEMS

**QF: What details about each dimension of each element are needed to specify how the solution we are creating will work?**

We all get frustrated when traffic flow is stopped too often by stoplights, invoices aren't paid on time, bus schedules aren't maintained, the furnace stops operating, social promotion in schools is discussed, or our physician is always late for an appointment.

"Someone ought to do something about this system," we cry.

But just calling it a system doesn't help solve the problem. After you've blamed the system or invoked the word, where do you go from there?

If we're actually trying to solve one of these problems, we might typically begin by deciding, "Let's start by getting all the details of the system." But how do you do that exactly (especially because Chapter 2 pointed out that it can't be done)? What questions do you ask to fix it or even describe it? Just using the word "system" doesn't mean you know what the system is or provide insight into what to do or how the right questions could be asked in developing a living solution.

**QF: What are all the elements and dimensions that need to be considered to develop an optimum and effective (say, traffic light sequencing) system?**

This is why you need some Questions Forward about "systems." The QF systems questions fit together as Foundation Questions with the Uniqueness and Purposeful Information ones (Chapters 1 and 2). It will lead you to many important questions to develop solutions (i.e., systems) that are "living," that is, ones that aren't static, but contain seeds of continuing change.

## The Systems Question Forward: What are all the elements and dimensions that need to be considered to develop a creative, workable, and integrated living solution?

Here's an example of how this Question Forward works in practice.

I was called by the president of an 1,800-employee advertising agency who described his problem as "why isn't anything positive happening based on the great strategic plan our management team developed at a two-day retreat a few months ago?" He said the group thought then that they had been very creative in developing a list of twenty-three values and beliefs they said would be all they needed as a strategic plan.

I asked questions about the purposes of the company, the various processes they used in the company's work, and the various resources they had to enable the work to be done. In effect, I was asking about what had been done to find out just how the "strategic plan" will work, an important prerequisite to getting it adopted. And did they consider the way the ideas get installed and implemented, both to help the ideas get adopted and to prepare for follow-up after getting broad-based acceptance and approval?

When he said they had done none of these things, I noted that my questions were raised from a systems perspective and that a strategic plan was a system that needed to be defined if the company was going to be effective in getting full benefits from a complete strategic plan. In short, just having a creative idea is insufficient, even if you have a whole list of them.

You need to systematically question the way things are going to fit together and figure out the details before you actually have a solution. That's when the light bulb went off in his head, and he set up the first meeting of the same team for me to facilitate.

After briefly describing the concept of the system matrix to the group, I asked them to determine what elements and dimensions each of their twenty-three values and beliefs concerned (each of them could be a part of one or more element/dimension combinations). They were surprised that their twenty-three statements (e.g. hire creative and cooperative people, establish a team-based partnership with clients, treat suppliers as members of "us") helped to define only two (of six) dimensions of five (of eight) elements. Acknowledging that they now saw why their retreat had not produced the results they had expected, they were motivated in the next several meetings to use the Question Forward approach of determining what the big picture strategic plan system ought to be.

## WHAT IS A SYSTEM?

*"Everything should be as simple as possible, but no simpler."*
Albert Einstein

Nothing exists in a vacuum—including an idea. Just like the forest is made of trees and each part of the universe is interconnected with every other part, so too are our ideas embedded in a vast universe or system. This system is made both of all the other ideas held by ourselves and our fellow workers and all the actual realities in the world—in which our answer or idea will have to play out.

Typically, someone generates an idea and presents it to the group. The idea is attacked; the person defends it; and if you're really unlucky, a bad idea gets taken up with no one having considered in detail its full implications.

Proposing *the* solution has similar difficulties. The immediate question that ought to be asked is "What arc all the system elements and dimensions that show how *the* solution would (or wouldn't) work?" And if you are the one who has the great idea, ask yourself this question before blurting out the idea. It will let you present the idea in a way that seeks the help of others in discussing how it would work.

51

Fortunately, you can use the idea of a system to help you structure the right questions. In fact, it lets you learn to generate questions you might otherwise have missed.

The idea of a system was invented when people (the word is credited to the Greeks) started to recognize that many descriptions of things were incomplete (as we discussed in Chapter 2). The word is used to describe a group of things that make a greater thing when they are connected together, like a system that accomplishes order fulfillment or health-care delivery, or makes up a larger whole, like a solar system or a political system.

In sum, this means that *everything is actually a system*—from a toothbrush, a kitchen, an organization, a car, an accounts payable procedure, a seminar, or a legislative bill. Just adding the word "system" to these illustrations—kitchen system, car system, seminar system—or any other so-called solution, however, doesn't mean it's workable. To determine that, you have to have a meaningful and understandable way to ask the right questions to create the system that you will call a solution. Nor can you assume something is complete, such as the advertising company's strategic plan, unless you consider it a system. It's like the old rhyme:

*The foot bone is connected to the ankle bone, the ankle bone is connected to the leg bone, the leg bone is connected to the thigh bone, the thigh bone is connected...*

Our studies of leading creators of solutions found that they had some sort of framework composed of elements (components, factors, constituent parts) and their dimensions (attributes, characteristics, properties) that they said led them to ask the right questions about potential solutions. If you don't ask the right questions, you increase the uncertainty about whether the solutions will actually work.

The elements of a system are usually described in economics, engineering, philosophy, and most disciplines as inputs, process, and outputs, with a feedback (of information about results) loop from outputs to inputs. The people we studied pointed out that these three may be satisfactory for the *analysis* purposes of those fields, but they were insufficient for determining what is needed to create answers that work in their *planning, design, improvement, development, and implementation* of assignments. In addition, they noted that each element needed to be specified in advance with other descriptors (dimensions) if their framework was to provide the basis for asking the right questions.

Beyond that, they noted that their idea of a framework goes far beyond the standard assumption about asking the commonly referenced *who, what, why, where, when,* and *how* questions for developing a complete description of something (what we are calling a system). They agreed that those six questions were better than nothing, but they emphasized that many more questions had to be asked to provide sufficient details about how a prospective system would work.

The system framework includes consideration of interactions among elements and dimensions of a proposed solution, priorities, passage of time, consequences (expected and unexpected) and has built-in ways to measure success or failure. It also has the usual specifications of basic operating conditions. It exposes the seven-eighths of every proposed solution or great idea that usually can't be seen—what we call the iceberg concept.

## What a system matrix is and how it is used

*QB: Why not just describe the critical outcomes of the proposal?*

Random and undisciplined asking of questions just gets you lost in byways and alleys; it won't get you to the thruway and take you home. Like a little child asking, "Why? Why? Why?" if you just keep on asking questions with no sense of direction or overall guiding framework, you will wind up lost in a maze of confusion.

There are many ways to organize your thoughts, as we discovered in our studies—every leading creator of solutions had a slightly different framework. Writers about systems and systems thinking also have different ways of describing such a framework, such as system dynamics modeling, functionalist systems approach, or critical systems thinking.

## Figure 3-1

## SYSTEM MATRIX

### DIMENSIONS

| | FUNDAMENTAL | VALUES | MEASURES | CONTROL | INTERFACE | FUTURE |
|---|---|---|---|---|---|---|
| PURPOSES | | | | | | |
| INPUTS | | | | | | |
| OUTPUTS | | | | | | |
| OPERATING STEPS | | | | | | |
| ENVIRONMENT | | | | | | |
| HUMAN ENABLERS | | | | | | |
| PHYSICAL ENABLERS | | | | | | |
| INFORMATION ENABLERS | | | | | | |

ELEMENTS

The most constructive way we have found to bring together their various perspectives is the system matrix (see Figure 3-1). It represents a picture that can become a part of your mental model about anything you are working on. The elements and dimensions, and the words or phrases used to capture their meaning, can be modified to fit the particular type of organization. In addition, the number of elements and dimensions, and the order in which they are presented, can be modified for your own needs. Some examples will be given after the following definitions of the elements and dimensions in Figure 3-1.

It is a checkerboard made up of rows of elements and columns of dimensions. Any of you who have taken a programming course will recognize that this is what is known in the business as a two-dimensional array. You can make things more complicated than this—for example, showing how each element, dimension, and even cell is a system that can be represented by a system matrix, a three-dimensional array in effect. But for most real-world purposes, the following elements and dimensions will stimulate your questions with a structured approach that leads to meaningful answers and viable solutions. And that's the point of a matrix.

A couple of other phrases in today's world that might be used to describe the point of creating a system matrix are "align strategies, processes, and technologies" and "manage fit across all activities." You may have heard these words coming out of the mouths of your team leaders before. The above matrix shows you how to do this aligning and managing with a minimum of fuss and unneeded complications.

### QF: What are the other elements needed to produce the proposal's critical outcome?

### A CLOSER LOOK AT THE MATRIX

To get a better feeling about the system matrix and how the cells help you generate the right questions, take a piece of paper and draw an 8-row-by-6-column checkerboard on it. At the top of the left hand side write "The Eight Elements" and directly above the main checkerboard, write "The Six Dimensions."

Down the left side by each row, write the following elements (just the titles) in this order (and make sure to include some of the six questions noted in parentheses as part of your question concerning each):

1. **Purposes**: missions, aims, needs, primary concern, function, what is to be accomplished (what); what are the purposes of creating, implementing, and operating the solution?
2. **Inputs**: people, things, and/or information to be worked on, made, or processed into outputs (who, what); who or what will be changed or modified by the solution?
3. **Outputs:** product, service, and/or response that achieves the purposes, desired and undesired consequences, outcomes

(who, what, where); what are the products, services, or outcomes of the solution?

4. **Process:** operating steps for changing inputs into outputs; flow, layout, unit operations; dynamic interactions among the other elements and process steps (how, where, who, when); what are the action steps required to create, implement, and operate the system?

5. **Environment:** physical and attitudinal, organizational policies, cultural setting, etc (where, why, what, when); what are the social, organizational, and political environments needed for creation, implementation, and operation of the solution?

6. **Human agents** (or enablers): skills, personnel, responsibilities, rewards, etc. (who, when, where, and how); who will enable the solution to be created, implemented, and operated?

7. **Physical catalysts** (or enablers): equipment, facilities, etc. (how, where, when); what physical things or technologies will enable the solution to be created, implemented, and operated?

8. **Information aids** (or enablers): books, instructions, Websites, etc. (where, how); what information will enable the solution to be created, implemented, and operated?

Now, along the top of the grid write above each column the following dimensions (and use the parenthetical words to aid in forming your questions):

1. **Fundamental:** basic or physical characteristics (what, where, when, how, who); what is it, where, who, how, when?

2. **Values:** goals, motivating beliefs, global desires, ethics, moral matters, quality and sustainability expectations (why, what, when); what values, beliefs, and principles should the solution encompass?

3. **Measures:** performance—criteria, merit and worth factors, objectives—how much, when, rates, performance specifications (when, why, where, how); how will success of attaining fundamental and values dimensions be measured?

4. **Controls:** how to set up feedback loops about and evaluate and modify the elements or system as it operates (what, where,

who, when, and how); how will we make sure the operation of the solution stays on track?

5.  **Interfaces:** relations and dynamics of all dimensions to other systems or elements (who, what, where, when, how, and why); who and what is affected by and can influence the successful design, implementation, and operation of the solution?

6.  **Future:** planned changes and research needs for all dimensions over time (who, what, where, when, how, and why); what are the implications we expect for the future?

This depiction of a system has distinctive features not included in the usual one offered in almost all other professions. In those, the outputs are usually *assumed* to be the purpose of the system, whereas this system framework shows that purposes are *not* the same as the outputs.

For instance, look at the book you are holding. What is the purpose of the system that has the book as an output? If you said "to produce books," you miss the huge advantage of considering the larger purposes of a book. For example, bigger purposes such as to convey information about its subject, to develop skills, and to gain knowledge are stimuli for generating other creative and living solutions where the information could have greater impact on its readers' lives.

In addition, the three enablers in the usual system definition are included as inputs whereas they are separate here to provide a basis for asking the right questions as you seek to create solutions. A human enabler, for example, needs many unique specifications in a living solution that differ from the specifications for the human customer (client, user, patient) inputs. Lumping the enablers into inputs almost always leads to assuming that "everybody knows what to do" about the enablers and, thus, postponing if not ignoring critical factors about the enablers in the detailing of a potential recommendation.

Even though the elements are presented as distinct categories (see Chapter 1), they are all interrelated. A specific product (output) of a company depends on and is related to the materials and design specifications (inputs), product operating instructions (another output) and the people who prepared them (human enablers), the steps taken to change the inputs into outputs, and the equipment used to produce it (physical enablers), to name a few. Then when considering the dimensions of each element, especially interfaces, a system is a network, composed of internal nodes and a node or hub among many external networks.

Furthermore, creating a solution does not necessarily proceed in the order the elements and dimensions are presented. Although the purposes element is the first and most important to be considered and specified, the others may be developed concurrently or in a different order.

Here's another example to better illustrate how this approach makes the development and acceptance of a solution easier.

The dean of a large midwestern public university's medical school asked me to help them develop a plan for a new medical center location on campus. As we proceeded to use all of the Question Forward methods, one of the early major milestones set up by the executive project team of twenty-two people (there were also twenty-nine project groups) was to prepare a proposal to the state legislature for funding of the building.

Because all of the twenty-nine groups were using the system matrix to describe their preliminary details, the executive project team was able to assemble them into an overall system framework. The executive team also used the system concept in developing a plan of presenting the proposal so that it would increase significantly the likelihood of it being approved, even though several legislative staff members were involved in the executive project meetings to help prepare the groundwork for such rapid acceptance by the "decision makers."

The proposal submitted to the legislature had eight tabs, one for each element, although different words were used for each element to make them more understandable to the general legislative reader.

Each of the eight sections included descriptions as needed of all of the dimensions of the system matrix.

The proposal was approved in the least amount of time on record for what was and still is the largest construction project in the history of the state. In addition, many legislators congratulated the dean and other university officials on submitting the most understandable and complete proposal they had ever seen.

## THE ELEMENTS

When you are looking for a successful plan, design, development, or improvement, your proposed system must—and can—be described in an easily understood approach that leads to effective questions as you are creating a solution. (Table 3-A1 at the end of the chapter is a "training-wheels" Starter Question Matrix to which you can add many more questions related to your area of concern.) In order for this effectiveness to happen, you have to aim for it from the beginning. So you have to start with questions about the most important element— your purpose or purposes. That is why it's first.

### QF: What are the purposes of the system that we are creating?

The purposes element develops your questions about what the system should be accomplishing.

You will quickly find out, if you let a little blue-sky into the process that the purposes get bigger and more encompassing fast. You'll go from "to get more storage around everyone's desks" to "to provide correct delivery schedule to customer at the time of taking the order" by continually asking "what is the purpose of that" for every suggested purpose.

The questions about purposes are so important that they form the basis of Chapter 5.

### QF: What inputs should our system have?

59

What people, things, and information do you need to be worked on, processed, or changed?

And what must you start with that will be included in any solution you come up with? Do you have to use coal and not natural gas? Are there people who are worked on by the process? Do you need specific information to start with to make your solution work?

Some physical items to ask about could be required amounts of steel, powdered plastic, money, a floppy disk, or a sales order form. Information could be a bank account balance, the location of an executive, knowledge content for a course, or production statistics.

The people who are "inputs" might be those who are sick on entering a hospital, a shopper in a store, a family looking for house plans, a student, or other customers or clients.

Every system requires at least two of these three types of input. The reason? A manufacturing system, for instance, might need information about the steel, such as the width and strength, as well as the metal itself. A patient would also be accompanied by information inputs—previous test results and the like.

### QF: What outputs that achieve our purposes do we want our system to have?

What type of physical items, information, people, and services do you want as the desired outputs or outcomes of your system? What are some possible undesired outputs or consequences of your system, such as pollution, dislocation of workers, scrap, waste, etc.? (The latter questions are meant to raise other questions at the earliest possible moment about what can be done to eliminate, minimize, and handle such outcomes.)

Outputs can also be properties such as performance, and physical and chemical characteristics of the output when actually being used. What sort of handling characteristics do you want the automobile (that is the output of your manufacturing process) to have? How much give do you want the shock absorber to have (which will affect ride and handling)? What should be the customer's (or user's) total experience of introduction, ownership, and communication?

You need to determine these desired outputs so you can anticipate the net gains in value that come from your solution and to prepare to deal with the undesirable side effects as part of your system specifications.

### QF: What are the processes we will use to create the outputs?

What are the necessary steps to convert the inputs into the outputs? How do they flow from one to the other? What are the unit operations or identifiable changes in the inputs as they are transformed into outputs? How do you lay out your work area to make these transitions move smoothly from one to the other?

Such steps include, but aren't limited to, causal bonds, movement, storage, meeting, decision, or control. Are there parallel channels for processing different inputs? Are there points at which such parallel channels interrelate and in what fashion do they come together? Do they merge? Do they intersect? Does one take over and the other stop? How do the steps affect the whole network?

### QF: What environment do we need to create within which the whole system will operate?

An environment is the psychological, political, cultural, legal, or economic factors that should be factored into solution creation. No human is an island, and no answer or solution takes place in a vacuum. What is the corporate culture, management style, organization ecology, and organizational climate that you want to create at your workplace? You need to address this aspect directly through direct questions—or your solutions won't actually work where the rubber meets the road.

Some of the sociological factors to ask about include the state of technology in the organization, the company culture and history that form the background of the present attitudes of its managerial and supervisory personnel, morale and reality of its workers, the operating

61

controls and rules for personnel, and the social interaction and communications of the people involved.

These factors concerning the environment don't just include those of the local workplace. They include the culture of the geographical and national area in which the workplace is located. Ask questions about any such particular cultural or historical issues by country or geography that may affect solutions to your problem. Are there any psychological, political, legal, or economic factors that should be factored into solution creation? *How could any of these factors be better specified to help achieve a more effective, creative, and living solution?*

What about physical environmental factors? Would climactic factors such as temperature, humidity, noise, dirt, light, colors of machines and walls play a role in an effective solution? Are accessibility, spatial aspects, shapes, and relationships issues of design of the physical facilities and equipment? What resources are to be used in the system that could be made available on a naturally sustainable basis rather than on continuing depletion of resource s. *How could any of these factors be arranged to achieve better outcomes and reduce residual impact on those working in the organization?*

## QF: Who are the human agents we need for operating our system?

These people are not the same people as those who might be "inputs" or "outputs" to your solution. That is, these are not the patients in the hospital example. Human agents are the nurses, orderlies, doctors, and others who enable the transformation of inputs (sick people) to outputs (healthy people).

What skills do these enablers need? What different types of personnel do you need to achieve your solution or to manipulate controls or change input items? Must they be able to reason, perform tasks with particular dexterity, make decisions, evaluate, learn, create or act as diligent monitors or sensors during the course of the process of changing inputs to outputs? What sort of rewards, punishments and other behavior modifiers should be applied to these human enablers?

There may be some overlap in individuals acting as both inputs and enablers (patients can help patients, for example). But the definitions of the two elements will help significantly in asking the right questions about the specific roles such individuals play in the system.

## QF: What sorts of physical catalysts do we need within our system?

What sort of equipment and facilities will you need? What physical resources will help you in each of the steps of transforming inputs to outputs that are not part of the outputs themselves (that is, they are not resources that become the outputs such as metal ingots and natural gas)?

Some typical items that you should explicitly ask if you need might include chalkboards, machines, vehicles, chairs, computers, filing cabinets, buildings, tools, jigs, automatic devices, paper, projectors, desks, sensors, and shipping pallets. You might also ask about energy and lubricating oil. But distinguish between what is needed to make the outputs and what is needed, for example, to heat the factory or offices—or lubricate machines that make the outputs but aren't part of the final product (such as the oil in a finished automobile motor).

A chicken on an egg farm is a physical catalyst or enabler. A chicken on a chicken farm is output. A computer may be a physical enabler in an accounts payable system, input in a maintenance system, and an output in a production system. Again, the definitions of the elements will help significantly in asking the right questions about the specific roles such items play in the system.

## QF: What sorts of information aids do we need within our system?

What knowledge and data resources will help at each step in the process (but that are not part of the outputs)? Do you need computer programming instructions, standard operating procedures, maintenance manuals, policy manuals, and Websites? Do you need expert guidance, such as a media consultant or legal advisor, to embody the role of information enabler?

## THE DIMENSIONS

The dimensions specify six properties or attributes for each element. (You may find that your particular situation requires that some of these be subdivided or that additional ones are added.)

### QF: What are the fundamental characteristics of the system (what, where, how, who)?

What are the tangible, overt, observable physical, or basic characteristics of the different elements of your answer or solution? What is it? Where will it take place? How will it answer the question or solve the problem? Who will be involved? Notice that the definitions of the elements in the previous heading are basically related to the fundamental dimension.

### QF: What are the values of the system—goals, motivating beliefs, quality perspectives, global desires, ethics, and moral matters—we want (why, who)?

What values are associated with the different elements? What is the value of (why) work on this project?

Values may be based on what you experience (that is, they may be feelings, emotions, desires, passions, and sentiments). They may also be related to your goals (for example, to have fun, to enliven living spaces, to eat gourmet foods, to improve productivity, to have a system based on naturally sustainable resources, to assure privacy of personal information, to make money). They may set ideals for living or practicing a profession such as law or medicine. They may also

64

relate to defining and preserving (or destroying) cultural and human values.

Values are almost always a guiding context within which the other dimensions are specified, so it is deeply tied to all the other dimensions. You can't even describe reality, the first dimension, without some underlying belief structure!

Focusing on this dimension lets you address whether or not to stick with existing values or to set out to change them. For example, your workplace might have a value that says a human enabler is "a hired hand." You might want to ask if that is as good as having someone who is "a participative and empowered employee." Answering with the latter value means you have to set up specifications in many elements and dimensions to move toward it as opposed to merely accepting what may already exist.

The values dimension and the following measures dimension are primary sources for determining the criteria to be used in decision making at many points of planning, design, development, and improvement. Conversely, the values of those involved in trying to create a solution should help determine what specifications ought to be included in the value dimension for each element. Whatever the solution seeks to enhance or promote (positively or negatively) are the values we're talking about here. For this reason, the values dimension is an indicator of the factors you will consider in determining how successful the system is when installed.

**QF: What are the measures we need to maintain our system and determine how successful it is—criteria, merit, and worth factors, and objectives of how much, when, rates, and performance specifications for the factors (what, how much, when)?**

How do you find out how you are doing in the attempt to translate the fundamental and values dimensions into specific measures (or objectives)? How do you measure the amounts of those factors to be achieved in a given time or for a given cost (performance measures or standards)?

Measures can be monetary or non-monetary. For example, you may have objectives such as: building employee or human enabler capital (a performance measure may be a 30 percent increase in training hours per employee within one year); building customer— part of output—satisfaction and loyalty (increase customer retention levels to 90 percent within two years); or contributing to corporate social responsibility—as part of environment (increase number of volunteers and hours from all levels of the company by 40 percent for each of the next three years) or as part of output (reduce by 33 percent per year the amount of toxic materials used in manufacturing).

Be careful to keep in mind the Question Forward of collecting only purposeful information here! As discussed in Chapter 2, too much unnecessary data can get you into as much trouble as inadequate amounts. So measure carefully and just what you need to if you can.

> *"Not everything that counts can be counted;*
> *and not everything that can be counted counts."*
> Albert Einstein

## QF: What are the controls we will need to maintain our system, as it operates, based on the measures (who, when, how, where)?

Since measures of the values and fundamental dimensions of the system elements can never be complete, accurate, and precise, the control dimension will similarly be incomplete. However, the control dimension is critical as a way of trying to avoid solution breakdowns and to foresee contingencies.

The basic maxim is to trust, but verify. What measurement methods can you put in place to determine what is occurring with the key fundamental, values, and measures dimensions of your solution while it is in operation? Will you be able to compare the actual measurements to the desired ones in real time (or enough time to deal with problems)? Are these measurements adequate to alert you to opportunities to correct the course mid-stream through human intervention, automated response, or advance modifications of equipment, by changing a desired specification or by designing an overall improvement on the fly? Are these measurements and controls adequate to alert you to upcoming catastrophic failures?

For example, computer networks are subject to all sorts of breakdowns and hacker attacks, and anticipating any number of disruption possibilities is a critical control specification for all parts of this dimension.

There are various techniques that can help you predict and manage these random problems. If you are dealing with a sophisticated problem, such as a computer network, you will find various probabilistic approaches to deal with such issues in the fields of chaos theory and adaptive systems.

In addition, the control dimension checks on the validity of the measures that are being made. For example, the value of customer satisfaction is often measured by customer surveys (as well as by specific data about response times for inquiries, on-time deliveries, customer turnover rate, returns and rejects, and referral rate). However, the response rate on surveys is often quite low, so the survey may not be valid as a good measure. Other ways of controlling the value of customer satisfaction, such as in-person visits and talks with as many customers as possible, may be better to find out their needs and their customers' needs. Such feedback is almost impossible to obtain with surveys.

But for more straightforward situations—what to do at the cafeteria during lunch hour when there is a huge rush, for example— you can use common sense and prior planning. What are the contingencies you need to think up solutions for ahead of time? How do you keep track of whether you are running out of something in time to make more? Put those questions here and then use the answers to build alternate plans.

**QF: What are the interfaces with other systems or elements we will need to operate and maintain our system (what, how, when, where, who)?**

No solution exists in a vacuum, so you have to make explicit the relationships between your solution and other systems, people, networks, and conditions in the world, and even between one element and another in the same system.

What are the consequences of implementing your solution? Will it change other systems? Does it affect other areas at your work or in the world at large? If you require overtime from workers, what impact will it have on traffic in your parking lot and child care costs? All these interfaces with other systems and issues outside of the immediate sphere of your solution should be questioned here.

Additionally, the interaction of different elements of your solution should also be questioned at this point. Some measures, such as costs, delays, and resource utilization, are most often considered only in terms of the particular system. Interface raises the question of the effects of the solution or its technology beyond its initial implementation. For example, the costs of poor quality start with those of rework, warranties, and scrap or discarded work.

There are four often hidden aspects of solutions that you should address in this interface dimension: hidden costs of unnecessary paperwork, wasted meeting times, and internal communications that ought to be the subject of a project to improve; lost revenues due to marketplace failures to meet customer needs; losses incurred by customers due to the poor quality of your outputs; and losses in the socioeconomic realm that affect a community such as products that can't be recycled, have harmful side effects, and whose production processes add to the toxicity of the environment.

Also consider the interfaces between your solution and the systems that are already out there. What sort of bridges can you build to connect or network your solution to other systems? What can be done to improve sustainability of resource usage by changing inputs, outputs, operating steps, environment, and physical enablers? A living solution frequently involves networks of connections among internal and external organizations and people that need to be established and/or continued in some form. Interface can also include such aspects or factors in order to ensure that your solution keeps working well.

## QF: What is the future of our system (what, when, how, who, where)?

Sometimes, it is worthwhile to examine the future of the solution if it were to be pushed to its extreme top or bottom limit. What, for example, would happen if the solution were wildly successful or depressingly ineffective?

Although the interface dimension addressed this question in the here and now, the questions that you ask about the future dimension aim to establish contingencies for your solution through time. Do relationships between elements and dimension stay the same as they are now or do they change because of predictable changes in the future (such as the evolution of the European Common Market or the move to hybrid electric automobiles)? What changes should be planned to occur when you have a future (living) solution target to guide you, as discussed in Section II? What research is needed to make the future solution target workable?

These definitions can help you set up a system matrix to suit your unique needs. Here is how one consultant did it: Elements—purposes, stakeholders, outputs/outcomes, inputs, process, physical catalysts human agents, environment, information aids, and capital; dimensions—physical, measures and specifications, control, interface, and future.

A product development department in a company did it this way: Elements—**purposes** (a) focus and (b) bigger ones of customers; **inputs** (a) humans, if any, and sources, (b) information and its suppliers, and (c) physical and suppliers; **outputs** (a) desired product or service (scale, size, shape, color, etc.) to accomplish purposes), (b) users and customers expectations of outputs, (c) post-output services, and (d) potential undesired outcomes of process and actions to eliminate them; **process** (a) human and/or physical flow and spatial orientation, (b) information flow, (c) feedback and feed-forward loops, and (d) post-output follow-ups; **environment** (a) attitudinal and organizational, and (b) physical and spatial; **human enablers** (a) operators and team qualifications and methods, (b) designer qualifications and methods, (c) manager qualifications and methods, (d) supplier and customer human links, and (e) services (maintenance, technologists, etc.); **physical enablers** (a) equipment, technology, tools, and (b) space requirements; and **information enablers** (a) manuals (maintenance, training, etc.), and (b) back-up documentation.

Their dimensions were **fundamental**; **values and quality** (a) external, (b) internal, and (c) regularities; **measures** (a) goals, (b) objectives, and (c) financial; **control** (a) how measure, (b) how compare with desired, and (c) possible actions if needed; **interfaces**; and **future** (a) next changes, and (b) R&D needs.

### llustration of How the System Matrix Can Clarify Meaning

Chapter 2 discussed the impossibility of words and information to describe any reality. Yet all of us exist in and deal with many realities, so some way of using descriptors of a reality is necessary. The system matrix helps significantly to fulfill this role.

The knowledge management movement mentioned in Chapter 2 does have merits organizations should consider. The following listing of system elements briefly illustrates some questions that need answers related to what knowledge management (KM) may mean in an organization. Section II provides the reasoning process to use in developing the answers for a specific organization. Notice how these and many other questions can be added to your Question Matrix (Table 3-A1) if you consider your field to be KM.

**Purposes:**
What should the KM system accomplish—make knowledge accessible to all employees, provide a resource for training, use knowledge as an asset, categorize project and customer knowledge, maintain a record of added value knowledge (patents, licenses, research reports, customer databases, parts descriptions and catalogs), and so on? What are the values of KM—generate new knowledge, leveraging our knowledge base, retain tacit knowledge of those

leaving the organization, transferability of knowledge, etc.? Questions for the other dimensions follow from these.

**Inputs:**
What level of information and knowledge should enter the KM system—project or work group, strategic decisions, related external knowledge, system matrix descriptions of competitors, and so on?

**Outputs:**
How should the KM system be organized—all entries are described in system matrix terms to provide a whole story and easy access by anyone seeking specific element-dimension information, types of technical know-how, and so on? What possible unintended consequences or unanticipated occurrences should be considered and handled?

**Processes:**
How and when will the inputs be handled to produce the outputs—gather reports and knowledge/information resources, prioritize them, determine the quality of the inputs, organize them into the output categories, enter the knowledge in the database, publicize availability of updates, etc.?

**Environment:**
What physical and organizational policies and procedures should we have to effectively set up and use KM—a separate department, organizational role definitions, top management commitments, internal or outsourced platform, and so on?

**Human Agents:**
Who will be assigned, trained, or hired to implement the process—content or KM skilled persons, capabilities as a coach or facilitator or consultant, full or part time, etc.?

**Physical Catalysts:**
How will the KM data be stored and handled—computer based, paper records, transparencies, microfiche, at what physical location will the equipment be located and outputs stored, are special temperature and humidity specifications necessary; and so on?

**Information Aids:**
What operating instructions, maintenance manuals, software packages, are needed for all the elements?

The many other questions not included above that could be generated by the dimensions of each element can be imagined (use

Table 3-A1 as a stimulator) given the nature of these questions. Also note the overlap with other elements and dimensions that occur among the questions listed for each element. And note that each question may not be needed in your activities. The Question Matrix is based on the premise that they are better to ask (than not) as a stimulus for you to consider all possible complexities of a system and to let other questions arise in your mind from those that are asked.

## PURPOSES AND GOALS OF THE SYSTEMS QUESTIONS

The system matrix helps you to develop questions that lead to creative, effective, and living answers by providing the following:

**1. A common language for discussing and describing problems, solution ideas and recommendations.** The elements and dimensions provide a language or imagery for forming questions everyone involved can understand. In addition, the matrix helps you focus any questions and possible answers on the important elements and dimensions.

It also helps to stimulate the development of complete stories. A story is a narrative of what a coherent solution might look like.

Stories are often used in several parts of creating solutions, such as generating options for a future solution target (Chapter 6) or describing a training plan (Chapter 7). A story is also a way of recounting what happened in, say, a project or incident (the cases in this book are a form of story). Because a story is supposed to be a representation of a past, present, or possible future reality, a system framework raises questions that help the narrator to consider the factors that may make the account more understandable.

**2. Detailed specifications of what your answer or solution will look like once it is put in place.** It will also help you to lay out the major activities and events needed to move from questions and answers—through approval of a solution and to implementation of the approved plan. There are many tools for depicting various aspects of a system, but they are inadequate because they fail to interrelate all of them. Rather than checklists and other isolated descriptions of what will take place, the systems Question Forward and its matrix lets you put all the different elements of any possible solution (and all the questions that you must get answered) into a context of all other implications and other aspects of a potential solution.

**3. Crucial information on how any solution will function over time.** Too often we come up with solutions that work now, but fail to take into account easily predictable changes in the future (faster computers for example) that may affect them. This provides protection against becoming complacent after you find your first solution. By forcing you to think of everything as part of a fluid, ever-changing system with dimensions and elements, trouble is avoided down the line. It also encourages you to define desirable future changes that might be made when you learn about newly available technology or information. If you continually review all the elements and dimensions while you are at a meeting, it lets you ask the right questions.

**4. Explicit documentation of the solution after this solution.** Too often, the idea that this solution will get us so far and then we will have to take other steps is lost along the way. The systems questions force you to clearly address what happens after this solution has served its purpose before you rush to implement it. This leads to rather thorough speculation about the future. The dimension of the matrix that talks about the future forces you to think about any possible answers to your questions with the future in mind.

**5. A reduction of the odds of failure.** Or at least the matrix can greatly reduce failure due to risks and unexpected causes. Too often we just hand-wave away the difficulties involved in any particular course of action, say, the adoption of a hot technology. Some failures can be protected against with redundancy, others can't. But you had better do your best to surface potential pitfalls and weak points in the initial planning phases. Systems and organizations should view such possibilities as a means of crisis leadership, that is, including within the solution methods for handling and managing crises (think Firestone tires) should they arise even though steps are taken to avoid them. The system matrix provides an excellent way to minimize unintended consequences, efforts at pushing technology for technology's sake, and unwanted side effects. The law of unintended consequences—any change or policy for the future will very likely produce unexpected reactions and/or unanticipated consequences—will continue to be a real-life factor to consider even though the odds of failure are significantly reduced with the system matrix. For example, the 911 emergency call system has been blocked to many legitimate emergencies because of an amazing number of weird calls, many of which might have been anticipated if questions about the fundamental, values, and measures dimension had been asked when it was being designed.

> *"A common mistake that people make when trying to design something completely foolproof is to underestimate the ingenuity of complete fools."* Douglas Adams

**6. Assistance in making decisions.** Because a decision involves selecting one alternative from several at each point where a choice is needed, the details made possible with the system framework presented here are often crucial. Several of the previous items above imply that a choice is required, and selecting the eventual recommendation is often considered *the* crucial decision where almost all details of system workability are supposed to be available.

**7. Simplification of control and correction procedures.** The matrix puts controls in the perspective of the larger system and lets you stop micromanaging and push decisions down to the appropriate levels. It also lets you simplify the complexity of a solution because it exposes all levels of possible interactions.

**8. Encouragement of continued learning.** Any organization must continue to learn in order to grow. The matrix, with its emphasis on solutions, fosters an environment of continued education and development, both of systems and workers.

Chapter 8 will discuss how these purposes and goals help to create a powerful dynamic perceptiveness in an organization.

# RECAP

## The Systems Question Forward: What are all the elements and dimensions that need to be considered to develop a creative, workable, and integrated living system?

A system is more than just a word—it is a way of approaching the world and forming the right questions about reality. A system model helps people to see the wholeness of their actions and the ways in which it interacts with other systems and with other people. It also lets you speculate with some reliability about both the eventual outcome of your proposed solution and the types of changes you will have to create new solutions for over time. A system matrix of eight elements and six dimensions provides a reasonably straightforward way to apply the Question Forward way of systems thinking and asking the right questions.

Developing these questions is a process that comes from exploring the meaning of each cell in the matrix (that is, the way the elements and the dimensions interact) when focused on a specific problem for which you wish to create a solution.

The exact wording of the questions will vary based on the specific circumstances and what form of the system matrix you are using (see Figure 3-1 and the wording used before by a consultant and a product development department).

As you review Table 3-A1, a question matrix, you can develop other questions for each cell that are more fine-tuned to your specific situation. Your particular arena of work (human resources, sales, accounting, manufacturing, marketing, career guidance, technology commercialization, project planning and management, zoning changes, office layout, organization design, teaching, negotiation, change agent, etc.) will bring particular words, phrases, concepts, techniques, and models into use in raising questions. Some right-brain or visual-oriented people may want to ask about the usefulness of pictures, drawings, scenarios, mind-maps, or tree diagrams in describing one or more cells.

## Reflective Question

After you identify all the elements and the dimensions of a system you work with, how would this information help you in describing what you do to a friend?

## Table 3-A1
## A Starter Question Matrix

# PURPOSES ELEMENT

## Fundamentals Dimension

What is the focus purposes in its most fundamental terms?
What purposes does it support? (What are its larger purposes, missions, and strategy?)
Do the focus and larger purposes help achieve customers' and customers' customers' purposes?

## Values Dimension

What are the values, qualities, culture, and beliefs that you and your organization want (not just what exists) to accompany the focus and larger purposes?
What organizational leadership is needed to support the focus purpose(s) and values?
Do the focus and larger purposes help achieve customers' and customers' customers' purposes?

## Controls Dimension

How will you measure what is happening related to your purpose as the system would be operating?
What early warning signals should there be so that you know if you're off or ahead of desired measures?
What contingency plans or actions are there to get back on track?
How will you know when the purposes are being achieved?

## Measures Dimension

What are the measures of purpose accomplishment (MPAs) or key success factors? How do they relate to the larger purposes?
How can they assess achievement of the values?

## Interfaces Dimension

How do your focus and larger purposes interface with the other elements and dimensions of your system?
Do your outputs support your purpose? Do you have proper inputs?

Are the larger purposes in the hierarchy consistent with the values of your future human enablers?

How do the purpose(s) interface with the elements and dimensions of other systems? What systems? Parallel? Parent? Subordinate? External?

## Future Dimension

What larger purposes in the hierarchy might become the focus in two or three years?

What other values, measures, controls, and interfaces might be developed for this or larger focus purposes?

# INPUTS ELEMENT

## Fundamentals Dimension

What are the inputs the solution will need to be worked on, converted, or processed – physical, human, monetary, information/data, outputs of other systems, feedback from this system (all inputs require at least two of the three types—physical items, information, or people)?

What specifications about the inputs will this system need?

How are competitors likely to affect inputs?

## Values Dimension

What inputs are consistent with the norm for your purpose values? What are the values, attitudes, etc. regarding your inputs?

What quality features are to be associated with the inputs?

What can be done to identify and resolve any value conflicts with other systems?

## Measures Dimension

What are the measures of the fundamental and values dimensions of inputs?
What variables would be measured?
How will they be obtained?
Is there a purpose to each measure?
If your inputs are goals/objectives, can these be measured or observed? How?

## Controls Dimension

How will you compare what happens when the system is operating to the input fundamentals, values, and measures?

What minimal/maximal thresholds should be determined?
What actions do you need to take (if anything) to get back to standard? Is there a feedback loop to the producer of your inputs? What is it?

## Interfaces Dimension

How do your inputs interface with the other elements and dimensions of this system?
Are your inputs related to someone else's inputs or outputs? What is the relationship?
What is the relationship between the way you measure your inputs and the way someone else measures them (such as a supplier)?
What are the factors about suppliers for which you want to develop learning (performance) data?

## Future Dimension

What input changes are you projecting for the future? How will you get there?
What input changes are likely to occur outside your system?
What will be the impact of the changes on your system (number of suppliers, quality, volume of input, change in fundamental dimension, etc.)?

# OUTPUTS ELEMENT

## Fundamentals Dimension

What are the output specifications for the solution idea?
Do they support the accomplishment of your purposes? How?
Are there undesired outputs? How will you minimize and cope with them?

## Values Dimension

How do your outputs stay consistent with the values of your system?
Do they support organizational philosophy?
Do they meet appropriate quality, appearance, production, etc. standards?

## Measures Dimension

What are the measures of the fundamentals and values of outputs? How will they be obtained? How will you measure the outputs?
What devices will you need to measure the outputs?

### Controls Dimension

How will you know when your outputs no longer meet your desired specifications?
What feedback loops have you built in?
What are the contingency plans in place and what will trigger them?

### Interfaces Dimension

Will the system share outputs with other business units? What's the relationship?
What potential unexpected outcomes might contingency plans be developed for?
What plans should you have to handle a crisis or unintended consequences?
What should be the relationship between the measurement of your inputs and outputs?
How do your outputs affect other systems? How do other systems affect your outputs?

### Future Dimension

What will be your future outputs (volume, designs and programs, systems supplied, customers)?
How are you capturing knowledge about "field" performance?
What kind of demand will there be in the future? How will this change your outputs?

## PROCESS ELEMENT

### Fundamentals Dimension

What will be the fundamental sequence of events, activities, operating steps, or processes that serve to convert, work on, or process inputs to outputs?
How can the sequence be mapped or diagramed to provide details?

### Values Dimension

Is the process consistent with the values of you and your organization? How can you make them fit the culture?
Can the people relate adequately to them (do they buy in)?
How critical is it to use the exact sequence or process you have described? How might it be changed?

## Measures Dimension

How will you measure the performance of the steps in the sequence or operating steps (time, number of items produced, result obtained, in quality, etc.?)
What are the measures?

## Controls Dimension

How will you know when the sequence is out of kilter? How will you identify where this problem might be?
Is there feedback built into the system to give you an early warning that the process is malfunctioning?
How will you learn from operating performances about finding improvements?
Are there contingency plans?

## Interfaces Dimension

How and where will the sequence steps affect other process in the system and/ or in other systems?
Are there bottlenecks, pinch points, etc. you can anticipate?
How do the sequence steps relate to the other elements of your system? Are the human enablers trained? Motivated? Are there enough now or in the future? Are there maintenance schedules? Are there instructional manuals and availability of data? How will timeless of information be ensured?

## Future Dimension

How is the process supposed to change in the future?

# ENVIRONMENT ELEMENT

## Fundamentals Dimension

What is the environment you want to surround your solution, idea or system? What is the physical facility? What are the physical conditions? What economic, demographic, and financial conditions are the basis of the system? What cultural and organizational policies do you want to establish?
What are the societal conditions and regulations surrounding the system?

## Values Dimension

How can the fundamental conditions be made consistent with the desired values surrounding this system?
What steps will be taken to ensure that this system keeps abreast of physical and organizational environmental requirements?

## Measures Dimension

What are the measures of the environmental (physical and organizational) factors? What impact do they have for operation of the system?

## Controls Dimension

How will you identify when an environmental factor changes significantly enough to affect this system?
How can this be done early enough?
Can an automatic feedback and control procedure be developed?

## Interfaces Dimension

What environmental factor interfaces with factors from other systems?
How can changes in the environment affect all systems equally? What will the differences be?
How can the same factors be arranged to affect all systems equally rather than by variations (geographically, time wise, by level, etc.)?

## Future Dimension

How will the environmental factors change in the future? What will the impact be on your system and other systems? How can any impact be mitigated to minimize the results of this system?


# HUMAN ENABLERS ELEMENT

## Fundamentals Dimension

Who are the people (by name, class, skill category, etc.) who will be needed to work in the system to help convert the inputs to outputs without becoming part of the output?
How will they work in the system in terms of such things as skills, knowledge, experience, sufficient numbers, etc.?
What roles, methods, and procedures (job description) will they each have?

## Values Dimension

How are your human enabler fundamentals consistent or inconsistent with the values of you and your organization?
What should be the organization values, culture, etc. regarding human enablers?
What should be the impact of outside human enablers on your system (such as sales representatives, suppliers, consultants, users)?

## Measures Dimension

How will human enabler fundamentals and values be measured (cost, headcount, types of people, job categories, training, performance time, quality of work, etc.)?

## Controls Dimension

How will you know when changes in your human enablers affect your system positively or negatively?
Do you have feedback loops built into your process to give early warning and accommodate for change?
How will you know when a change becomes a problem or opportunity?.How will you know when you need to take action if performances do not match desired levels of measures?

## Interfaces Dimension

How will your human enablers interface with other systems?
How will they interface with the human enablers of other systems?
How do they impact the other elements and dimensions of your system? (For instance, an intersect with information enablers future may tell you about future need for updated training, manuals, job aids, or other material.)
How can each person (team) get involved with others who may have had similar experiences?

## Future Dimension

What changes will occur in the future and how will they affect the system?
Will human enablers be older, younger, better or worse educated, speak English, have lower or higher turnover, be motivated by different factors, have different problems, etc.?
What skill levels will the solution idea need in the future?

## PHYSICAL ENABLERS ELEMENT

### Fundamentals Dimension

What physical items (machines, electronic resources, furniture, fixtures, tools, buildings, etc.) facilitate the conversion of or work on inputs to outputs but don't become inherent parts of the outputs?
What specifications are needed for the physical enablers in this system?
What non-electrical and non-mechanical physical enablers (posters, easel pads, marking pens, etc.) are needed for this system?

### Values Dimension

What qualities should the physical enablers have to fit in with the maintenance, benefit/cost, and other support systems of the organization? Or should the support systems themselves be changed?
What esthetic values about physical enablers are needed to enhance the organization's image?

### Measures Dimension

What should the performance measurements of physical enablers be (time per cycle, maintenance schedule, cost per unit, etc.)?

### Controls Dimension

How will you know when negative change occurs in a physical enabler that could affect your system? Or positive change that should be incorporated in the system?
Is there a feedback loop regarding physical enabler performance?
What contingency plans are needed to handle unforeseen mishaps with physical enablers?

### Interfaces Dimension

How should your physical enablers interface with other systems - maintenance, capital investment, training, etc.?
Are there shared resources that may cause availability, quality, quantity problems?
Is there adequate supply of new resources should a problem occur?
How do the physical enablers interface with other elements and dimensions?
Do human enablers know how to use the physical enablers? Are they set up

properly in the process (sequence)? If your inputs change in the future, how will that affect the use of the physical enablers (resources)?

## Future Dimension

What changes in the physical enablers will be needed to move the system closer to the future solution target?
How will new technology, obsolescence, atrophy, financial conditions affect the physical enablers in the future?

# INFORMATION ENABLERS ELEMENT

## Fundamentals Dimension

What information enablers are needed to make your system work—job enablers, training and instruction manuals, technical manuals, maintenance documentation, computer programming, public relations internally and externally, advertising, standard operating procedures, reports, etc?

## Values Dimension

Who or what department sets up the information enablers?
How understandable are the information enablers?
How often should they be updated?

## Measures Dimension

What measures of quality and quantity are needed for the information enablers? (Perhaps not only the quality of the information enablers themselves but the degree to which they achieve their desired results.)

## Controls Dimension

How will you know when information enablers are not achieving your desired outcome? How will you know what to do and when to do it?
Is there a feedback and control loop that can be built in for the information enablers? Would a "sunset rule" be appropriate?

## Interfaces Dimension

Are the information enablers used in other systems?
Are they produced by other systems?
How do they support your purposes and outcomes?

What is the impact on Human Enablers values (e.g., people may need video and you are producing print material)?

## Future Dimension

What future changes (new needs, technologies, change in users) are planned for the information enablers?
What will you do about the enablers that become obsolete?

# SECTION II. ACTION QUESTIONS

*"Minds are like parachutes. They work best when they are open."*
Anon. (Japan)

What are the "right" questions that should be asked in what "right" way in what "right" order at what "right" time to create living solutions?

The real power of Question Forward is that it is a framework that lets you take any situation, problem, or even popular management theory, such as change management, total quality management, or lean manufacturing, to create powerful results. For example, it is wonderful to read management books and self-help books, but you are always left with the question of whether it is the answer you need and, if suitable, how to apply it in your own situation or organization. Thus, the idea behind Question Forward is that we must be dynamic—we must take what we are working on and create momentum that carries it forward, into the future and achieves the results that we desire.

The chapters in this section describe four Question Forward actions that rely heavily on the three presented in Section I and lead to three organizational questions in Section III. This section provides a practical action "road map" for asking the right questions that lets you tailor and use techniques to develop creative and effective living solutions.

The four action questions are abbreviated in the practice and application of Question Forward as PPTR (people, purposes, target, results), the names of the chapters in this section. PPTR is a framework that can be used repeatedly at all stages of creating solutions. It is a simple, but powerful and iterative framework to help you in the heat of battle. It helps you recognize good questioning and good thinking (or lack of it). It helps you and your groups to overcome the usual problem orientation. (The basic People-Purposes-Target-Results action questions can have different word variants—for example, (1) stakeholders-mission-vision-action, or (2) who can contribute and is affected—determine what really needs to be done—visualize the ideal—stay close to the ideal and do it.) What the PPTR process described in these four chapters shows is how to do it, rather than presenting mere exhortations.

> *"All the serious mistakes are made in the first day"*
> Eberhart Rechtin

Each action Question Forward is described in terms of three specific sets of questions: List or generate many possible stakeholders in people in Chapter 4 (or purposes in 5, or future solution ideas in 6, or ways to stay close to the target in 7), build or organize them into a form that presents good alternatives to consider, and select or choose the one (or combination) that is best for that action. In this way, creativity through exploring or divergence, developing many options (list), occurs in all actions before convergence or choosing (select). Much research in identifying the characteristics of successful decision-making points to early development of competing options (the list questions) from many types of tools and techniques.

PPTR is far more a way of thinking about issues than a dogmatic prescription. The Foundation and Organizational questions presented in Sections I and III are integrated through PPTR, a framework that permits and encourages starting at P, P, T, or R, or going back and forth among them without fear of leaving something out, knowing that the Action questions have a well-defined purpose and rationality for existence. It recognizes that any living solution you develop must be considered a system within larger systems. It thus introduces the barriers-constraints-limitations-obstacles-restrictions of the larger systems only if and when needed in each of the PPTR actions.

Figure II–1 illustrates PPTR in terms of list-build-select that makes creativity a built-in part of asking the right questions. It also shows how returning to a previous step, as occurs in many solution creation situations, refers to specific types of questions to ask, not just the generic "get more facts" or "be more creative" or "be sure to think systems." Use the simplicity of PPTR to make it an ingrained habit.

FIGURE II-1    **P P T R   ACTION QUESTIONS**

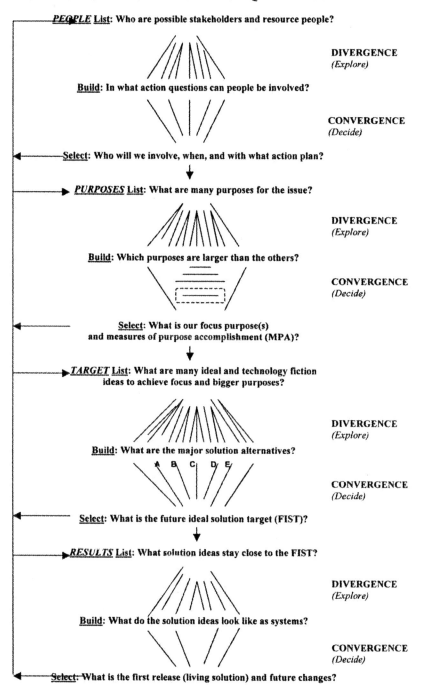

*PEOPLE* List: Who are possible stakeholders and resource people?

**DIVERGENCE**
*(Explore)*

Build: In what action questions can people be involved?

**CONVERGENCE**
*(Decide)*

Select: Who will we involve, when, and with what action plan?

*PURPOSES* List: What are many purposes for the issue?

**DIVERGENCE**
*(Explore)*

Build: Which purposes are larger than the others?

**CONVERGENCE**
*(Decide)*

Select: What is our focus purpose(s)
and measures of purpose accomplishment (MPA)?

*TARGET* List: What are many ideal and technology fiction
ideas to achieve focus and bigger purposes?

**DIVERGENCE**
*(Explore)*

Build: What are the major solution alternatives?

**CONVERGENCE**
*(Decide)*

Select: What is the future ideal solution target (FIST)?

*RESULTS* List: What solution ideas stay close to the FIST?

**DIVERGENCE**
*(Explore)*

Build: What do the solution ideas look like as systems?

**CONVERGENCE**
*(Decide)*

Select: What is the first release (living solution) and future changes?

PPTR is the essence of the approach taken by those leaders we studied and have worked with throughout the years. They all stated many times that the questions you ask determine the range of answers that are possible. And the questions should be raised within a structured and iterative process that fosters creativity, effectiveness and workability, implementability, and built-in seeds of continuing improvement (a living solution).

The value of a structured process, such as PPTR, is illustrated by a recent case. The CEO of a long-established and profitable company brought an international group of twenty-five people to one location to develop much better distribution practices. He exhorted them at the kick-off meeting to be creative and develop the most far-sighted ideas. No other structure was set up for the project and the team. Each representative was encouraged to feel free to apply himself/herself to reach the goal. There was confidence on the part of everyone. After three months, the project fell apart, canceled after over a million dollars in costs and consulting fees and uprooted families. Expecting cross-fertilization by allowing the team to float in an unstructured approach, however much creativity was emphasized, was fatal.

Question Forward gives you a road map for the journey so that you and your organization don't wander aimlessly in search of solutions. The odds of you achieving a desirable destination are in your favor. PPTR is a "common" language and a way of getting it together that provides clarity to the fuzzy front end and the remaining process of creating a solution.

*"The beginning is the most important part of the work."* Plato

Our answer to the opening question of this section explains why we put quotation marks around the word *right* at each of its appearances—there is no single answer, just as there is never just one solution that could be used for a situation. Rather, our answer repeats the criteria we offered before for selecting a "right" question:

- Does it align with foundation, action, and organization Question Forward questions?

- Does it open and expand look-to-the-future responses and possibilities?
- Does it create new Question Forward-type metaphors?
- Does it feel like an interesting or important Question Forward?
- Does it spark creative responses (many options, other Question Forward-type questions)?
- Is it likely to bring people together enthusiastically and with commitment to focus on building a desired future and getting results?

*Gerald Nadler and William J. Chandon*

# Chapter 4

# PEOPLE INVOLVEMENT

*If it weren't for people, planning would be a science.*

**LOU** (a consultant, receives a telephone call): Hello, this is Lou Neptune of Planning Associates, Inc.

**MARIE** (who placed the call): Hi. I'm glad I reached you. You were recommended to me. I'm Marie Goodrich, CEO of the Medical Forensics Company. We have 1,800 employees, and I want to grow the company. The market prospects look very good, but I don't think our company is prepared to take advantage of the potential. I've talked to several executives at other companies, and they are unanimous in saying that we need to do strategic planning to effectively position ourselves. Several of them gave me your name as one well versed in strategic planning. Would you be willing to come to my office and talk with me about developing a strategic plan?

**LOU:** Of course. How about next week on Wednesday afternoon?

**MARIE:** Good. Let's plan on two o'clock.

Lou is impressed with the posters, photographs, and charts on the walls of the MFC office. The company has been a pioneer in developing forensic tools and their growth has been quite good. When Lou enters Marie's office, he congratulates her on the progress of the company, and she tells him how delighted she is to have the strategic planning consultant so strongly recommended to her to visit her company about its needs.

**MARIE:** Perhaps you could sense from the materials you've seen how proud we are of our developments. The problem I sense is that our growth has been based more on being at the right place at the right time than on knowingly plotting a path to achieve better results.

Gerald Nadler and William J. Chandon

We've done very well in the past but our future is more uncertain and I want to be sure we continue to grow and develop new services. A lot of companies are using the Internet. We don't have a strategy for that. From what I've learned about strategic planning, I have concluded that we should use it to become more proactive in knowing where we should be going. I returned a couple of weeks ago from a conference where a speaker defined his model of strategic planning. I'd like to use it here. Can you help us?

**LOU:** Setting up a strategic planning process is very desirable for your company, and the sooner the better. I have had quite a few assignments to do this, so I think I can be of significant help.

**MARIE:** Good. I'll send a memo to my eight executives telling them we are going to start a strategic planning process in a couple of weeks, and you will be setting up appointments with them to let them know what is going to happen.

*QB: Doesn't everyone know how good strategic planning would be for our company?*

Consider the impact on each of the executives when they are confronted with the memo (Reductionist thinking that says here is the answer, do it, an expert will guide us, etc.). Each is likely to wonder what the problem is, wonder if his or her job is in jeopardy, defend his or her own "planning" actions, call for more data about why strategic planning is needed, protect their "turf" in all activities, curse the CEO for forcing another one of her "programs" down our throats, question why an outsider is brought in, and otherwise behave in a negative way. These consequences aggravate whatever current issues exist as well as generate additional ones in future interactions with the CEO

.

**LOU:** Getting the executives involved is essential. Based on my experience with getting organizations to use strategic planning, as a beginning point to have everyone think strategically all the time, I'd like to suggest your memo only invite them to a meeting where the issue of strategic planning, and not the problems you face, will be discussed. I would be glad to facilitate the meeting where our expected outcome would be a plan of action to do strategic planning in the company.

**MARIE:** That sounds like a reasonable way to proceed. I'll have my assistant set up time for… (asking Lou) how long?

**LOU:** Make it for two to two-and-a-half hours one morning or afternoon.

At the meeting a week-and-a-half later, the executives, including the CEO, sat around a conference table. After being introduced by the CEO, Lou started.

**QF: What are the purposes of doing strategic planning?**

**LOU:** Strategic planning is a technique that all of you have probably heard about. However, that doesn't mean that everyone agrees on what it is supposed to accomplish. So let's start by having each of you record individually as many purposes as you can think of for strategic planning.

Thirty-six purpose statements were identified by the group. Lou asked them to arrange the purposes from small to large scope, and then select the focus purpose to be achieved by strategic planning in their company.

**QF: What are some ideal ways of accomplishing our key purposes?**

**LOU**: Now let's develop some ideal ways the company should organize efforts to achieve the focus and larger strategic planning purposes. From them, we will set up a plan of action that stays as close as possible to what you select as a good future target way of doing strategic planning.

In about three hours, the group had determined the specifics (where to start, form of the outcomes, time schedule, series of steps to follow or questions to ask, who would be involved, what type of computer systems would be needed, and what other resources would be needed) of the plan of action to do strategic planning and what each of their responsibilities were.

Consider the reactions of the executives when asked these kinds of questions: Each saw an opportunity to contribute, found a sense of meaning in what was to be done, was challenged to be creative, became willing to implement the solution (developed a buy-in to action), understood that change is always going to occur, was motivated, developed trust in the process and with others, saw the whole picture, and found a way to communicate easily with others. Many future organizational concerns and issues would be significantly minimized as result.

**MARIE** (the next week, in reviewing the outcomes of the meeting): Lou, now I understand why you are so highly recommended. The strategic planning framework we will be using is not the same as the model I heard about; it fits us better. And your insights about my executives were right on target. Getting our top people together with the agenda you had in developing a plan of action was much better than telling them that strategic planning was going to start in two weeks.

**QF: How can we get the right people involved, with their unique proclivities, understanding, and mental models, to appreciate the benefits of strategic planning?**

**The People Involvement Question Forward: How can we give people who will be affected by, or are possible contributors to, the solution many opportunities to take part in the solution creating process?**

This chapter addresses the often-overlooked reality that it is real people who have the needs and concerns for which solutions are sought. People create the breakthroughs; they find the technologies. People are the ones who apply technology, information, and innovations to achieve the often seemingly impossible. Creativity can only be found in individuals. People quest for meaning and seek progress—they want better lives. Breakthroughs and solutions begin and end with people.

> *"A question cannot be asked until there is someone to ask it."*
> Anthropic Principle, as restated by Theodore Roszak in
> *The Voice of the Earth.*

Would there be problems if no humans existed? At this point in the book, we assume that someone is looking for a different way to do something, that a group finds some problem occurring in what was expected from a system or other performance, or that some issue or possible opportunity leads to an activity for creating a solution. Change starts when someone (the problem owner, at least initially) believes it is necessary to move from now to what might be. When you look at Figure 4-1, it is easy to visualize why problems do arise, needs are identified, and desires for new systems and relationships are expressed. YOU, the center of the graphic, are unique, and the perceptions of each of the YOUs about the complex setting Figure 4-1 portrays are different. Creating a solution for any sort of situation means as many as possible of the YOUs that can affect the possibility of a successful and innovative outcome should be involved as early as possible in developing the solution.

> *We cannot talk people into accepting the future*
> *if they haven't been there.*

Figure 4-1

By Jesse Gordon and Natasha Tibbott

**ARTIFACT**: TOOLS FOR SELF DISCOVERY

What We Use to Learn About Ourselves

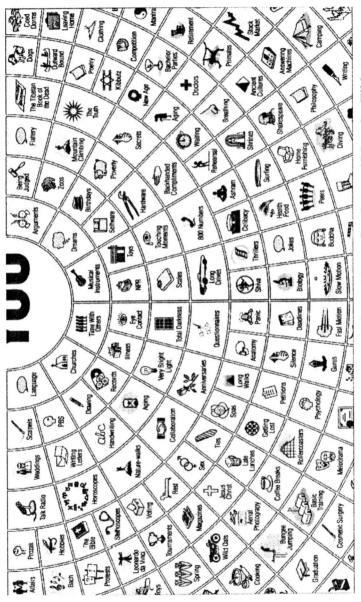

Reproduced with permission of Jesse Gordon and Natasha Tibbott

## PEOPLE NEEDS

*QB: Why should I pay attention to your request when you already have so much?*

Got it all?

Well, it's a rare person, living a very lucky life, who can say "yes" to that question. That much is always true—now, or a thousand years ago. Human nature has not altered since human history began. And you can bet it'll be the same a thousand years from now, too. People have wants they may not recognize as well as needs. People, not organizations, seek innovations.

The point is there's an apparently unstoppable human urge to seek solutions to a usually endless—and steady—stream of needs, wants, and desires. If all the needs in the world were miraculously met tomorrow, we'd have a long list of new ones in very, very short order. A brief review of any portion of history shows that people always find new problems. These create the need for new solutions and new systems (in the broader sense).

Now for those living that lucky life, whose every question is the right one, who have solutions to meet all their needs, maybe you don't need to pause for a moment before plunging into your solution-creating process.

For the rest of us, posing the issue of what questions ought to be asked in trying to find solutions assumes some overriding difficulties or unexpressed desires exist in the way we're doing it now. If you aren't satisfied with your solutions, then you're a likely candidate for a review of your question-asking approach, starting with the idea of motivations. That's because your needs and desires are a major reason you ask the questions that you do. And if you don't recognize the importance of these underlying needs and desires in yourself—and in others—you'll be stuck with the same sort of solutions you come up with now. Time after time. That's why it's so important to start by noting it is only people who perceive needs and seek solutions.

Solutions are the visible part or outcome of the questioning process, whatever specifically happens as a result of the solution-achieving process.

That isn't to say that anything goes, though. It is the specific new or revised *implemented* method, process, product, answer, service, format of a meeting, strategy, decision, resolution of a conflict, response, pact, action, system, or policy we are talking about. The thing by any name you choose that solves a problem, achieves a need, satisfies a want, takes advantage of an opportunity, or resolves an issue.

**How do people affect solutions? Let us count the ways.**

The emphasis on an *implemented solution* (or whatever you call it) includes the recognition that some change of behaviors and actions is expected to improve something specific to a particular place and time, and still influence and interact positively with its larger communities in terms of being economically, politically, and culturally acceptable.

**QF: What sorts of intellectual horsepower do we need to develop in ourselves and our organizations to really create what we want?**

Involving people is the only way of handling and coping with all these factors to incorporate all aspects of a living solution, *the change of today that contains seeds of its own continuing change.* In addition, it is still people who are the fount of new ideas and creations. There is also another reason that people should be involved early and frequently in the solution creation activities. It involves the fact that

> "the world is becoming increasingly complex, that the demands of modern life are fundamentally different than they were even just a few years ago. The human response to the complexity is to become more complex ourselves, more capable of dealing with the demands of modern life. The capability that we need is not physical capability—the capability to work longer

hours, to lift heavier objects, to dig deeper ditches. The capability that we need to increase is intellectual. We need increasing levels of intellectual development."[18]

(Chapter 8 explores in more detail the types of intellectual developments needed to meet the mental demands for the modern workforce.)

A major part of the solution to generating more intellectual horsepower is to learn to ask the right questions.

## QF: What are the bigger purposes that we might consider and who else might be involved in trying to achieve those purposes?

Human beings have developed and used particular ways of doing things and interrelating to others (call them systems) over long periods of time. Systems' long history often causes individuals and communities to forget the purpose of the systems' existence. At least, the rationale for their existence and modes of operation is placed below the waterline of people's mental models.

The last millennium brought a tectonic-plate change in the perceptions of the place of each human in the world. It started with aristocracy and serfdom, religious predominance, and individual submission, artistic splendor amidst squalor and poverty, and ended with an admonition about "me, my brand, and I." Whether or not you agree that this shift is good, the fact remains that, for the next century if not for all time, creative and effective change must start with recognizing that solutions and systems are for the people, by the people, and of the people.

Whether product, governmental process, a home, laws, family relationships, education, health care, transportation, finances in retirement, and so on, every creative and living system that is sought and proposed always involves a change in the beliefs and actions of people. At the same time, life goes on pretty much as it did before the new solution is used regardless of how brilliant the change or technology may be. The more things change, the more they stay the same. Science, whatever progress is being made in studies of the brain, is really no closer to understanding the human mind. It, not faster computers, defines what people productivity is.

*"We are not seats or eyeballs or end users or consumers. We are human beings—and our reach exceeds your grasp. Deal with it."*[19]

Even if the publishing technologies had been available 1,000 years ago, the likelihood that anyone in Western society would raise in a book the issue of effective and creative questions to ask in developing solutions is virtually zero. The culture was both a religious hierarchy (God will tell the Pope what to do, he will tell the cardinals, the cardinals will tell the bishops, the bishops will tell the priest, and the priests will tell the people what to do) and autocratically ruled by inherited power, thus relegating the vast majority of the population to non-person status. Would a farmhand or shop worker then dare raise the question of "what about me"?

A thousand years makes a huge difference. So many people today can aspire to individuality. Even as recently as 150 years ago we saw the rapid rise of utilitarian individualism based on self-reliance and achievement. Today it is expressive individualism, which is about emotional gratification, expressing personal needs, and self-help. And consider the huge change in the status and role of women in just the last 50 years.

### QF: What is unique about the people we want to involve in the solution creation process?

Recognizing the need for people involvement emphasizes the Uniqueness Question Forward. People uniqueness is now being "discovered" in the distinct way each person learns from infanthood on,[20] reacts to medicines, tastes food, and interacts with other people. However much testing, for example, tries to put an individual into a particular "intelligence" category or personality group, there is no escaping the fact that no person really fits the label developed by the values and experiences of the elite group that produced the test. Each person has a different combination of the emotional drives that influence his or her behavior and actions—"the drive to acquire, to bond, to learn, and to defend."[21] Individualism is here to stay, and will

103

even expand; economic prosperity causes each person to seek ways to express individuality.

Technological developments, initially predicted to remove the human from so many systems and solutions, ignore the crucial fact that people and their organizations are key to effective and creative use of those technologies. Humans can and do accumulate history, have some ability to understand what others believe and desire, and acquire insights into another's emotions and intentions.

The inescapable conclusion for today (and, in our view, for many decades to come) is that the relatively high autonomy of humans should govern the way technology is used and solutions are created.

## WHAT IS THE ISSUE STIMULATING THE DESIRE FOR A CREATIVE AND EFFECTIVE SOLUTION?

*QB: Who should we assign to get data about the problem?*

Some question, problem, idea, customer complaint, desire, data on costs, quality, bottlenecks, turnover rates, waste, etc., or confrontation is usually the stimulus for initiating a solution creation effort, whether called planning, problem solving, improving, development, design, or issue resolution. These are almost always sufficient to motivate a person or group to start "doing something about it." The Question Forward process does not provide for this initial identification because PPTR is a reasoning approach that shows you how to know you are working on the right issue *regardless of the topic that gets the effort started.*

To illustrate with a case that will be described in more detail in the next chapter, a thirty-three member hospital council in a large metropolitan area was trying to cope with a shortage of nurses in the community. One of the ways they decided to look into was how to increase the utilization of nurses already in the hospitals. A highly diverse team was set up by the project director using the People Involvement Question Forward.

By getting the team to approach the topic with the Purposes questions rather than the question backward thinking of finding out how nurses currently utilize their time, the team determined they should focus on designing a system to provide nursing services to patients. By developing, with Target questions, an ideal way to achieving that purpose, the team recommended a first release from the Results questions that stayed as close as possible to the target. When a 500 bed hospital was used as a pilot of the first release, the utilization of nurses was improved by 48 percent, an astounding outcome compared to the usual 3-4 percent improvement found in hundreds of other nurse utilization studies around the country. In addition, the nurses were delighted with the change they had helped to develop because they were able to practice the skills for which they had been trained instead of performing many non-nursing activities. That acceptance contrasts sharply with the resistance of nurses when presented with the changes suggested from conventional questioning approaches, and with the longer term negative relations of nurses and administration resulting from the imposition of changes found by correcting the faults of the present system.

In addition to the above usual tackling of problems that walk in the door, you can always take advantage of and seek opportunities for planning, design, development, and improvement by priming yourself and others with questions such as these:

- What's bothering you?
- What's too complicated?
- What have you done lately that you'd like to do better?
- What have suppliers, employees and customers been complaining about?
- Where might a new technology be used in system XYZ?
- How might someone's "creative" idea be used in system ABC?
- How can we use to our advantage the revised tax (patent, trade, employment, etc.) regulations?
- What is an unmet desire of our customers or constituency?
- What is an "outlandish" goal you have for the system or for yourself?

- How can I capitalize on the idea I dreamed about last night?
- How should our products/services change due to demographic patterns in the country?
- Have I ever asked why a particular product or service can't be made easier to use or provide?

Since we have no way of knowing the issues you, the reader, face, these few paragraphs and questions should provide a way for you to identify what may be ripe topics for you to use Question Forward. There are almost always pressures for change that arise from the above type of questions. The PPTR process starts after an issue has been designated for planning, design, development, or improvement, and then provides a thinking approach that lets you identify what real issues ought to be addressed.

### QF: What stakeholders should we involve to help determine the real issue?

## ASKING THE RIGHT QUESTIONS IN DECIDING WHAT PEOPLE TO INVOLVE

When conventional thinking questions are the guide to seeking solutions, resistance to change is an almost assured consequence. Yet it's not change people resist; it's conventional change. Asking the right questions should virtually retire the phrase "resistance to change."

*"People resist change when it is not understood, is imposed, is perceived as threatening, has risks greater than its potential benefits or interferes with other priorities."*
Andy van de Ven

There are many purposes for involving people in Question Forward solution creating efforts:
- Cope with the realities of individuals and groups
- Share meanings and interpretations of reality
- Develop champions and a winning attitude

- Develop the capability of each individual
- Build the teamwork capability of each group
- Secure needed information from a wide variety of sources
- Produce creative ideas
- Account for human factors
- Overcome the arrogance of who is in charge
- Avoid past mistakes
- Overcome emotional, cultural, and environmental blocks
- Avoid the tendency to overcontrol solution systems
- Establish a basis for acceptance (buy-in) of the eventual recommendation
- Set up early commitment to meet time and budget requirements

Getting the key leverage points, people at all levels, involved from the beginning and throughout solution creation is a major turning point in achieving transformation and transitions. "…[P]eople want shared values—truth, trust, mentoring, openness, risk-taking, giving credit, honesty, and caring—in their work environment to be more productive and to perform at the top of their game."[22]

A recent report on resistance to change[23] provides a compelling reason for involving people in the Question Forward solution creating efforts. The authors, professors at the Harvard University Graduate School of Education, show that people often have a hidden competing commitment and big assumption that prevent them from actually accomplishing change however much they may claim to favor change. For example, one manager discovered he was committed "to not learning about things I can't do anything about," which was based on his big assumption that he "should be able to address all problems [or] be seen as incompetent if I can't solve all problems that come up." This unveiling occurred through many questions backward that may still be necessary in extremely stubborn resistance cases. However, asking the right questions would almost always let them surface their commitments and assumptions in a way that avoids such "revelations…feel[ing] embarrassing [and covered up] again once they are on the table." The key is to get them involved right away with the Question Forward approach, especially with Purposes and

Gerald Nadler and William J. Chandon

Target questions, to give them the *opportunity* to take part without the fears of exposure of what they may feel are their weaknesses.

> *"Let's not forget that the little emotions are the great captains of our lives, and we obey them without realizing it."*
> Vincent van Gogh

Another critical reason for involving people is the increasing recognition that change does not always start at the top of an organization. Many of the cases in this book demonstrate that people involved in working on an operational issue develop strategic proposals by asking the right questions. Conversely, studies of unsuccessful change programs trace their failures to inadequate involvement of people and attention to people issues, or to a lack of management commitment (in many ways demonstrated by the inadequacies of attention to people). And the effective team-building process for generating change is accomplished by working on a real problem or issue where the team members establish their synergy by asking the right questions.

> *"People are the common denominator of progress. No improvement is possible with unimproved people."*
> John Kenneth Galbraith

Figure II–1 provided an overview of the whole PPTR process. To translate the people involvement type of questions into operation means that the action plans developed for the entire solution creating effort need to consider PPTR and each of its list-build-select questions. List-build-select is also needed for this phase to determine who should be involved, the purposes for involving each stakeholder, how each will be engaged, and when will their involvement be needed (and what the scheduled timeline is for the whole effort). The list-build-select questions in People Involvement as in all of the Question Forward process, is an iterative one that lets you deal with later questions before earlier ones, return to questions you may have considered answered, and refine your answers.

Deciding on what people to involve, in effect, starts the implementation of whatever solution emerges. *Implementation starts from the beginning.* This is a key component of the Question Forward approach. Whether or not a project will be successful depends primarily on people-related issues—internal, customer and market needs, internal people and customer perceptions of values and risks, and available and accessible people competencies and skills, for example. Other possible success factors, such as commercial, technical, and resource availability, will be introduced with Purposes, Target, and Results questions.

**QF: Who should be involved in the List-Build-Select questions of PPTR, and how will they be involved, when, and for what purposes?**

## LIST QUESTIONS

## QF: Who should we possibly involve?

First, ask what the purposes are for tackling the issue. This lets the group relate the following questions to the overall purpose for making the list.

Who are the many stakeholder groups, possible individuals within each group, and other people and resources that may be needed? For which one(s) of the Purposes, Target, and Results questions should they be considered? Are shareholders and institutional investors to be included? Who are the users and customers and customers' customers? Are there partners, suppliers, or alliance members to consider? What management groups or functions ought to be represented? What employee groups should be involved to ensure cross-functional views? What experts (engineers, scientists, information technologists, community representatives, consultants, etc.) might be needed to help the group be creative? What community and societal groups need to be considered? What governmental agencies, media groups, creditors, and possibly competitors ought to be considered? When considering individuals within any stakeholder group, ask what are his or her attributes, what ends do they apparently want, and what means might they have to get their ends (intelligence and psychological type are not important—a widely diverse group is desirable)?

The list questions are meant to be open to a variety of possibilities (divergence) with no attempt to be judgmental about who will get involved (convergence). Even people antagonistic to changing the situation should be involved early—it is better to know and learn right at the beginning about the positions of those who can negatively influence any potential results. Doing so with PPTR lets them contribute to purposes to be achieved and future solution targets and become committed to the recommendations that are developed.

Reggie White, the outstanding former defensive end of the Green Bay Packers, donated $1 million to his hometown to set up a Knoxville Community Investment Bank to assist in the economic development of the inner city. The city then added $250,000 to the gift. A colleague of his knew about the PPTR process and suggested he arrange for me to facilitate an all-day planning meeting to determine how the bank should be organized and operated.

When his associates in Knoxville asked about who should be involved in the meeting, some of the obvious stakeholders were mentioned: educators, health-care providers, residents of the inner city, commercial bank leaders, ministers, and social workers to name a few. The associates mentioned an urban activist who gave talks about the inner city problems and presented petitions to the city council and government officials on behalf of the residents. They suggested he not be included because he had filed suit against the three major commercial banks that would likely have representatives at the meeting. I asked the associates if the activist could affect and influence the implementation of the meeting's outcome. They said he could and would. So my response was simple—of course he has to be included.

The group of twenty-six did include the presidents of the three banks as well as the activist. Even though there was polite hostility between them at the beginning of the meeting, I launched into the

Purposes phase. By the end of the day after going through the Purposes-Target-Results questions, *everyone* agreed on the way the bank ought to be set up, the timeline of and milestones for activities needed to implement the first release, and who would be responsible for each activity. The activist had his assignments along with those for the other group members. You can easily imagine what his negative reaction would have been to any plan developed by a group in which he was not included.

Of course, it would be very nice if all the people who might be involved were committed to the need for creating a solution for that issue, and would be willing to enlarge their zone of comfort and creative space (Chapter 5). And that they were able to think at a systems level (Chapter 3), and had mental model assumptions that let them take a positive role in discussions. However, at this point in the solution creation process, the basic People Involvement Question Forward should be used. Engaging those who don't have these desirable participant characteristics in the remaining Question Forward PTR process very often produces the conversion of those, such as in the above case, into a much closer fit.

Some *techniques* for the list questions are: scan the organization chart, go over the job descriptions of positions and functions, who works in the system where the issue has arisen, review the mailing list of the organization used for notices sent to those not in the organization (customers, suppliers, shareholders, regulators, etc.), community groups, obtain lists of experts regarding the presumed issue, union representatives, ask peers in your field at other organizations about types of people to involve.

*"Light is the task where many share the toil."* Homer

**QF: Who are the people that can contribute to creating a living solution, will be affected by any solution, and could influence the implementation of any solution?**

## BUILD QUESTIONS

**QF: How and when shall we involve people?**

## Figure 4-2

## QUESTION FORWARD<sup>SM</sup> PROCESS WORKSHEET

| CORE STEPS | WHO should be involved | PURPOSES of the involvement | HOW to involve them | WHEN to involve them |
|---|---|---|---|---|
| Use core steps for each need and opportunity: Set up a program, Solve a problem, Planning, Perform an activity or any step of phase | Users, managers, influencers, customers, vendors, users of related systems, people who think they will be giving up something, community activists, etc. (List step of People Involvement phase) | Generate ideas, communicate, make decisions, gain approval, get expert opinions, etc. (Part of Build step of People Involvement phase) | Presentation, one-on-one interview, brainstorm, survey, computer group support, nominal group, Delphi technique, etc. (Part of Build step of People Involvement phase) | Dates, milestones, project tasks, measures of project performance, etc. (Select step of People involvement phase) |
| 1. List many purposes | | | | |
| 2. Build a purpose hierarchy | | | | |
| 3. Select focus purpose(s) and measures of accomplishment | | | | |
| 4. List many ideal and technology fiction ideas | | | | |

| | | | | |
|---|---|---|---|---|
| 5. Build alternative future solutions | | | | |
| 6. Select future solution target (for regularities, if necessary) | | | | |
| 7. List ideas that stay close to the target (for irregularities) | | | | |
| 8. Build alternative living solutions using the Systems Matrix | | | | |
| 9. Select "first release" and plan for betterment | | | | |

The Question Forward Process Worksheet, shown in Figure 4-2, is what is to be "built" from the list responses. After deciding (the upper left hand corner) regarding what the project is, the Worksheet lets you sort out the list of stakeholder alternatives and group them in the "Who" column.

As each stakeholder group is considered, ask about the purpose(s) (the "Purposes" column) each would serve: Develop serendipity? Represent a financial, top management, labor, user, etc. constituency? Present regulatory perspectives? Relate the project to human resources policies and/or seek appropriate changes in them? Make decisions? Provide big picture, flexible, communication, and option development creative skills? Enlarge the perspectives to be considered, even if they may be initially antagonistic? (Prior to Bill Gates' decision at Microsoft to reject the Department of Justice's 2000 final offer in its antitrust case, he assembled the same group of people he had relied on all along for advice–all high level Microsoft executive insiders. Even though he asked some of them to play the role of devil's advocates, they were all imbued with the Microsoft culture that it could do no wrong. Consider what competitors, customers, legislators, other government officials, suppliers, and outside financial advisors could have added.[24])

The "How" column recognizes that a face-to-face meeting is not always the best way to get people involved. Some people are at different sites, others have busy schedules, still others hesitate to speak up in big meetings, and some feel they don't want to use their position as a way to influence the group. Furthermore, because each person has a preferred learning style (auditory, visual, kinesthetic) even though most can learn through all three, tailor the contacts to allow different modes of presenting the questions and recording responses – tell stories, use graphs and charts, have a way to try things out, scribble pads, etc. In addition, the How column could involve developing a sense of the environment in which the involvement will take place – separate meeting room, piped– in music, meals, etc.

**Some *techniques* for "How" include one-on-one interviews, meetings of the team, several small group meetings, lunch or breakfast meeting,**mail minutes and ask for comments, send questionnaire, e-mail, set up Web site (which theoretically lets everyone be involved), etc. Which technique to use with which person(s) should be based on the purposes for which the person is involved, his/her preferences and attributes, and where you are in the PPTR process.

The "When" column puts some time frame on the whole effort and provides some guidance to the individuals about approximate amount of involvement and when. There is always an overall time frame for arriving at a solution. The "When" column requires an allocation of that "deadline" to the various list-build-select questions. Although most motivated people work harder to meet a deadline, an unrealistically short deadline could also burn-out people and cause too many corners to be cut. In addition, the amount of budget for the effort or requested by the team affects the resources available for the estimated time. Figure 4-A3 at the end of the chapter is a way of developing more detail for the "When" column by using a time scale for the questions of PPTR and by noting who is responsible for doing what. Larger and longer time range timeframe efforts usually need this type of detail or that available with project management software.

Two or more worksheets could be used to reflect alternatives that may appear. Each may have different groups of people and "How" methods that produce different "When" timelines, which allows alternatives to be considered before a final decision is made.

Some *techniques* for "When" include work programs, Gantt charts, project management software, asking people what they estimate the time allocation should be, system matrix to describe the whole project, work schedules for team members, and overall priority for this and other solution creation efforts.

## SELECT QUESTIONS

**QF: What stakeholder groups and people might be involved to represent the broadest range of organizational functions, geographic locations, customers, suppliers, community interests, and solution idea stimulators?**

115

How many people, what budget and time, or how much of each to ask for are additional aspects to "Select," beyond who specifically to include. Choosing which alternative Process Worksheet that appears most effective could be subject to very stringent decision process rules. However, the details needed for the Process Worksheet are almost always quite subjective for these Select questions. In general, the individual or group making the selection does so without the more formal decision methods presented with select questions of Purposes, Target, and Results. The Question Forward Decision Worksheet specifically will be introduced in Chapter 6 and expanded in Chapter 7 where more detailed decisions are to be made).

Some *techniques* for "Select" include the Question Forward Decision Worksheet if a formal method is deemed necessary, arbitrary selection, random number selection, self selection, group software, ensuring that technical people never outnumber all the other stakeholders, and do it yourself.

Whatever selection of people is made at this point should always be considered open for change. For example, the Purposes phase may find that the focus should be at a different level than the one that got the project started, as the nurse utilization case illustrated, and thus different people may need to be involved. The Question Forward Process Worksheet is almost always updated throughout a project.

## THE INVOLVEMENT PARADOX

The proposed solutions for most issues and problems will very likely affect far more people than could possibly be involved in the development effort. The paradox is simply expressed:

How can all the concerned people be involved in developing a solution and still get something accomplished?

The simple answer is that all people can get involved in some way at some point (see Chapters 7 and 8 for illustrations of how, even during installation and training activities, people can be exposed to show how the decisions were made and to get them to contribute ideas for improving the living solution). A more action-type answer is to try to determine how everyone might ideally be involved, and then use that target as the basis for identifying when, even in the installation activities, to involve them and how. Communications with all those who can't take part initially in the development activities is essential for successful implementation as well as their learning the Question Forward way of thinking to create solutions of their own.

## RECAP

**The People Involvement Question Forward: How can we give people who will be affected by, or are possible contributors to, the living solution many opportunities to take part in the solution creating process?**

We started this chapter describing broad human needs and that each individual is one in an almost infinite number of combinations of characteristics that form the person's life. The impact of the larger whole on the specific individual will similarly vary in an almost infinite number of ways. The conclusion about people and involvement is straightforward: Each person is different, there is no way to know what transpires in each person's mind, and each person affected even tangentially by or who could influence a solution creation effort must be involved in some way. In addition, getting them involved early provides a powerful way through the remaining Purposes-Target-Results questions to ensure you are tackling the right issue. The list-build-select questions are the critical way to ensure that implementation really starts at the beginning of a project.

*"Things don't turn up in this world until somebody turns them up."*
Garfield

## Reflective Question

Who are the stakeholders you should consider getting involved with a project (kitchen remodel, forming a basketball round robin, improving the productivity of your department at work) you are leading, what purposes would each one serve, how will you get them involved, and when in the timeline do you think each should be engaged?

*Gerald Nadler and William J. Chandon*

# Figure 4-A3

**SOME DETAILS FOR THE "WHEN" COLUMN ON THE
QUESTION FORWARD PROCESS WORKSHEET**

Project _____ Persons on Team _____

Date of Version 1, 2, 3, 4, 5, 6 (Circle appropriate version) _____

| STEP, WORK TO DO; ACTION TO TAKE | Resp. of | CALENDAR TIME | OTHER DETAILS |
|---|---|---|---|
| 1. List purposes | | | |
| 2. Build hierarchy(ies) | | | |
| 3. Select focus purpose(s) and MPAS | | | |

If the project is to have subgroups or task forces, start each one with PPTR and the Question Forward Process Worksheet. Indicate on this sheet when each subgroup or task force is to report back, and indicate similar dates on each separate sheet.

| | | | |
|---|---|---|---|
| 4. List many ideas | | | |
| 5. Build major alternatives | | | |
| 6. Select future solution target | | | |

If the project is to have subgroups or task forces, start each one with PPTR and the Question Forward Process Worksheet. Indicate on this sheet when each subgroup or task force is to report back, and indicate similar dates on each separate sheet.

| | | | |
|---|---|---|---|
| 7. List ideas to incorporate irregularities | | | |
| 8. Build system matrices | | | |
| 9. Select "first release | | | |

Give reference to other Question Forward Process Worksheets and "when" sheets for:

A. Subgroups and/or task forces

_____
_____
_____

B. Follow up activities to this project:
   I. Presentation to get approval _____
   ii. Installation plan _____
   iii. Purchase hardware and software _____
   iv. Train people _____
   v. Transition plan _____
   vi. Normalization _____
   vii. Betterment plan _____
   viii. Performance review _____

# Chapter 5

# PURPOSES

**The Purposes Question Forward: How can we consider and expand a number of possible purposes and choose those that provide the largest feasible "creative thinking space"?**

*QB: What is the most pressing problem that we need to fix?*

Life should be more than solving problems. Many people, perhaps most, get up in the morning and head to work with an undercurrent of dread. Work seems to be an endless of supply of problems or fires to put out. The minute they walk into the office, the message light on their phone is blinking and they know that when they check their voicemail and e-mail there will be a fresh batch of problems for them to solve, probably more than they can solve in one day.

Some people are energized by a problem-solving lifestyle, but in our experience, they are the minority. To most people, it feels more like the life of Sisyphus, who for all eternity rolls a stone to the top of a hill, only to near the top, then have the stone roll back to the bottom. The compelling question is, can there be any other way to live and work in the modern world?

I was working with a client, "Michelle," who walked into the office on Monday, talked about her fitful night of sleep, how her migraine headache had kept her up most of the night. There were so many things on her mind, so many problems to solve, that she felt overwhelmed and didn't even know where to begin to apply her dwindling supply of energy. Every trip, rolling the stone up the hill, left her with less energy. All she could see were problems and it was only a matter of time before she was going to burn out and then quit or transfer to another job.

Michelle and I had a conversation about her situation. I empathized with her situation, that it really is lousy to begin a workweek feeling overwhelmed, and we both agreed that for her own wellbeing, there had to be another way to operate. We talked about her adopting a "purpose orientation" rather than a problem orientation. A purpose orientation is a fundamentally different way of thinking and being at work. Rather than trying to figure out which are the most pressing, urgent, or even the most important problems to work on, a purpose orientation always begins with questions about the purposes of solving any particular problem.

Here's how I helped Michelle get a handle on what was important to her in her present situation.

We started by talking about the various problems she felt she had to solve. Instead of talking about which problems were most urgent, we began to talk about the purposes of solving the various problems. Shifting the conversation to purposes and not problems made it clearer to her which problems were more meaningful and relevant.

This led to her first insight: There are always more problems than can be solved.

But instead of being overwhelmed by this realization and thrown into a funk, she was able to arrive at her second insight: She didn't have to solve every problem to be effective and to achieve what she thought needed to happen in her organization.

Take away the following lessons from the story of Michelle:

1. The process of backing away from the problems that first appear and looking toward the purposes hiding behind them is the first action.
2. There are always more problems than can—or need to be—solved.
3. Your purposes determine what problems need solving and help you figure out if the problems that first arose are really the important problems—or just symptoms of some other underlying trouble that's the real culprit. ("Be sure you are

achieving the right purposes" is the Question Forward metaphor to replace the conventional "Be sure you work on the right problem.")

## QF: What are the purposes of solving this problem(s)?

### Purposes and Creative Space

We all have habitual patterns of thinking. Some people are naturally more expansive in their thinking and consider a broader range of possibilities than others. However, it's our observation that most people begin a problem-solving or design opportunity with a "creative space" that is too small.

Creative space is a metaphor for how expansive we are in our thinking, how well we see the bigger purposes to be achieved, how many possibilities we consider as viable. You can think of creative space as a type of mental playground.

Some people begin a problem-solving opportunity with a large playground full of interesting people, lush grassy areas, picnic tables, slides, trees, games to play, and sand to play in. Others begin problem solving efforts in playgrounds that are small, have patchy grass, have no interesting games to play, and are unpopulated. They believe that there are many barriers, constraints, limitations, obstacles, or restrictions they aren't allowed to ignore. The range of possibilities is limited.

Many, perhaps most, people have been socialized out of their childhood's big creative space. Kids are naturally curious, inventive, and playful. But by adulthood, almost all of us have found out the hard way to be more serious and restricted in giving in to our creative impulses and go-for-it spirit.

We've been socialized to live in small playgrounds where the risks are lower and the rewards are too. We get used to these small, uninteresting playgrounds where large expansive thinking and possibilities are limited.

The purpose of focusing on purposes is to help you move to a bigger creative space, to childhood's lush and varied playground, so to speak.

Take a moment to think: How big is your playground? How interesting and unusual are its components? Expanding your use of purposes is the first step in building a rich mental playground.

In this way you can expand the creative space of your problem solving efforts, to bring you back to the original, younger, less rigidly socialized mindset. With this attitude you will find more possibilities and can approach problems playfully—not with the tense, constrained anxiety that so often accompanies our efforts to create solutions, to take chances, and to change.

## Expressing the Inexpressible

Our minds have a wonderful power to simplify life for us. We have ways of doing complex tasks essentially without thinking about them if we have done them long enough. There are literally hundreds of tasks that we do every day without conscious though, or intention. We get up in the morning, make our beds (sometimes), shower, shave or put on makeup, brush our teeth, make the coffee, without giving it any thought. In fact, all the while we're thinking about something else entirely—from the news to how to rebalance our 401(k).

Our unconscious handling of myriad activities is both good and bad, an illustration of the uniqueness paradox. We get so locked into routines we don't even consider that we could live life very differently if we chose to do so.

Take a case of mid-career crisis, for example. I was coaching a client, helping him consider what he wanted to do with the remainder of his career. We began a purposes conversation to help him to expand into a larger creative space.

At first he talked about being interested in working less hours and working more with others rather than working so much as an independent consultant. He also wanted to do work that was more fun and interesting.

I asked him what that work might look like and he talked about work that would be more meaningful. But he had no idea what that would actually be. As the conversation continued, he began to describe how his life and career had drifted over the years away from work that was more spiritual.

What he meant was that earlier in his life he had wanted to help people find a deeper sense of their talents and purpose in the world. He had aspired to help people find their calling in life. That is, to do work that was both of service to others and was deeply meaningful for him.

After about an hour of conversation, he stopped in mid-sentence and looked at me with a sense of wonderment and said, "You know, I had forgotten about this. I'd forgotten that this is what I once wanted and didn't think was possible any more. I guess I just didn't think it was even possible to talk about this with anyone, that anyone would understand."

That is the power of purpose, to help people move into a larger creative space, to consider ideas that were, perhaps, once compelling and that have been buried in our unconscious. Focusing on purposes helps us to make the inexpressible, expressible.

*Most people tend to jump to solutions without considering purposes to find the real need.*

## LIST QUESTIONS: How can we make what was unthinkable, thinkable?

By thinking about purposes, we are beginning to expand the creative space to think in. You can think of it as a type of retreat where you are putting people into a new context to stimulate thought and creativity, perspective and relationship, and meaning and passion for purposes.

*Gerald Nadler and William J. Chandon*

> *"The mind, once expanded to the dimensions of larger ideas,*
> *never returns to its original size."*
> Oliver Wendell Holmes

The main point is that one purpose is larger than another—and the bigger of two is the one that has the greater range of possible solutions.

For example, a purpose of having transportation is larger than a purpose of having a car. A car, public transportation, an airplane, a bicycle, a scooter, or a decent pair of walking or running shoes can satisfy a purpose of having transportation. Only a car, albeit a number of different types of cars, can satisfy a purpose of having a car.

The concept of working with purposes is to help people think of larger purposes that expand the range of solutions available to them.

As explained in the Section II introduction, each of the People, Purposes, Target, and Results questions are accomplished by using list, build, and select questions. We list a broad range of purposes. We build or refine the purposes into a coherent whole. We then select the purpose or purposes that are the most appropriate for the problem or design task that we are working on. This section explains how to list purposes.

There are many possible ways of eliciting purposes. Which method you choose depends on both the capabilities and style of the facilitator, the audience, and the setting for the conversation. With time and experimentation, you will find ways that feel most comfortable and get the kinds of results you desire.

There are two general approaches for listing purposes, a structured method and a conversational method. Structured methods use chart pads, note pads, and/or computers and projection screens to list and document purposes. Conversational methods are more intuitive and informal, more like telling a story and may or may not document the purposes formally.

**Structured Methods**

Any situation, problem, design task, conversation, or event is a candidate for listing of purposes. The place to begin is by asking a few key questions, that is, to Question Forward.

### QF: What's the purpose of solving this problem (or creating this solution)?

This is the key question for the people involved in beginning any solution creation effort. It shifts the creative space so you begin to consider what is needed or desired. The question helps people resist the powerful urge to move immediately from problem to solution.

This urge, to move directly from problem to solution, is not uncommon with people—especially in management. It is a double-edged sword.

On one side, good managers or leaders are decisive and action oriented. On the other, the bias toward decisiveness and action can also shortcut the consideration of different purposes and the expansion of the creative space.

Those who are particularly biased toward decisiveness and action, should put this useful impulse to work by first using it to create the right creative space to work in.

### QF: What's the purpose of that?

The next Question Forward expands purposes and enlarges the creative space. Purposes always have larger purposes.

In one session with a client we were working on creating purposes for an organization that was in part responsible for helping a large multi-functioned organization become more integrated. Various groups were working in silos designing information systems and were having problems with rework because of the non-integrated approach. As a part of the integration effort, they were installing a computer system to support their new high-tech manufacturing plant.

125

Rather than develop a solution such as "have a daily integration meeting," (or some other obvious solution) we had them consider purposes. The first purpose that they came up with was:

- To have someone be appointed the "integration czar."

This is a reasonable starting point for a purpose, but, as in most purpose conversations, it is probably too small a creative space. One powerful way of creating a larger creative space is to simply ask the question, "What's the purpose of that?" In the work with the integration problem, when we asked this question, it stimulated the following responses:

- To have the "integration czar" create an integration approach.

And we asked them the purpose of having an integration approach. They answered:

- To have people know when they need to work together on something.

After a couple times of asking "What's the purpose of that?" the group started asking it themselves and started expanding purposes spontaneously. They listed more purposes:

- To have people working together when appropriate.
- To eliminate rework.
- To have people knowledgeable about one another's work.
- To clearly define points of integration.
- To create subsystems that work together.
- To create a system that meets the needs of our organization.

After some discussion, the group decided that the purpose that created the right creative space for them was "to clearly define points of integration." They realized that they were only discovering points of integration after something went wrong.

They decided to be more proactive about discovering them beforehand. Eventually they created a small cross-functional team, which defined the key interface points, held weekly integration meetings, and assigned a team member to manage particular interface issues.

## QF: If there were no constraints of any kind, what is needed here?

Sometimes people or groups of people get stuck because they are too immersed in current realities or constraints or perceived obstacles of the organization they are working in. In addition, some individuals have habituated patterns of thought that lead them to unconsciously accept a range of barriers as being immutable. Rather than think about the possibilities of something working, they think of all the reasons why something can't work.

This point of view can be very useful when you are looking at risks of particular solutions, but is not helpful during the purpose expansion phase. One way to shift the conversation to one of possibility is to ask the Question Forward, "If there were no constraints of any, kind, what is needed here?"

## QF: What is the purpose of this constraint and what is its purpose?

In reality, there are always barriers, constraints, limitations, obstacles, and restrictions surrounding any solution you develop (recall that every system is part of larger systems). The advantage of the Question Forward approach is that it, first, gets rid of many supposed constraints by expanding purposes where they won't exist, and, second, introduces them only as needed in the PPTR process. For example, with the purposes questions, we will show how to determine those that are really needed in the step of selecting the focus purpose, and in setting up measures of success in achieving the focus purpose.

## QF: What do your customers need or want to get accomplished?

Some individuals or organizations can be intently internally focused on optimizing work systems, cutting costs, improving productivity. These are all good things that are incorporated in the other dimensions of the system matrix.

However, focusing on these issues at this point (when we are expanding the creative space) is premature. It is our experience that only when we hear groups and individuals begin to talk about the purposes and possible purposes of their customers that they are beginning to build a large enough creative space.

*"There is only one valid definition of business purpose: to create a satisfied customer."* Peter Drucker

## QF: What do your customers' customers need or want to get accomplished?

To go even one step further, it is useful to consider your customers' customers. This builds a very large creative space and opens up possibilities of major breakthroughs, such as alliances between airlines in their award programs, which allows travelers a much broader range of choices about how they use their awards. In this case, you might consider the airlines customers' customers to be the families of frequent travelers. What might they want from an airline's frequent traveler program? They might indeed want a broader range of choices for a family vacation. These types of breakthroughs are not likely to be thought of and considered until you ask questions that consider the purposes of the customer's customers.

One technique we have found very useful to stimulate individuals and groups to generate many purposes is the list of some verbs shown in Table 5-1. In a one-on-one discussion, each verb could be used as a talking point to obtain possibilities. In a group, each person goes over the list silently to generate and record as many purposes as possible for the issue. This permits each individual to contribute independently without group pressure.

## Table 5-1
## Some verbs to stimulate thinking about purposes

| | | | | |
|---|---|---|---|---|
| acquire | adapt | administer | adopt | allow |
| analyze | apply | appraise | argue | arrange |
| assess | be | build | calculate | change |
| choose | cite | classify | collect | combine |
| compare | compile | complete | compute | conclude |
| confront | construct | contrast | control | convert |
| coordinate; | copy | create | critique; | debate |
| define | demonstrate | develop | drive | describe |
| design | detect | determine | develop | diagnose |
| diagram | differentiate | discuss | distinguish | do |
| document | draw | educate | employ | enable |
| encourage | engineer | establish | estimate | evaluate |
| examine | expand | explain | express | extrapolate |
| find | fix | frame | generate | get |
| give | group | have | identify | illustrate |
| implement | indicate | inspect | institute | integrate |
| interpret | inventory | invest | investigate | involve |
| judge | keep | know | label | learn |
| list | listen | locate | make | manage |
| match | measure | modify | name | operate |
| order | organize | outline | perform | plan |
| point | practice | predict | prepare | prescribe |
| present | produce | project | promote | propose |
| provide | question | quote | rank | rate |
| read | rearrange | recite | recognize | recommend |
| record | re-engineer | relate | reorder | repeat |
| rephrase | reply | research | resolve | restate |
| restructure | review | schedule | select | separate |
| sequence | set | up | solve | sort |
| specify | state | structure | supervise | tabulate |
| teach | tests | trace | train | transfer |
| translate | use | write | | |

## Illustration of verb-noun purpose statements :
## To make marks; To recite poetry

## Avoid these verbs that are measures and values

| | | |
|---|---|---|
| To improve... | To reduce... | To optimize... |
| To maximize... | To lower... | To summarize... |
| To increase... | To simplify... | To generalize... |
| To minimize... | To enchance... | |

## ...all verbs that imply "rate-of-change."

Then each person, one after another, reads one purpose that a facilitator records without any discussion. The reciting out loud continues round robin until each person has no more to add. This permits piggybacking on anyone's statement because the group is encouraged to record any other purposes that occur when someone else reads a purpose statement.

Then clarifying each purpose statement on the list helps everyone understand the perspectives of the others. Changes in wording and addition or deletion of some purposes often occur as the purpose statements are discussed. Because of the larger-looking view that focusing on purposes provides, rather than faultfinding or massive data collection, the group usually starts to coalesce as a team.

This focus lets them perceive how their individual perspectives are included under the hierarchy umbrella. And the overconfident ones who thought they knew what the problem really is get a good dose of humility when they learn that they don't know what they don't know.

*"The fool doth think he is wise, but the wise man knows himself a fool."*
William Shakespeare

## Conversational Methods

In some cases, particularly when working with one person, less formal and more conversational methods of expanding purposes are appropriate. This is particularly true in coaching conversations, where the context is more personal, intimate, and free-flowing. The purposes conversation becomes more like helping someone tell a story about what is important to him or her, rather than brainstorming a list of purposes.

There are a number of good purpose questions for conversations in addition to using Table 5-1. Which one(s) you choose depends on what type of response you get from the person being coached.

As a general rule, a question is a good one if it is evocative for the person being coached and if it expands the creative space. Some particular words or language will work for some people and not for others depending on the meanings that the people you are working with assign to the words.

Here are some typical, constructive questions:

### QF: What's missing for you?

This is useful to ask when someone is upset, but is not exactly clear about what is not working. It can lead to reflection about how we might really want our lives or a particular situation to be different.

### QF: What are you committed to?

This is a useful question when you are coaching someone whose actions or behaviors seem out of alignment with what that person tells you he or she wants or desires. Because our actions flow from our deepest commitments, it is often useful to ask people we are working with to be explicit about their commitments.

### QF: What's your purpose or mission?

Purpose or mission suggests something deeper or more enduring than vision. For some people, they are reasons for being. Others may find the word "calling" to be a similarly evocative word. In this way, we can identify purposes that anticipate our and our stakeholders' needs in the future.

### QF: What do you want to do?

One small but significant point about the above, and most all purpose questions: use the word "what," not "why." "Why did you do that," "why do you want that," and "why are you saying that is a problem" are questions that cause defensiveness on the part of the person being asked. "Why" also tends to lead to subdivision rather than expansion responses about the issue.

## SETTING OF CONVERSATIONS

In addition to paying attention to your choice of words used to evoke purposes and expanded purposes, the setting for the conversation can also be an important factor.

For example, once we were in a multi-day workshop in a building with no open windows. We needed to have a conversation with a colleague about the possibilities of working together in the future. We left the building and took a walk on a nature trail woven in among a number of buildings.

The conversation was relaxed and refreshing, enabling us to talk about what both of us really desired and what was currently missing for us. This led to a conversation about the kinds of work that we could do together and was very energizing for both of us.

After the walk, the colleague gave the name "Zen walk" to the conversation that we had had. She felt refreshed and we had a very productive talk and ended up working together for a couple years.

### Self and Purpose

### QF: What purposes describe my quest for meaning in this system?

It is often appropriate to have a dialogue with oneself when beginning a problem solving or solution creating endeavor. Although it may seem strange to you initially, it is a useful practice to have an internal dialogue around purpose.

### BUILD QUESTIONS

### QF: How do we make sense of the various purposes?

Once we have listed some purposes and expanded the creative space, we need to somehow make sense of the many purposes that we have generated into some coherent whole, the purposes hierarchy. In addition to helping you to select a focus purpose, the hierarchy provides an important way for you to always keep the larger context of purposes in mind as you go through the rest of the PPTR process.

A major advantage of building a purposes hierarchy stems from one of its important properties the larger. The purpose, the more solution options are theoretically possible. Chapter 6 will use this larger context property to stimulate the generation of more future solution ideas.

There are two general categories of methods that we use to build purposes hierarchy, logical and intuitive methods. Both methods arrange or array purposes from small to large, relative to how much creative space they create for the people engaged in the problem-solving/design effort.

## Logical Method

### QF: Which purpose is larger than the next?

The most common and powerful logical approach is to arrange purposes into a hierarchy from small to large. One simple way of telling whether one purpose is larger than another is to use the "couplet test." In the case that we used earlier about the organization charged with integration, we had the following two purposes:

- To have people working together when appropriate.
- To create a system that meets the needs of our organization.

The question is, which one is larger in scope or in number of possible alternatives (creative space)? The couplet method determines which is larger by comparing the purposes by using two questions.

For these two purposes we ask: (1) Is the purpose of having people working together when appropriate so that we can create a system that meets the need of our organization? Or, (2) Is the purpose of creating a system that meets the needs of our organization so that we have people working together when appropriate?

In this case, (1) makes more sense. The purpose of having people work together is in service of (or is smaller than) creating a system that meets the needs of the organization.

On occasion, a group may not agree initially on which purpose is larger. Even though purposes seem simple because they are framed in simple sentence fragments, everyone sees them through their own lenses and can have understood them very differently.

This difference is resolved by asking those with one opinion to describe what they think each statement means, and then the other individuals do the same. This leads, in many cases, to defining the terms in the statement more carefully and often changing the wording to make sense to everyone and to agreement about which is larger.

Asking about meaning and defining terms, similar to continually asking "what is the purpose of that," are ways that can also be used anywhere in the purposes phase. An important consequence of this type of exchange is the encouragement of discussion about purposes to be achieved rather than the usual faultfinding, blaming, and defensiveness. In addition, the discussions stimulate easy-to-resolve conflicts about positive topics and purposes, which build collective intuition.

We continue to use the couplet method until we have arranged the purposes into a hierarchy, from small to large. As the hierarchy is being developed, especially after discussions about meaning and definition, other purpose statements almost always are added to the list and some are even eliminated. All additions are treated in the same way to arrive at the hierarchy. In the case of the organization in the above example, the purpose hierarchy looked like the one in Figure 5-1.

There is a common recognition that comes out of building the first version of the hierarchy. You find that there ought to be some other incrementally larger purposes between two or more purposes.

Figure 5-1. A purposes hierarchy for issue of integrating a multi-functional organization.

To create a system that meets the needs of our organization

To create subsystems that work together

To eliminate re-work

To have people working together when appropriate

To have people know when they need to work together on something

To have people knowledgeable about one another's work

To clearly define points of integration

To have someone be appointed to be the "integration czar"

As an illustration, if the purpose of "to have someone be appointed the 'integration czar'" was listed as "to have people working together when appropriate," most people would sense that the latter purpose was a "large jump." Such large jumps are often discernable by some people claiming they can't see the connection between the two purposes.

Inserting other purpose statements between the two almost always occurs. A key Question Forward to clarify the purposes and fill in the gaps would be "What are some incrementally small larger purposes of this one that will eventually have the second one as its purpose as well?" And some listed originally are deleted.

In effect, this process is a major way to be sure you are phrasing the purpose (problem) correctly. Over the many years of our experience with Question Forward, we have never had a case where the final hierarchy, such as the illustration, was the same as the first one.

Once you have built the purposes into a hierarchy, you are ready to select which one or ones are most appropriate for your problem solving/design task. Before we discuss that we'll talk about an intuitive method for building purposes.

### Intuitive Method

*"Great minds have purposes; others have wishes"*
Washington Irving

At times, the list questions will produce a very large number of purpose statements.

For example, in one instance, over 150 statements came up when a school was developing individually guided education. In another situation, nearly 90 arose when arranging an inner city economic investment partnership.

This is especially common when working with an individual or groups of people who are not professional or organizational members or are from broad-based, general public groups. In such cases, the intuitive method for building purposes may be more effective.

A simple intuitive method is to explain to the group that you are going to ask them to decide if each purpose is small, medium, or large. Usually a simple example will help them understand what these terms might mean. One example is shown in Figure 5-2.

Figure 5-2. Simple example of a small-medium-large purposes hierarchy.

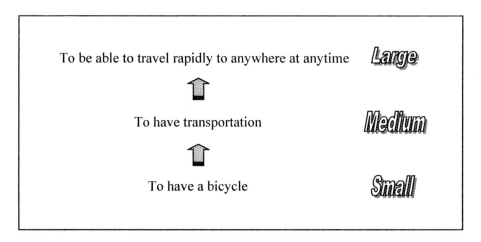

The purposes are not objectively small, medium, or large, but what matters is that they are arranged relative to one another as small, medium, and large. In the case with the organization charged with integration, the group could cluster the list of purposes as shown in Figure 5-3.

Likewise, there is no "right" way to build the purposes hierarchy. As noted before in discussing the logical method, there are inevitably disagreements about whether a purpose is small, medium, or large. Most often, the group helps itself in making an assignment of a purpose statement as it discusses meaning and definitions of words and adds other cluster labels, especially when a large number of purposes are listed, such as the 90 or 150 illustrated before. Small-medium and medium-large, and very large, big, and huge are illustrations of such additions.

Once the group has labeled a few purpose statements, they usually can assign the remaining purposes using the couplet test between a new one and one or more of the already-classified purposes. And don't be surprised to find new purposes and reclassified or clarified statements as the process proceeds. The point of arranging them into some coherent whole is that it enables us to more easily select which one or ones we want to have as our focus.

Figure 5-3. A cluster hierarchy for issue of integrating organizational functions.

## Large

To create a system that meets the needs of our organization

To create subsystems that work together

## Medium

To eliminate re-work

To have people working together when appropriate

## Small

To have people know when they need to work together on something

To have people knowledgeable about one another's work

To clearly define points of integration

To have someone be appointed to be the "integration czar"

*There is no "right" way to determine the purposes.*

A general note about all hierarchies. The caveat at the bottom of Table 5-1 about avoiding certain change-of-state verbs arose because we found so many hierarchies in all types of organizations, but especially companies, having the largest purposes state such items as increase market share, make a profit, improve competitive position, create shareholder value, and so on. Such "purpose" statements are not the customer's and customers' customers purposes, what big purposes are supposed to reflect. Customers, up to the point where they want you to stay in existence for service and upgrades, don't care about your measures of success. A hierarchy should deal with purpose statements that you as well as your customers or users and customers' customers or users want accomplished. Organizations of all types need the large purposes of all its hierarchies to be customer related if they are to get on the path to success. This will also inculcate strategic thinking in most of the organization's behavior.

*"Never solve a problem from its original perspective."*
Charles "Chic" Thompson

## SELECT QUESTIONS

### QF: What purpose provides the right creative space for us in which to think and design?

Once we have built the purposes into a coherent whole, the task then becomes one of selecting which purpose or purposes on which to focus. We want to determine which purpose generates the best creative space for us to accomplish our problem-solving/design effort. We want to choose a focus purpose.

A focus purpose (sometimes "purposes" when the scope of two or three purposes next to each other in a hierarchy seem to be very similar) is the key purpose that we choose among all the purposes that we have listed and built. The focus purpose within its setting of larger purposes frames the context for our thinking effort; it is what we continually refer back to, like a sailor would to the North Star, to make sure that we are on course to our destination. The focus purpose frames the creative space that we think in.

The most common mistake that people make is to use purposes, usually implicitly, that are too small. This biases us to focus on solving this tiny problem as stated because it is definable, and those involved think it is the only one over which they have some power to affect change.

For instance, a special project team was given the task of designing a manufacturing facility that would double the factory capacity. The company president and executive team took eight months in studying the problems causing late deliveries of almost all their orders and decided that increased capacity was needed. The team believed initially that this was *the* problem (although not tiny) to work on. I was asked to facilitate the team at its meetings. Although several team members insisted right away that any change they could make had to concentrate on the new facility design, the selection of a focus purpose for the team's work from its hierarchy was "to develop management control systems." The questioning that led to this selection also led to making a persuasive case to the executives to change their initial decision. Their resulting proposal avoided the huge cost of building a new facility (a great solution for the wrong problem) by an almost complete change in the organizational arrangement and business processes. Asking the right questions showed the team how it could enlarge the creative space over which they did have power to make changes.

Similar to the build questions, there are two general approaches to selecting a focus, a logical method and an intuitive method.

## Logical Method

### QF: What criteria can we use to select the right focus purpose?

The logical method that we use to determine the focus purpose is to develop criteria that help us decide when we have found the appropriate focus purpose. We can determine what criteria by asking what the critical success factors are for the problem-solving or design effort. There are always a certain number of critical success factors or "givens" that help us frame the thinking that we engage in.

Continuing with the organization charged with the integration effort, there were two key critical success factors or criteria that they decided upon.

1. They knew that had to have a successful launch of their new manufacturing facility and computer system. They had

invested millions dollars in their new of system. They needed the additional capacity and had to justify the expense to stockholders.

2. They knew that they had to overcome long-standing organizational barriers of working across functional boundaries. It was clear that the old ways of working in silos no longer worked with new manufacturing methods and technologies.

Having decided on these two criteria, they began to apply them to the purpose hierarchy to determine the focus purpose. Always begin with the largest purpose in the hierarchy.

They considered their largest purpose: To create a system that meets the needs of our organization. Does it meet the first criterion? Yes, because a key part of the new manufacturing facility was the new computer system. Does the largest purpose also meet the second criterion? No, because just implementing the new system would not necessarily solve the people problem of working across boundaries. So, the first purpose met one of the criteria, but not the other.

They turned to the next largest purpose: To create subsystems that work together. It also did not meet the second criterion. So, they looked at the next largest purpose: To eliminate rework. It also did not address the second criterion. They then examined the next largest purpose: To have people working together when appropriate. It did meet the second criterion. So, the group chose two focus purposes to guide their design effort. They chose:

- To create a system that meets the needs of our organization.
- To have people working together when appropriate.

As a general rule, the fewer focus purposes the better. Having a small number allows the focus to be crisp and clear. We wouldn't advise more than three. One is ideal.

Most cases will involve more than two criteria in selecting a focus purpose. These could be things like: the cost of doing the project, due date for a recommendation, availability of resources to do the project, impact on long-term trust relationships, and eagerness of the organization to be a trend setter.

A decision of any sort involves four major aspects—1.) the purpose of the decision (select a focus purpose in this case), 2.) alternatives to consider for that purpose, 3.) criteria, factors, or considerations to frame the selection process, and 4.) a method for assessing the alternatives in terms of the criteria. In the integration effort, the method for assessing the alternatives was basically intuitive.

More formal decision-making techniques for the select questions may be necessary for complex situations. A decision worksheet, introduced in Chapter 6, is one of them. It embodies the four aspects plus other techniques and the questioning process briefly illustrated by the integration effort.

## Intuitive Method

### QF: Do any of the larger purposes stand out as being the right focus?

The intuitive method of choosing the focus purpose is simple and fast. The simplest method is to ask the group if any of the larger purposes stands out for them as being a viable focus purpose. If so, and if the rest of the group agrees, you can quickly decide on a focus purpose. If the person or group identifies up to three purposes that stand out, that is a good indication that they have chosen the right purposes. This method is particularly reliable when there has been a lot of good discussion about the purposes and we are confident that everyone is aligned about what each purpose means.

Another intuitive method is to use a multi-voting process. Multi-voting provides each of the participants in the purpose definition effort with a number of votes that they can use to determine which purpose(s) should be the focus.

As a general rule, we give participants a third of the number of votes as there are purposes. For example, it there are thirty total purposes, we give the participants ten votes each. They can vote for any purpose that they think should be the focus. They can use the ten votes any way they want, placing multiple votes on one purpose if they chose.

After each person has placed his or her votes, we tally the total votes for each purpose. It usually happens that a relatively small number of purposes gets the most votes.

As a general rule, if the top three votes are relatively close, we will use all three as the focus purposes. If one or two of the purposes have significantly more votes, we will ask the group to decide if the top purpose or two feels like a sufficient focus purpose to guide the solution creation or design effort.

If the group is not able to align on the focus purpose, you can always use the logical method to select the focus. It is important, however, to select a focus purpose within its context of larger purposes because it establishes "true north" for the solution creation efforts.

### QF: How will we know if we're making progress?

One of the keys to success is being able to define continuing factors of success or purpose accomplishment.

Unless you know these factors and say how much is enough for this particular initial effort, you are forever chasing rainbows to find the elusive pot of gold. The way in which we like to define success is by measuring, that is, being objective about what success looks like.

For each of the focus purposes, we ask the people we work with to define measures to track progress and to define expectation levels for each measure, that is, what a "most challenging" number would be good enough to declare success in what period of time. Because the big picture set up by the hierarchy is also available to the group, possible factors to consider as a basis of measuring big success are often identified to keep the whole context in mind. Some questions that help elicit possible measures of purpose accomplishment (MPAs) are which change-of-state items mentioned above might apply, what measures would we consider for our wish list, what indicators do we care about; what are our aspirations; what factors are competitors emphasizing, what environmental, safety, health, and other social factors ought to be considered, how do we measure the contribution of this focus purpose to our larger and strategic purposes, and what do all of our stakeholders noted in Chapter 4 want? There is always more than one measure of purpose accomplishment, as is to be expected from the purposeful information questions.

In the example of the organization with the integration problem that we have used throughout this chapter, we asked the group to develop measures for each of their two focus purposes. For the purpose, "To create a system that meets the needs of our organization," they chose to have a yearly survey of key users and they also chose to track the number of problem tickets that were generated by the help desk for the system.

The initial level that they chose for the user satisfaction survey was 90 percent satisfaction for the first year and 95 percent for the next two years. They figured that if they could achieve 95% satisfaction for two years, they might be able to end the yearly surveys and declare the system a success.

For the purpose, "To have people working together when appropriate," the group decided that the best way to measure that was to have a monthly meeting of the cross-functional managers. In the meeting they would discuss and tally breakdowns (and define resolutions) in key defined integration tasks that had been reported by their employees.

Their objective for the first year was fifty or less per month. The whole manufacturing organization was approximately 5,000 employees. They figured that if less than one percent of employees were having significant problems in a month, it was a good objective. Their goal after two years was ten or fewer breakdowns per month. They agreed that they would declare success and might cancel the regular integration meeting if they had six consecutive months of less than ten breakdowns. They figured that they could deal with sporadic breakdowns as needed after that.

Because the selected focus purpose in many situations is often bigger than the originally assigned problem would indicate, the measures, which may have stimulated the identification of the problem, often become insufficient or even inappropriate for determining success in achieving the focus purpose. The additional and possibly new measures may identify where needed information about the current situation has to be collected to become the basis for knowing when success is achieved and even to get approval to proceed with the project.

As an example, a hospital faced with a shortage of nurses defined its problem as improving the utilization of nurses. The measure it selected for declaring success of achieving its assumed purpose of "to utilize current nurses on staff" was a 15 percent improvement.

But when the focus purpose became "to provide nursing services to patients," several other measures became more important. For example, response time to patient calls, on-time delivery of medications, rate of secondary infections, and number of patient complaints.

A couple of the factors did not have currently available measures upon which to base the evaluation of possible solution options. Data was collected about them while the design effort went forward. The solution that was recommended and installed achieved significant improvements in all the measures, including a 48 percent increase in nurse utilization.

As measures are being identified, techniques for obtaining information about those measurement factors as the future solution operates are proposed. Because any measurement is only a representation of the reality, it is quite important to consider as many other factors that can round out your perspectives of that factor. For example, customer satisfaction is often a factor to measure success, and almost everyone jumps to the technique of customer surveys to get that information. However, that data is far from enough, even if the response rate is high. Visiting with a number of customers is another technique that may provide greater insights about future needs or purposes of the customer to keep your hierarchy up to date as well as some indicators of current satisfaction.

Another way to help you identify the factors that will indicate success is to remember that the focus purpose must be a part of the system that the solution is to become. The focus purpose is the fundamental dimension of the purpose of the system. Asking about the values, measures, and controls dimensions of the purpose will help in many cases to surface factors to determine overall system success.

### QF: How do I keep a focus on purpose in the trenches?

It is easy to think about purposes when you are in a workshop. There you have a trained facilitator and you're isolated from the hectic environment of answering voicemail, e-mail, and the constant interruptions of the modern businessperson, teacher, or parent.

But in reality, the questions are more like, "Can you continue to focus on purposes in the heat of battle, when you are most pressed for time and creative space?" Or, "Should an organization, even at the top levels, re-examine purposes of a project, unfinished after many millions of dollars have been expended and many deadlines missed, especially when the union states that it will go on strike if the recommendations are installed?"

We would suggest that the answer is yes. Not only is it possible; it's necessary.

It is when you are most absorbed in fighting fires or in an adversarial position that you need to focus on purposes. Without the focus of purposes you can easily end up spending a day being incredibly busy, working very hard, but in reality, accomplishing very little significant results. A focus on purpose is a focus on results, what is most important, what will feel most satisfying at the end of the day.

I was working with one client who worked in an organization whose various departments, to put it politely, were at war with one another. They were all working very hard with tight timelines in order to finish a project, which was already six months behind. They all wanted to do the right things and get the project back on track, but couldn't seem to break out of the cycle of constant conflict.

I suggested that they take just an hour or two and talk about the purposes of what they were trying to achieve. I held a mini-workshop on purposes, which allowed them to surface some of their reasons for behaving the way they were. They realized that they were a lot more aligned about what they were trying to accomplish.

This purposes mini-workshop allowed them to surface their intentions, which created more understanding and generosity about how they interpreted one another's behavior. They established a better foundation for their relationships, which opened up avenues for dialogue that had been previously unavailable.

Similarly, in the heat of battle, remember the difference between the fundamental and the other dimensions. We constantly ask executives, for example, when they insist that the organization's purpose is "to make a 15 percent yearly profit," to tell us, make a profit *accomplishing what?* This question is also a reminder that individuals in the organization, suppliers and customer population sense a disrespectful, exploitative, and manipulative relationship with the organization if "to make a profit" is its mission.

*Breathing is to life as profit is to business: both are necessary to exist but are not the purposes of our existence.* Unknown

**QF: What purposes, arising from considering the initial issue, should we really seek to achieve to make sure we are working on the right issue?**

What do you do if you don't happen to have a Question Forward coach handy? I am a fanatical golfer. I would rather golf than do just about anything else in the world. Golfing metaphors are a wonderful source of education, plus I get to think about golf when I am working.

Let us suggest that, if you don't have a Question Forward coach to help you focus on purposes in the heat of battle, that you use a daily "swing thought."

A swing thought in golf is one idea that you keep in mind during every swing. Good golf instructors realize that you can't hold a number of ideas in your head at one time. It becomes counter-productive because it is too complex to try to manage the information in the heat of battle. Use one appropriate swing thought to keep your focus on what is going to make a difference for you.

In the Question Forward approach this means to keep your mind on *one key purpose* throughout the day. For example, in coaching one colleague, after some conversation, the swing thought that he needed was to "have peace."

Another colleague used a swing thought of "find a place where I can make a difference." This helped her to avoid getting drawn into the various conflicts and problems that arose throughout the day, but to stay focused on finding places where she could do something to help move the action ahead in her project.

In another client project, the executives of a large hydroelectric company had to decide what course of action to take when they were about to install a new work standards program for constructing and maintaining transmission towers. The several-million-dollar project proposed results that would increase significantly the amount of work each crew was supposed to do. Should the company proceed to install the measurement program when the union said its members would strike if that were done?

The executives did not react to the challenge by insisting management had the prerogative, claiming it was inappropriate to throw away so much money (the sunk cost fallacy), or trying to demonstrate the accuracy of the work standards. Instead, they were facilitated in developing a hierarchy of purposes for installing the program, starting with the small purpose of "to set workload standards for construction." From the eight purposes in the hierarchy, they selected levels 4 and 5 as their focus—to produce estimates of the construction work required, and to plan construction of towers.

Increasing the creative space of purposes the executives could see allowed them to consider several other options to achieve those purposes, including one the workers' requested—to set their own workloads. The executives decided to set up a trial of the workers' idea.

Within a year, the management quietly extricated itself from the measurement program because the workloads being set by the workers themselves were greater than what the program would have required. In addition to the productivity improvements that exceeded what the company had originally thought they would get, the huge costs, reduced customer service, and long-term animosities certain to result from a strike were averted.

## RECAP

**The Purposes Question Forward: How can we consider and expand a number of possible purposes and choose those that provide the largest feasible "creative thinking space"?**

Purposes frame our solution creation efforts. It is critical that we begin with the right purposes that give us a large enough creative space or mental playground to do our problem solving or design.

A consideration of purposes also helps us articulate what is often hidden to us in our thinking. We learn to express the inexpressible.

The process of refining purposes follows the Question Forward approach of list, build, select. We list many possible purposes, we build them into a coherent whole, and then we select the appropriate purpose(s) to guide the thinking effort.

Once we have selected the appropriate purpose, we chose a few key measures to make sure we are making progress toward our chosen purposes. Finally, it is important to keep purposes in mind in the heat of battle. Purposes help us keep our focus on what really matters.

## Reflective Question

What is your swing thought for purposes in the heat of battle?

# Chapter 6

# TARGET

**The Target Question Forward: How can we develop a target solution for the future that will guide what changes or designs to adopt today to achieve our focus and larger purposes?**

*"Focus on what we want instead of settling for what we can get."*
Anon.

When you stopped focusing just on the problem at hand, you started expanding your purposes. That led to creating a much wider range of potential solutions—that creative space we talked about in Chapter 5. Great, but now how do you take advantage of all these possibilities?

The short answer is what we call *targeting*.

The Purposes questions of the Question Forward process led to an orderly course of actions concerning *what* to achieve. Now the question is *how* to achieve all these focus and bigger purposes. That's what the Target questions covered in this chapter let you figure out.

We accomplish our targeting with the three list, build, and select questions using both structured and conversational techniques. The list questions use any of the creativity techniques as the second stimulator thought or phrase to "intersect" with the focus and larger purposes. "How can we ideally accomplish (purposes) by means of (creativity stimulator)? This lets you generate as many solution ideas as possible for how to achieve the purposes. The build step sorts these ideas into major alternatives to consider as the future solution target. The select questions usually involve more formal decision procedures than for the People Involvement and Purposes questions because what is selected will become the direction of continuing change.

In the Question Forward process, then, a "future ideal solution target" (FIST) helps us come up with and organize a series of changes—the living solution—that move smoothly into the future towards the target for achieving the focus purposes. At first it is an idealized or mental model. But with the Target and Results questions, we work out the details that turn this ideal model into an explicit plan of action.

How this works is illustrated by Figure 6-1. Let's go over the details of this schematic now. Assume that the distance between the legs of the triangle represents one (or more) measure of accomplishment of the focus and larger purposes, say, time taken for fulfilling a customer's order.

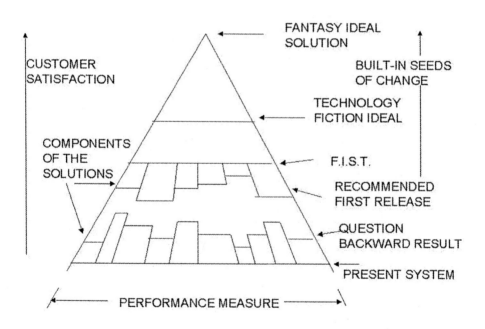

Figure 6-1. Ideal Solution Concept

*QB: How can we reduce the time taken by 25 percent?*

Now let's look at this QB in terms of Figure 6-1. The line at the open end of the triangle represents the current time for achieving the purpose. If the question of reducing the time by 25 percent is considered in the conventional fashion, then various segments of the present system are looked at to determine where time can be saved. For example, a team would go over the details of component 1 and ask how much time can we save here? The horizontal line at the top of the bar for component 1 represents the new time that change would take, and the team would note the percentage of total time saved by that component. The team then asks the same question about the other components until they total up savings of 25 percent.

### QF: How can we reduce the time taken by 100 percent?

However, the following illustrates what can happen when you start with an ideal result. We always ask a client who engages us for a project where the assignment is stated in, say, time reduction percentage terms, "Would you be happy if we achieved 100 percent time reduction?" After getting a quizzical expression, we explain. "Looking at the triangle, the only reasonable response to the question of what is the most ideal solution is the apex, or zero time." We call this the fantasy solution because in almost all cases, this is impossible to achieve. We keep trying, though, by asking the question.

Here's an example of a case that shows how dramatically different and successful this approach can be:

I was asked by the president of HealthCaring, a chain of eighteen hospitals located in six states, to help them develop a productivity improvement program as a means of reducing overall costs by 15 percent, an amount he considered a BHAG, a "big, hairy, audacious goal,"[25] for hospitals. He felt that such a program would have a better chance of being accepted by hospital personnel than would a cost reduction program. I asked QF's two: would you be happy if the costs were reduced by 100 percent? Would you be glad to have to an infinite improvement in productivity?

153

After he stopped laughing (and hinting he would throw me out of his office), I asked: what would be the impact on the organization of his measure of 15 percent cost reduction, even though disguised in the cloth of a productivity improvement program? Short answer: Much resistance and unhappiness throughout the organization.

We used the PPTR questions as discussed in earlier chapters and wound up with focus purposes of a chain-wide program to provide patient care services and to have patients return to self-sufficiency in the community. The Target solution for the plan of action was to set up a program on "attaining excellence among peer groups in providing patient care and returning patients to self-sufficiency in the community." Most interesting though was the group's measures of purpose accomplishment and the "big, hairy, audacious goals" they set up: zero hospital-based infection rate, 200 percent productivity level based on industry-wide standards, and have the highest market share in the respective communities, among others. Question Forward was taught to and used by facilitators, initially as a pilot in what was considered a poor performing hospital.

**QF: How can we achieve a purpose larger than the focus that would eliminate the need for the focus purpose (in effect, reducing the time to achieve it by 100 percent)?**

One illustration of the impact of "thinking ideally" concerned this hospital that was physically divided into two sites four miles apart in one city. A team was working on the issue of allocating capital improvement funds between the two sites. The team had not been able in about a year and a half to reach a decision even though it had spent nearly $300,000 to have an architect draw up seven master plans based on different splits of the money. When Question Forward was used by a new facilitator, the team decided, *in a day and a half*, to consolidate the hospital at one site and convert the second site into a retirement home, a new line of business and revenue stream for HealthCaring!

## LIST QUESTIONS

List questions focus on developing as many technology-fiction, ideal ideas as possible, even seeking fantasy solutions (as shown in Figure 6-1). Emphasizing technology fiction (imagine technology that doesn't yet exist, but would be useful in solving a problem) helps to avoid the availability bias (use ideas currently available). Instead, you think blue-sky or with a clean sheet, put yourself in the future from which you can work backward in action steps.

**QF: How can we ideally achieve the focus and larger purposes by means of [the creativity technique's stimulus]...?**

These blue-sky thinking approaches (used with Target questions and also next in with Results questions of our PPTR approach) are "creative," so let's discuss that much studied but little understood human characteristic. Bisociation is a widely accepted theory about the way the human mind develops creative (or any) ideas. It suggests that breakthrough ideas are born in the brain when two thoughts, two models, or two statements are forced to intersect. This intersection somehow stimulates the development of an idea that the person can then present. No one knows just how the brain does it, but it is the essence of all the creativity techniques. Instead of using the original problem statement as one of these thoughts to force an intersection with the stimulus provided by the creativity technique, the focus and larger purposes are the thoughts to use to force an intersection with the creativity technique's stimulus.

*"Thinking free from all prior restraints...allow[s] your mind to contemplate really outrageous ideas..."*[26]

Here are some Question Forward illustrations you might apply to get this intersection going:

- QF: How can we ideally achieve the focus and larger purposes by means of doing something that is impossible today?
- QF: How can we ideally achieve the focus and larger purposes by means of what the flash card says? (Flash cards each with a

word or phrase or picture/drawing or cartoon are shown as stimulators.)

- QF: How can we ideally achieve the focus purposes by means of an ideal way to do the first (then second, third, and so on) larger purposes, all the way to the purposes and total experiences of the customer and the customers' customers to anticipate their needs?
- QF: How can we ideally achieve the focus and larger purposes by means of the analogy of a telephone system (or a computer chip, DNA double helix, can opener, fuel cells, GPS, etc.)?
- QF: How can we ideally achieve the focus and larger purposes by means of a Rube Goldberg contraption or by a "reverse salient," that is, considering, one at a time, smaller purposes in the hierarchy?
- QF: How can we ideally achieve the focus and larger purposes by means of each of the phrases in the computer-based technique (use a computer program that randomly selects words for bisociation)?
- QF: How can we ideally achieve the focus and larger purposes by means of a metaphor, such as play a golf game?
- QF: How can we ideally achieve the focus and larger purposes by means of a zebra, mechanic, yacht, rubbish, comb (or any randomly selected word from the dictionary)?

*"Do not go where the path may lead, go instead*
*where there is no path and leave a trail."*
Ralph Waldo Emerson

There are plenty of other "creativity" techniques you could also try for the second bisociation thought, such as random dictionary words, checklists or principles from various fields, best practices databases, being the world leader, starting all over again, technology award winners, forecasts of breakthrough technologies in the next ten years, a clean slate or green field, the worst possible solution, doing it automatically, and "what ifs."

## QF: How would we imagine the future for achieving the focus and larger purposes?

Even though the process of expanding purposes and the creative space very likely elicited some ideas the participants considered "great," the Target questions help avoid the tendency to latch on to one of those ideas as constituting *the* solution. Developing Target ideas continues the expansion idea—notice the continuing reference to "focus and larger purposes"—introduces the deliberate use of idea generating stimulators to enlarge the scope of possible solution ideas to consider beyond the intuitively developed great idea with the Purposes questions. A recent case illustrates how this occurs.

A large company had me facilitate the one-and-a-half day strategic planning retreat it had planned for its nine top executives. Of the forty-five statements that emerged, it seemed to me that there were many solution ideas listed and not many real purpose or mission statements. In the statement clarification part of the phase, I asked the group to decide what each statement represented—a real purpose, a solution idea, or a measure of accomplishment. Only twelve were purposes. After further work clarifying this confusion, only five of these purposes wound up on the final list of seventeen. And those early solutions? After the Target phase was done, only two of the great ideas originally listed were included in the eventual strategic mission and vision target.

### "Completing" the List Questions

How many ideas are enough in either method? Most creativity techniques are concerned with generating a large number of ideas, and the methods proposed with list questions do seek a large number. Always have many options, including those that would make you the innovative leader.[27] The one important distinction that Question Forward makes in using any of the methods is the tie-in to the focus and larger purposes and to the *how* question – how can it ideally work eventually? The *how* emphasis continues the critical direction of Question Forward to arrive at implementable results, actual changes, real products and services, and living solutions. This orientation tends to reduce the number of total ideas unrelated to all the purposes to be achieved. On occasion, some of these way-off ideas can be useful to other creation solution efforts and should be sent to them.

So the answer to the number is a lot but not too overwhelming. In one project concerning missing files in an insurance company, 131 ideas were developed and the group did not consider them too many. In another project regarding the design of a knowledge management system, nineteen were "more than we can handle." The group and outside reviewers (the approval person or group, professionals in the field, etc.) will be the unique determiners of how many to develop. More is almost always better, and ideas will almost always be added (and some deleted) however much you think this step is completed.

## List Methods

### Structured Methods

In a one-on-one discussion, any number of the Questions Forward can be used as talking points to obtain possibilities, always in the context of *how* ideally to achieve the focus purposes. In a group, each person can use this basic question to generate silently and record as many as possible, so there's no group pressure. Then each can offer up his or her solutions for the facilitator to record without discussion.

Beyond that, outside experts with particular competencies relevant to these ideas can be added to the team as list questions are being asked.

Some additional QFs to ask might include:

- QF: How can we achieve the focus and larger purposes by having ideal inputs (then outputs, processes, environment, human enablers, physical enablers, and information enablers)?
- QF: How would an ideal solution for achieving the focus and larger purposes smell (look, sound, feel, taste)?
- QF: How can we make the overall environment of the organization conducive to generating creative ideas in specific projects and in general to fostering creativity?

- QF: What if we used a robot (jet engine, camera, watch, scanner, car, or any other technology) to achieve ideally the focus and larger purpose—how would it work?
- QF: How could we ideally achieve our focus and larger purposes by means of what is currently considered the best practice in similar or unrelated types of organizations?

In addition to the main concepts of a Question Forward Organization discussed in Chapters 8 and 9, several techniques may be useful in establishing a creativity-friendly environment—idea boards in meeting and break rooms, speakers on creativity techniques, regularly having "exchange your problem" days when someone else can work on the issue, motivating posters, field trips for team members to zoos and museums for inspiration, and "blue sky" days for everyone about a problem or project or two.

It is quite useful to record the ideas because each can be detailed later by asking the system matrix questions.

**Conversational and Intuitive Methods**

In some cases, particularly when working with one person, less formal and more conversational methods of developing possible future solution ideas are appropriate. Once the focus and larger purposes are set up, the conversation becomes more like helping someone tell several alternative stories about what the future solution target might be to achieve the purposes.

There are a number of good questions for conversations in addition to those already noted. As a general rule, a question is a good one if it is evocative for the person being coached and it if it leads to a larger creative space.

Some QFs that are particularly useful when coaching an individual include:

- QF: How do you envision a way in the future to achieve your focus and larger purposes?

- QF: How do we want our world (and our organization) to look in the future?
- QF: How would my world work look if I could invent the future?
- QF: How would our ideal organization operate?
- QF: How would you try to achieve your focus purposes if you started all over again?
- QF: How can you encompass activities you enjoy into an ideal system for achieving your focus purposes?
- QF: Where do you want to be in three years?

## BUILD QUESTIONS

Build questions put some order into often widely variable solution ideas that were developed with list questions. Some of the ideas conflict with others, some are possible components in several possible living solutions, and the rest are usually snippets of ideas that might be useful in some of the alternatives. Build helps you sort them all out and develop the three to five major alternatives (MA) substantial enough to consider as candidates for the FIST, to be determined with select questions.

The outcome of the build questions is identifying each idea as:
- either a plausible major future alternative (MA)
- a possible component (C) that could be incorporated in more than one major alternative
- or a detail (D) that may or may not be useful in creating this solution and may even have some value in other projects.

## QF: Is the idea a potential self-contained means of achieving the focus and larger purposes (major alternative)?

This is the main question to pose in reviewing the idea on the list to determine if it might be a major alternative. Follow-up questions to add to this one are:

- Is the idea describable in system matrix terms (inputs, outputs, operating steps, etc.) to assure workability?

- Is the idea more than a "flag and apple pie" statement (e.g., automate it, train people better, stop the waste, increase market share)?
- Is the idea more than just a component or detail that could be incorporated in several other major alternatives?

The idea is considered a major alternative if there are three yes answers out of the above four questions. If you or the group do not consider it a major alternative, then the idea will be labeled a component or detail depending on your perception of its possible usage in other major alternatives or some other project.

If the idea is a component or a detail, it will need to be combined with other ideas or expanded into a major alternative. Component and detail ideas are not a complete solution. They do not stand on their own.

Combinations such as MA/C and C/D occasionally occur. There is no formula to determine how many MAs there ought to be in any list created, but our experience is that 15 percent to 25 percent can be considered major alternatives. Regardless of number, each review of an idea is an opportunity to raise questions about making it more ideal and/or trying to develop new ideas to add to the list.

**QF: How can the regularity concept keep a solution idea viable with build questions?**

"Can't do that because 10 percent of the time we need a hard copy invoice..." or other barrier, constraint, limitation, obstacle, or restriction (BCLOR) words to that effect kill many a fine idea. When this comes up, rely on the regularity concept, namely that if the idea of, say, electronic invoicing works for 90 percent of the customers you can always create a special solution for dealing with the other 10 percent as "irregularities." That way the baby (your best idea) doesn't get thrown out with the bathwater. This way also helps to identify which BCLORs are conditions the bigger systems within which our solution will exist are really necessary.

Gerald Nadler and William J. Chandon

Designing a hospital emergency room might consider the most critical condition it faces, life-threatening accident or heart attack patients, as a regularity even though other types of patients may constitute a much larger percentage of the cases. In another case, designers of a cellular telephone considered the regularity condition to be the 97% of the people who have full touch, mobility, vision, and hearing, leaving the irregularity of potential users with disabilities to be considered with Results questions. More than one regularity condition may be identified for a project.

The purpose of regularities is to assume they exist 100 percent of the time while developing possible major alternatives and in selecting the FIST. The regularity concept does not proclaim the BCLOR irregularities as unnecessary because the valid irregularities will be considered with Results questions to determine how close the recommended solution can stay to the target.

**QF: How would the solution idea ideally work?**

**Building Major Alternatives**

The outcome of the build questions should be a brief description of the major alternatives and roughly how they would work with ideal and/or regularity conditions. A description can take many forms, but the main way of getting enough detail about how each MA would work and potentially minimize its unintended consequences or unexpected outcomes (see Chapter 3) so a decision can be made with select questions is to develop a rough systems description. Additional details may be needed in select questions to help clarify the alternative before selecting the target. (This is one of many points in PPTR where the foundation question about purposeful information is used—collect only the information you need.)

**Build Methods**

**Structured Methods**

During the build questions, you can add more structure by asking each person to do the classification into major alternative, component, or detail independently. Then the facilitator could call out the first idea and ask the whole group to state what assignment of MA, C, or D they made and record the result. Those ideas with the greatest consensus of a classification are put into that category.

Other techniques, such as flowcharts, activity networks, operator charts, organization charts,[28] dynamic flow and feedback loop models, and layout diagrams, are sometimes used to add some content and meaning to *how* the ideal alternative would work. These techniques can all be incorporated in the system matrix format. For example, flowcharts, activity networks, and relationship networks are possible ways of describing the fundamental, measures, control, and interfaces dimensions of the operating steps element. Operator charts relate to various dimensions of human enablers, and layout diagrams to physical enablers and sometimes environment elements.

**QF: What other creative ideas can I get by expanding each system element in this solution idea?**

Other details may depend on asking this question. Just as purposes were expanded, the other elements can also be expanded. If a suggested input appears to limit the opportunities for describing an outstanding technology-fiction solution, ask what the input to that input is, and then the input to it, and so on. If a suggested set of operating steps seems to limit the ideal nature of an idea, ask what the operating steps are before and after that set. Expanding the elements will be used much more with Results questions.

A rough system matrix description is another structured way of building a major alternative. The word "rough" is used because the purpose of doing any detailing of an idea here is to have enough information for making the selection of a target. The questions to ask are based on the systems matrix and question matrix presented in Chapter 3. Many more details will be obtained with the system matrix with Results questions.

Another benefit of thinking about the major alternatives from a systems perspective is that the matrix poses questions that should let you consider the total customer/consumer experience as part of the output element. Customer total experience, for example, from the initial exposure through contact, purchase, use, and disposal is more likely to be considered by the system framework of thinking.

### Conversational and Intuitive Methods

An imagined ideal scenario can be a structured process or a conversational, informal method that looks more like a story. In the structured format, some of the details from the other methods are usually put into a story format. Many people can understand the story of an alternative while having difficulty in interpreting the details in a systems format.

The essence of a story or scenario for purposes of building major alternatives (scenarios are also prepared to present a projection of the confluence of current trends) is to describe roughly how an idea would play out and what the consequences would be. It should describe a picture or image of the unique ideal forward-looking aspects of the idea, and try to identify what additional information may be needed if the idea is selected as the target. Because the select questions will need reasonable background about all the major alternatives, the most likely conditions that would prevail if each idea were used should be included in a scenario.

### QF: What future alternatives would work to achieve your purposes?

Almost all of the techniques available in the structured method can be used as mental guides in discussing what ideas are major alternatives. They just are used in a conversational mode. The discussion is likely to be more fluid and free flowing without the formal structure of technique.

Similarly, a conversational scenario is a story patterned to some extent on using parts of the structured method as well as some parts of the system matrix. The emphasis is on telling a story about the future each idea identified as a major alternative would entail.

*"Act as if it were impossible to fail."* Dorothea Brande

## SELECT QUESTIONS

Although each of the major alternatives could be considered a possible target, the aim with select questions is to identify the preferred future, the FIST, for achieving focus and bigger purposes. Even though one of the alternatives is selected, the others remain options to consider should developments with Results questions or in pilot projects show that the FIST may not be appropriate, or should external conditions and contingencies change enough to invalidate the evaluation of these select questions.

The major attributes to keep in mind when getting some detail to enable you to select a target are the measures of purpose accomplishment—what information do you need about each of the major alternatives to enable you to assess each alternative's benefits and consequences for each measure? The information is primarily related to *how* it will work. It is also not unusual to have other factors or measures to consider in comparison with the benefits of the potential target idea —associated risk, environmental friendliness, ease of use and convenience to user, simplicity, and image the alternative might create are just illustrations of what may not have been identified with Purposes questions. Depending on the solution creation situation, other factors may need to be considered—the ethics related to the alternative, demographics of population age groups, number of skilled people being trained, and equal rights for disabled workers.

### Select Methods

### Structured Methods

Using the Question Forward Decision Worksheet (Figure 6-2) as the guide to ask the necessary questions and record the responses is a straight-forward structured method. The scope and complexity of the alternatives being considered will determine the depth you go in using the Question Forward Decision Worksheet. Alternatives that could lead to significant changes, a new product or service, a major change in the accounts receivable system, or the purchase and installation of equipment, usually require a thorough assessment.

## QF: How much of the measures can be achieved by this alternative?

The worksheet provides a basis for asking many questions that are related to this one:

- What scale best represents this measure of purposes accomplishment?
- How important is this measure relative to the other measures?

Figure 6-2

Who Involved in Making Decision _____ Date _____

QUESTION FORWARD DECISION WORKSHEET
PROJECT _____

| | | |
|---|---|---|
| **PURPOSE** | A \| B | A = Rating of alternative |
| ☐ Select people to involve | | B = Risk, probability of occurrence |
| ☐ Select focus purpose(s) | C | C = A × B × Weighting |
| ☐ Select measures of purpose accomplishment (MPA) | | Scale used for rating: (A) |
| ☐ Select major solution alternatives | | ☐ 5 (excellent), 4 (very good), 3 (good), 2 (fair), 1 (poor), 0 (not acceptable) |
| ☐ Select future solution target | | ☐ 100 points to be divided up among alternatives, with higher amounts for preference |
| ☐ Select _____ | | ☐ _____ |
| ☐ Select _____ | | |
| **WEIGHTING** | | Risk or probability of occurrence (B) |
| ☐ 1 = Least important, 1.5 = 1-1/2 times as important as 1, 3 = 3 times as least important | | ☐ 0 to 1 (ex. 0.25, 0.75) probability, with higher probability value = very likely occurrence |
| ☐ Divide 100 points among factors with higher amounts for greater weighting | | ☐ 1 to 0 (ex. 0.90, 0.10) risk, with higher number = less risk |
| ☐ 5 (absolutely needed), 4 (very important), 3 (important), 2 (worthwhile), 1 (desirable) | | ☐ _____ |
| ☐ _____ | | COST = Investment + expected life + annual operating cost |

| FACTOR/CONSIDERATION/CRITERIA | WT. | ALTERNATIVE | | | | | |
|---|---|---|---|---|---|---|---|
| | | A | B | C | D | E | F |
| 1. | | | | | | | |
| 2. | | | | | | | |
| 3. | | | | | | | |
| 4. | | | | | | | |
| 5. | | | | | | | |
| 6. | | | | | | | |
| 7. | | | | | | | |
| 8. | | | | | | | |
| 9. | | | | | | | |
| 10. | | | | | | | |
| TOTAL OF MULTIPLIED VALUES | | | | | | | |

Alternatives:
A _____    D _____
B _____    E _____
C _____    F _____

- How much do we know about how the alternative might work in the future?
- Should we make a physical prototype or pilot facility or set up a computer simulation of the performances of the two (or three) alternatives that look promising?
- What impact would a change in external factors have on the workability of this alternative?
- How can we measure the impact of the alternative on the rest of the organization?

Another structured method involves using available software packages.[29] They prompt you to enter almost the same information needed by the Question Forward Decision Worksheet. They do not in any way change the need for you or the group to provide the answers to the kinds of questions already noted. The software does not produce better decisions; it simply helps you keep track of the answers you supply and, thus, probably lets you make decisions more quickly.

**Conversational and Intuitive Methods**

It is not too unusual to find a group making a decision by just scanning the Target alternatives and then arriving at a consensus as to which one is best for them in the long term. Many times, such a decision is made quickly because the group knows that it can return to Target questions and have the other major alternatives still available. A variety of ideal alternatives is also an excellent anticipatory tool.

**QF: Which major alternative best meets the measures of purpose accomplishment and related factors if it were selected as the future ideal solution target (FIST)?**

*"Neither man nor nation can prosper unless, in dealing with the present, thought is steadily taken for the future."* Theodore Roosevelt

The three basic considerations in making the selection of a FIST are the same as those in any decision making, such as is involved with all the select questions of PPTR—measures of purpose accomplishment and other indicators (criteria or factors to serve as desired attributes to consider in evaluating options), major alternatives (list of options from which a choice is to be made), and methods to assess the degree to which a major alternative satisfies the measures of purpose accomplishment (evaluation techniques).

Other considerations usually enter the picture with these and the Results questions—the importance or weighting of each measure of purpose accomplishment (each one usually is not equal to the others), likelihood of occurrence of particular conditions, the scales used to assess the alternative in terms of the criteria, the risks to assets from threats and vulnerabilities and possible countermeasures, and complexity of implementation, as illustrations. The Question Forward Decision Worksheet tends to be used more formally and completely with Target and Results questions. It contains all of the above considerations in a format that aids the orderly selection.

The worksheet is a reminder to everyone about what a decision involves as well as a convenient form to fill out as the decision process proceeds. But it contains nothing about the key ingredient in doing an evaluation—how each alternative would work. The details provide some basis for helping the individual or group to make the assessment of how much the alternative contributes to the measure. Many methods are available for making this assessment—rating scales of 0 to 100; yes or no; five points from "completely accomplishes" to "does not accomplish it at all;" and estimates of weight, dimensions, and costs. If weighting of importance of the factors is used, multiple assessments may be needed as the weightings are adjusted to reflect different trade-offs and uncertainties.

An important benefit of the QF Decision Worksheet is the increasing likelihood of avoiding the "technological imperative" in selecting a FIST—the tendency to focus on the beauty of the technology involved instead of considering all of the factors that will make a solution work.

# OTHER ISSUES HAVING TO DO WITH TARGET QUESTIONS

## What To Do with Ideas not Used?

Many of the components and details, even some major alternatives, not incorporated in the FIST may well be considered useful at a later time, in other departments or solution creation activities you are working on, and possibly included in the organization's knowledge management data base to make them available for other projects. Those that are potentially valuable for the living solution you will be developing could be listed as "parking lot" topics to consider in the continuing changes developed with Results questions.

One advantage of Target questions when considering ideas to incorporate in, say, a knowledge management database is that the system matrix description of many of them provides a basis for classifying them for easy accessibility. Someone looking for ideas about product ideas could search for entries in the output elements of those in the database. In addition, all the ideas and the FIST itself should be used as a learning experience for the people involved as well as for the whole organization, even if the later Results questions show the FIST is a mistake or the eventual outcome fails.

## Defining a FIST in the Heat of Battle

It is easy to think about future solution targets when you are in a workshop with a trained facilitator, isolated from the hectic environment of answering voicemail, e-mail, and the constant interruptions of the modern businessperson, teacher, or parent. The question is, is it reasonable to believe that you can continue in the heat of battle to focus on how a long-term Target solution for achieving the purposes could benefit you now, when you are most pressed for time?

We would suggest that the answer is yes. Not only is it possible, we think it is necessary.

169

It is the times where you are most absorbed in fire fighting or in an adversarial position that you need to focus on a target solution to achieve focus and larger purposes. Without the direction of a target, you can end up wasting time and blocking continuing change because of what you do on the spur of the moment. A focus on a target, even though its time horizon may be shortened from three years to eight months because of the heated battle, is a focus on results, on what is an important guide.

We were facilitating a manufacturing company's strategic planning activities. The executives had done very well in developing its focus and larger purposes. They were starting to develop ideas about the ideal way of organizing the company and producing its products and services when two different government-owned manufacturing facilities, located in opposite sections of the city, were put up for sale. The company had already decided that some new manufacturing facility would be needed if the product line was to be developed, expanded, and marketed as the strategic plan indicated, but had not designed a future manufacturing system target. The executives were delighted such space was available and discussed various pros and cons of each facility—location in relation to where employees lived, cost per square foot, maintenance history, utility of the current transportation arrangements, ease or difficulty of installing the current manufacturing system, and so on.

The executive group told us about the opportunity and said they were definitely leaning toward facility A because it was the best bargain, based on cost per square foot purchase price, requirements and costs of grounds and building upkeep, and related cost considerations. Since they were talking about moving the current manufacturing system to the facility, we asked, "What system would that lead to?" and "How would the new product line be incorporated?" We spent a couple of hours listing some "ideal" ideas to answer those questions, quickly reviewing them to determine possible workability, and estimating the impact of the ideas on achieving the company's long-term mission and vision. The one definitive outcome of discussing possible future solution targets was the decision to purchase facility B. The configuration of the two buildings were different (A was U-shaped and B was rectangular), with facility B having much greater flexibility than A for change to new products and state-of-the-art manufacturing equipment and only a five percent higher purchase cost basis.

### Benefits of Target questions

Ideal solutions are talked about often, usually without major results. The Target in PPTR carries on this creative thinking within an overall process that brings many stakeholders to the task and makes sure the right purpose is being sought. This thinking brings many benefits to the Target questions:

- Having a Target frequently improves the results you can get today.
- Trade-offs and compromises needed for selecting a solution are made in a forward-looking mode, especially helpful in accepting the sunk cost concept, that is, not letting the amount of money already spent on doing something stop you from walking away from that expenditure.
- What you do today is done within a framework of continual improvement.
- So-called resistance to change gives way to acceptance and even anticipation of change.
- Valuable lead time is gained for future changes because you know where you are headed.
- You can leap beyond competition, not just catch up.
- Contingency or back-up alternatives are already available.
- A creative environment is far more likely to exist when discussions deal with "what's the future solution?"
- Creating solutions with purposes and targets helps to establish a fun atmosphere.
- You do not let current knowledge limit your thinking.

*Make change with a FIST.*

### RECAP

**The Target Question Forward: How can we develop a target solution for the future that will guide what changes or designs to adopt today to achieve our focus and larger purposes?**

Taking advantage of the creative space developed by People Involvement with the Purposes questions is the aim of the Target questions. The focus purpose is usually bigger in scope, and the larger purposes of the focus open possible routes to *how* most ideally to achieve them. Four notions are the basis of the Target questions: (1.) A fantasy ideal system (100 percent reduction in costs, 0 percent waste, etc.) should always be the motivating goal in any solution creation effort—in other words, there is no such thing as *the* solution, just living solutions; (2.) the bisociation concept of creativity is much more effective when one of the thoughts or phrases used to "force an intersection" with the second stimulator thought or phrase is the focus and larger purposes; (3.) you can develop many technology fiction ideas from which a future solution target can be selected; and (4.) the regularity concept is used to keep an idea viable for as long as possible.

Structured and conversational techniques are presented for the list, build, and select questions. List is where many creativity techniques can be used as the second stimulator thought or phrase to generate as many solution ideas as possible in achieving the focus and larger purposes. Build sorts these ideas into major alternatives to consider as the future solution target. Select usually involves more formal decision procedures than for the People Involvement and Purposes questions because what is selected will become the direction of continuing change.

The focus and larger purposes along with the future solution target are what Question Forward calls a vision for the organization or individual. Both comprise a picture of what you would prefer to have occur. At the same time, they recognize the need to have anticipatory options available for contingency purposes—there is no certainty in the world (Chapter 2).

## Reflective Question

Think about a major problem or solution that you worked on in the past. What major alternatives did you consider before selecting the future solution target for achieving your focus and larger purposes, and how would the target work if ideal conditions were available?

# Chapter 7

# RESULTS

**The Results Question Forward: How can we develop a living solution(s) and implementation plans that work within their surrounding environments and systems for achieving the focus and larger purposes and also stay as close as possible to the target?**

## GETTING RESULTS

*"An idealist believes the short run doesn't count. A cynic believes the long run doesn't matter. A realist believes that what is done or left undone in the short run determines the long run."*
Sydney J. Harris

Heroic efforts. Giving your all. The commitment and dedication. We all appreciate the thrill of victory. Likewise, however, we all recognize the agony of defeat, of failing to deliver the intended results.

I remember as a Washington State student going to a basketball game in the 1970s between my school and UCLA. We took perennial favorite UCLA to three overtimes—but lost anyway. It was a great game and a great spectacle. But there was still a twinge of disappointment that we hadn't ultimately won. Was it a great game? Yes. Did I appreciate the effort by my team? Sure, but in the end we lost.

The point is that results matter, and the question addressed in this book is, "How can we give ourselves the best chance of getting effective and creative results now and continuing in the future from the solutions that we develop and implement?" Results questions recognize that seeking to install all of the perfection of a FIST right away is an almost certain road to getting nothing done, and, worse in

173

many ways, dampening future interest in developing creative and ideal ideas in the organization because of the illustration of such failures. Results questions are meant to get the recommended changes to reflect as far you can go now while retaining the built-in changes the FIST provides.

In Chapter 3, we talked about the concept of systems. Now we focus on creating and implementing solutions, not as isolated things, but as systems themselves. Why? Because the real result we want is always to solve tomorrow's as well as today's problems.

This process of developing solutions with Results questions is similar to the process of creating ideal solutions with Target questions, as discussed in Chapter 6. The key difference: Target solutions are ideal—and not necessarily implementable now. Results questions are meant to come up with solutions that *can* be done now—and yet will still keep us on the path to our desired target future.

The purpose of Results questions is to translate the work of the People, Purposes, and Target questions into both the recommended change for now and the projected future changes (and assignments of responsibility to develop them). This purpose will advance the solution toward the FIST. (So even though we cover Results in only one chapter, just like we covered People, Purposes, and Target questions, be warned! Getting results almost always takes far longer than any other.)

One reason results takes more time is that, for example, it might require several ad hoc task groups to work on detailing parts of a solution, including:

- To prepare proposals to get the resources for development and follow-up of parts of the target
- To address involvement in parts of the approval process
- To handle purchasing of equipment
- To prepare and implement organizational change activities
- To monitor outcomes of the changes

Our major comment concerning how these other possible parts of a project should be thought about is simple—use all QF questions, especially the PPTR ones, when taking responsibility for any and all of the above kinds of assignments or tasks.[30]

## LIST QUESTIONS

### QF: What are some ideas we can use to keep the solution as close to the target as possible?

*"It is a bad plan that admits of no modification."* Publius Syrus

The sky was the limit for the Target list questions, but with Results questions it is time to face the so-called barriers, constraints, limitations, obstacles, and restrictions that we didn't get rid of then. we will try again with Results questions to eliminate barriers, constraints, etc., that we face *now* in the real world.

Some of the reasons that our FIST can't be implemented now might include:
- Technology is not available
- Skills will need to be developed over a long time frame
- The attitudes of various players in the pending change need to be "handled carefully"
- Irregularities have to be handled
- All the required resources will not be allocated right away
- The likelihood of unexpected outcomes or unanticipated consequences seems to be risky
- Key decision makers are skeptical about the target ever working

Even though our FIST faces such impediments, try to minimize their influence during the Results list and build questions; let them come into play with the select questions instead.

In essence, the list questions for Results are the same as those for developing the Target list. The aim is to develop many options about

175

how the recommended change can stay as close as possible to the FIST. Bisociation is quite effective. Only the wording changes:

**QF: What ideal ways can we think of to achieve the purposes of this FIST component (service, action, process, etc.) by means of a "zebra" (dictionary, flashcard, robot, a specific technology or patent, etc.) that will be as close as possible target solution?**

Let's look at a quick example of how Results questions work to lead us to the best Results list:

### *The OTC Case: Outsourcing the IT Function*

A client, Outsourcing Technology Company (OTC), does a multi-billion dollar business supplying of outsourcing information technology (IT) workers and services to other companies. That is, OTC workers do the computer work in-house for a company, and OTC manages the department or division. IT is not the only activity that can be outsourced. Other examples include accounting, payroll, manufacturing, research and development or marketing.

Usually, OTC actually hires the IT professionals at the company as a way of outsourcing the IT function. Getting workers to happily leave their company to work for the outsourcer is almost always a volatile process that takes a good deal of care to manage.

**Structured Methods**

In the case of OTC, there were a number of major target alternatives. Let's just look at how we handled one of them.

Overall, as with Target questions, we used both structured methods and conversational and intuitive methods to list Results solution ideas. Along with the Question Forward approach, we also used ideas from the Target list as a spark to help us develop our Results list.

One major target alternative was to create an "expert system." (These systems are like an elaborate, interactive help menu, only more so. They can give answers to any question on a certain topic. In this case, the topic was outsourcing transitions.)

At the meeting of the project team, I set the context and clearly focused them by posing the basic Results question: What are some possible solutions that stay as close to the target as possible?

The team members were savvy computer geeks and knew that a true expert system was beyond their practical ability to produce (some experimental ones for medicine, for example, have been decades in development). The main reason that expert systems have been so difficult to develop is that our brain has incredible power, handling hundreds and thousands of variables.

However, the expert system ideal target was a good springboard to come up with a more practical result. They could develop a living methodology for transitioning, if they worked out a scheme for a database of ever-evolving best practices, tools, and techniques that could be searched (queried) by people involved in outsourcing transitions. Sure, it wasn't as elegant as a real expert system, but it got them most of the way there. Moreover, it supported their main purpose of having outsourcing transitions that helped outsourced employees feel welcomed and valued in their new company.

Having come up with this living methodology idea, we then used the systems matrix and its Questions Forward to list its possible elements. The following is an excerpt of a detailed listing of result ideas for the elements that could lead to the expert system FIST:

**QF: What are other potential purposes of the living methodology system in addition to those determined with the Purposes questions?**

- To have an updated and evolving record of outsourcing methodology
- To enable change agents with practices and tools
- To have a state-of-the-art practice of outsourcing transitions

**QF: What are potential inputs that stay close to the target?**

- Current outsourcing transition practices
- Change agents
- Outsourced employees
- OTC

**QF: What are potential outputs that stay close to the target?**

- Updated methodology, practices, and tools
- Empowered change agents
- Outsourced employees who feel more valued and empowered
- More successful outsourcing business for OTC

**QF: What are potential processes for converting the inputs to outputs that stay close to the target?**

- Ensure the project team has all the resources needed
- Decide on an approach to creating the methodology
- Create a draft of the methodology
- Review draft with sponsors and other impacted change agents
- Create tools, templates, to support the methodology in the field
- Publish the methodology
- Train change agents in the use of the methodology
- Determine next revision schedule

**QF: What are potential environmental elements that stay close to the target?**

- Use a virtual team approach to developing the methodology since this will save on travel expense
- Have a project team that is clear about its task, roles and responsibilities, budget, and the deadlines for completing the project
- Have a methodology that breaks new ground, not simply best practice (copying what others are doing).

**QF: Who are potential human agents that stay close to the target?**

- Question Forward coach
- Sponsors of the project
- Change agents who have been outsourced and understand the experience
- Project team members

**QF: What are potential physical catalysts
that stay close to the target?**

- Computers
- Internet infrastructure
- Telecommunication equipment
- Word processing software

**QF: What are potential information enablers
that stay close to the target?**

- Social scientific research about what makes human transitions or major changes most successful
- Experience of outsourced employees
- Outsourcing best practices

Some of the elements listed above were generated by expanding the elements of the Target solution. That is, the expansion concept for purposes is used for the other system elements—what are the inputs to the target inputs, the inputs to that, and so on, what outputs will the Target outputs produce, what are the outputs of that, and so on.

For example, in the Target solution expert system, one of the inputs, outputs, and human agents was employees who had been outsourced were recognized as a key part of the expert system because they would be users of the system and their experience of being outsourced would be captured by the expert system and would be used to help the system be ever evolving and learning. It turns out that the same human agents were also key to creating and updating the living methodology solution.

## Conversational and Intuitive Methods

Conversational and intuitive methods of listing solution ideas can be very powerful in the Results questioning. This is especially true when practitioners use the systems matrix, having memorized, over time, its elements and dimensions and many of their questions.

Each of the forty-eight cells (see Figure 3-1) contains a number of possible questions (see Table 3-A1) that can be used to guide a conversation to list elements of a solution. Knowing which cell or which questions to ask at a particular time becomes a matter of intuition, experience, and judgment.

As a rule of thumb, in any conversation or meeting that I attend, I am always paying attention to what elements of a solution participants are talking about. Even more so, however, I pay attention to the elements that are not being discussed and will, when appropriate, ask a Question Forward of the group or person to stimulate more systems thinking around a particular solution.

### QF: What is the "best" way we could use the target to achieve the best purpose?

For example, one part of the target in a project was to hold a communication fair. The idea was to achieve the purpose of creating buzz (marketing) for a new system. But after a good deal of discussion about purposes and the complexities of some of the list ideas, and after some team members met with the fair idea's sponsor again to discuss his purposes, the communication event was canceled. From a systems perspective, it was not feasible because of the early stages of the project and the amount of resources it would have taken.

## Handling Irregularities

Back to the outsourcing idea. The team determined that the regular use of the outsourcing practice guide would be via the Internet via a secure corporate Web site. The most important irregularity was that 10 percent—20 percent of the time, users would be at client sites and unable to access the corporate site. The team listed some possible solutions, including:

- Have a CD version of the guide and tools available for employees who traveled regularly
- Publish a hard copy version of the guide and tools
- Have portions of the guide and tools that could be downloaded via modem connections

**QF: What ideal solution would take care of this irregularity?**

One of the main purposes of the Results list questions is to find ways to accommodate the exceptions. Asking this Question Forward about the irregularity often leads to ways to eliminate the "cause" of the exception and even be able to use the target as designed. Customers of your organization are often the source of the irregularity. So ask the customer(s) "What purpose does this irregularity serve or what do you want to accomplish with it, and what's the purpose of that?" And then "How would you achieve that purpose if you started over again?" And then, "How would the start-over-again solution work in system terms?" This approach treats an irregularity as any problem you have to solve. You begin by asking about the purposes dealing with irregularity.

You may come up with even better ideas this way. So the "irregular" customer can become a part of the solution you are developing and of what it may become in the future.

## BUILD QUESTIONS

**QF: What do the solutions look like as a system?**

Once you've developed the ideas and elements of the results, it's time to add enough detail to the solution ideas so they can be examined for workability and implementability. Once again, there are both structured, and conversational and intuitive methods.

**Structured Methods**

The most common structured method for building or "detailing" the options for Results solutions is to use the systems matrix and especially its dimension questions (see Table 3-A1 for the starter question matrix). This type of information is needed to let you make the best possible decision with the Select questions.

Each of the 6 dimensions for each of the 8 elements can be used to build a detailed picture of the possible Results solutions. However, it is not always necessary to explore all six dimensions for all 8 system elements. As a general rule, for very large and complex systems, it is a good idea to explore all six of the dimensions for each of the eight elements. As systems decrease in terms of size and complexity, more limited exploration of dimensions questions is generally appropriate.

**QF: What dimensions should we explore?**

In addition to size and complexity of systems, a QF practitioner should use the uniqueness principle to help determine which dimensions are most likely to be most relevant for the solution design effort. For example, in the outsourcing case, when they considered the uniqueness of the system they were designing, they determined that the values dimension was particularly important because one of the key issues that the team was dealing with was how to help the newly outsourced employees feel they were valued members of the outsourcing company. This consideration led them to explore the values dimension with particularly close attention.

They considered the values dimension by asking questions for each of the elements. For example, for the output element they asked the following question, Figure 7-1 illustrates some of the responses.

Figure 7-1. Illustrative Values dimensions of the
Output element of the OTC case.

| Output Components | Values to Build into the Solution |
|---|---|
| Updated methodology, practices, and tools | In the methodology and practices, there should be explicit instructions, samples communication events and messages about how to communicate that the outsourced employees are valued by their new company. |
| Empowered change agents | Change agents who are facilitating the outsourcing process should be instructed on the importance of communicating to outsourced employees about the issue of valued employees. |
| Outsourced employees who feel more valued and empowered | There should also be a workshop developed that could help the new employees participate in designing their own future within the outsourced company. |
| More successful outsourcing business for OTC | It is believed that outsourced employees who feel more valued will result in more successful business practices and could also result in some future marketing messages to potential clients. |

**QF: What sort of values do we want to design into our outputs?**

In addition to considering uniqueness, size, and complexity of systems, there are other factors that can be used to determine which dimension questions should be asked and answered.

## QF: How can we make the output product or system user friendly?

The technological developments of the last decade or so have occurred at a rapid rate. The emphasis in the late 1990s was often focused on getting the technology out there as fast as possible (the technological imperative). Part of the so-called collapse of the new economy is due to the lack of consideration of how the user would be able to effectively get the benefits of the product or system. Simple example: You now have a 20 gig hard drive with all your work for the last year on it. Have you backed it up lately? Why? Because it is so time-consuming and typically difficult to do reliably. If you still had floppies, you would probably be at less risk of total loss of your data. (Maybe you should back up that disk now!)

This general user-friendly Question Forward can lead to others, including:

- QF: How will the solution option improve the user's productivity?
- QF: Does the option project simplicity?
- QF: Is the option convenient to use or follow?
- QF: Does the option pose any risks to the user?
- QF: If appropriate, is the option fun to use and project a good image?

Will it be possible to eliminate all undesirable and unfriendly outcomes? Of course not. But it helps to expand the output element and its dimensions to reduce the likelihood of them.

## QF: How can we minimize the impact of negative and potential unintended consequences of the option if used?

Every change is part of one or more larger systems. Every system is a node on a relationship network. Almost every solution poses a possible workability conflict even at this point between certain element/dimension desired conditions, say a physical enabler and a human agent. And consequences of the change will occur, as Chapter

3 discussed and, however we've maximized the benefits, there are always things that will go wrong (remember Murphy's law).

The system matrix elements and dimensions and the many questions raised by each element/dimension cell are the critical form for probing such seeming imponderables in the decision process. Will the system matrix always provide the information needed? No, but it does significantly increase the likelihood of "catching" many of the glitches that could affect the decision and the eventual installation and success of a change and its future changes.

**QF: What resources are at our disposal to build the system?**

If the project team is large, the funding large, materials plentiful, and the talent pool rich, more dimension issues can be explored with Build questions

For example, the environment element and its dimensions may take on major significance to the workability today and in the future of a particular option. So expertise in the group concerning major world trends might be important, for example, people or information on the aging of the population, the seemingly contradictory new baby boom that will be occurring, the growth of entrepreneurship at all age levels, the rate of technological developments, greater threats of terrorism, and increasing population and cultural diversity.

**QF: How much time is available for building the system?**

In setting up the time to allocate to a particular task, especially if in weeks or months, also set up interim, weekly deadlines for completion milestones of particular portions of the task. Each of the options for staying close to the target may have much different tasks and times needed for each that will have to be detailed with build questions. Each option may also need to consider the way it might be implemented—whether to seek a big one-time installation or to install smaller segments to generate incremental successes.

Time (and resources) will also shape one of the most important interim build decisions. To determine workability of an option, should we develop a prototype model, or set up a pilot facility to test the operating steps, or do an extensive computer simulation, or draw extensive charts[31] and flow process graphs, or do focus group studies, or in some way test the workability of the option?

### QF: How will the interfaces with other systems work?

Because every solution or system is part of larger systems, you'll always have to work out the details for the "fit" between your solution and the "bigger picture." Since Results includes the issue of ensuring workability, some of the other build questions that help detail a description of the options are:

- What buffering aspects or factors to avoid are needed to keep this option working?
- How can we develop bridge-building aspects with other systems to increase the likelihood of success and improvement of this option and its utility to other systems?
- What specific external systems interactions are needed for the particular element of this option to maintain the option's effective operation within its larger context?
- Can we identify several orders of consequences of the option and its technology beyond its initial implementation, and how might those consequences be ameliorated, handled, or, if positive, enhanced in building the details of the option?
- What priorities should be set up for work to be done if the assignment of parts of the option for development is given to task subgroups?

### QF: How do we know when we have answered enough of the QF build questions?

One good test: Determine if the team feels they can move forward to the select questions. It is also important to remember that all list, build, and select questions of the Question Forward PPTR process are iterative (like a feedback loop), so a team or individual can revisit earlier questions.

## Conversational and Intuitive Methods

As a QF consultant or coach, there are always numerous meetings that occur in the process of doing work. All meetings need planning to some degree to ensure success. However, in some cases the meetings occur in an ad hoc fashion, which leaves little or no time for planning. These types of meetings provide an ideal setting for using conversational and intuitive methods for doing QF.

Keeping in mind the systems framework, you can use it to construct an ad hoc agenda that is more likely to give you the results that will make a difference. Below is a sample of one agenda that was created in the first ten minutes of the meeting.

### QF: What are the purposes of the meeting?

- Prepare for strategic planning workshop
- Lay the groundwork for eventual use of the strategic plan

### QF: What are the main outcomes you want from the meeting?

- Have an agenda, logistics, and responsibilities assigned for conducting the upcoming strategic planning meeting
- Commitment of time and resources to make the strategic planning meeting successful

### QF: What are the ground rules (environment) for this meeting?

- Record action items
- Allow everyone the chance to participate in the planning
- No sidebar conversations
- Allow the facilitator to do his/her job

### QF: Who will play what roles in the meeting (people enablers)?

- Facilitator: Mary
- Scribe to take meeting notes: James

## QF: What will be the next steps (process, future dimension) for the team after the meeting?

- The team will decide this during the meeting and record future action items

## QF: What are the agenda items for this meeting (process steps) and how much time do we allocate to them?

- Check in (5 minutes to allow people to say what's on their mind in order to "get present")
- Determine purposes of strategic planning meeting (15 minutes)
- Determine desired outcomes for strategic planning meeting (15 minutes)
- Determine attendees invite list (10 minutes)
- Decide time and location (10 minutes)
- Determine pre-work required (20 minutes)
- Assign responsibilities for logistics (10 minutes)
- Determine next steps (10 minutes)
- Process check: How did the meeting work? Did we get the results that we were looking for? (5 minutes)

## SELECT QUESTIONS

### QF: What is the first release?

In software, first release (or version 1.0) pretty much implies that it "ain't" perfect yet...and there will be new versions coming to address the bugs and make improvements.

The idea of releases is useful and you can apply it to any solution. In Question Forward, no solution is ever viewed as final and complete. We assume there are always future releases (or versions) of the solution. In the Results select questions, we identify both the first release and subsequent releases that should move toward the Target solution and eventually redesign the FIST itself.

**Structured Methods**

Once enough detail had been provided for the various possible build solutions, it is time to select which solution or solutions will actually be implemented. There are a number of formal methodologies that can be used as an aid for decision making such as the following:

- Multi-attribute utility models (MAU)

- Cost effectiveness analysis

- Pair comparison

- Sensitivity analysis

- Contingency analysis

- Variance analysis

- Subjective probability assessment

- Expert consensus

Many software packages[32] based on one or more of these methods are available, supposedly to help you make a decision. They almost always ask you to enter or develop the type of information you have already prepared through the PPTR questions to this point. That is, what are the alternatives you are considering, what criteria/factors/measures are to be considered in making the selection, and how much importance do you assign to each of those factors? Then, the package asks about issues that pertain to one or more of the above techniques. The software then makes its particular calculations and most often says "Alternative B is best" and claims that the risk has been removed from making that selection.

Our advice from the hundreds of projects we have worked on and know about is simple—don't believe that claim or even assume the calculations from the Question Forward Decision Worksheet, even though they are relatively simple to use and sufficiently robust to handle most complex decisions, give you *the* answer. Bargaining about and negotiating the trade-offs that are often needed, especially concerning probabilities of occurrences of certain events, risk assessment, and values and ethics issues, is common.

## QF: What political and social factors may need to be considered in selecting the first release?

> *"Politics, not technology, sets the limits*
> *of what technology is allowed to achieve."*
> Brenda Forman

Many of these possible considerations may have surfaced with the Target select questions, but were probably set aside to let a good future ideal solution target be selected as the guide. These Select questions form the basis of where the decision is supposed to be putting the rubber to the road. That aspect may produce some probing and hesitation about accepting the numbers about *the* best alternative because some of the following factors and Questions Forward are raised:

- QF: Which alternative provides a unique and valuable strategy others will find difficult to match?
- QF: Would we be better off just tinkering with what we have rather than embarking on a diffcrent path?
- QF: Does our management team have a shared appreciation of where the alternative is leading?
- QF: Do we know if the plan balances its direction with particular high business impact areas?
- QF: How do we know we have the skill sets necessary to move ahead with this alternative?
- QF: What are the ethical and social issues that we should be considering about each alternative?
- QF: Aren't there interpersonal and social issues that might interfere with using this solution?
- QF: If we select this alternative, what is the likelihood that R&D will be able to accomplish the needed developments to let us move toward the FIST?

- QF: Will the costs of and time needed for implementing this option make it very difficult to obtain the expected benefits of the solution?
- QF: How will we be able to acquire the money to be able to install the solution even if the benefits of it far exceed the costs?
- QF: Will the risk tolerance of our management and R&D departments play a role?

*"Money does not make the world go round...[Political events, sex, and power shape modern life and are] individually or together capable of over-riding money."*[33]

Coping with these kinds of questions at this point requires that you ask about the purpose of the factor (such as R&D for designing future solutions) and then, what's the purpose of that factor? In many situations, the factor sort of disappears or becomes irrelevant and in other situations the factor may be useful. If it is indeed worth considering, add it to the list of criteria. However, the measures of purpose accomplishment ought to remain the key decision factors.

### QF: What solution or solutions will best fit our decision criteria (mainly the measures of purpose accomplishment)?

In the OTC outsourcing case, the sponsors of the project were very clear about the criteria that were used to help select the solutions. Since OTC was getting large, signing new outsourcing deals on a regular basis, there was a good deal of urgency to get a solution in place. The time frame the sponsors had in mind was four months to create and implement a solution. In addition, there was a fixed budget created for the project even before the solution was defined. Finally, the solution had to be supportive of the focus purpose of the project, which was to help newly outsourced employees feel valued, welcomed, and be productive team members. The solution or solutions that could best meet the requirements of the time frame, budget, and focus purpose would be selected.

Selecting a first release will in many cases require that formal standards of expected performance be set up for it. The values, measures, and control dimensions of the system matrix should have alerted you to this need when detailing the release. Part of setting up of such expectations will also be carried over to the implementation planning activities where certain changes are to be scheduled for accomplishment within certain time and cost amounts. Such implementation amounts may in some cases be a part of the cost/time tradeoff considerations for selecting the first release.

### Conversational and Intuitive Methods

### QF: What solution or solutions make the most sense for us to implement?

*Beware of the technological imperative and the sunk cost fallacy.*

In the case of OTC, the process of selecting the Results solutions was structured in that there were decision criteria. It was also intuitive as there were a number of conversations that led to the adoption of viable solutions. The technical experts advised a Web-based outsourcing guide and tools, with hyperlinks and downloadable tools was too complicated to do within the budget and time constraints.

After consultation, the project team, through conversations among themselves and with sponsors, decided that what was doable was to create the outsourcing guide and tools using standard office software that was readily available to all team members and consultants in the field. Eventually, the office software could be used to create the Web-based version of the guide and tools. It was also decided that the guide and tools would be available for download on the Internet and that a CD version of the guide and tools would be created and distributed to meet the irregularity conditions of consultants at client sites without Internet access.

### INSTALLATION PLANNING

### QF: Who needs to do what in order to have a successful installation of the living solution?

One of the key mistakes unsuccessful project managers of change efforts make is to leave consideration of implementation until the solution has been fully designed. The assumption is that you cannot know how you will implement something until you have designed "the something." There are many great ideas, but it takes the creativity and discipline of Question Forward, and time, to translate the recommended solution into usable results.

In addition, there are many other aspects of installation each of which must be designed with PPTR to be the most effective—getting a champion and other persuaders for the recommended change and its FIST, preparing a proposal to get financing, transitioning or phasing in the plan; ordering equipment, tools, and facilities; arranging for construction, if needed; training, monitoring of initial use of the solution; normalizing or optimizing the solution while in operation. And so on. Presentations about the project status may be needed at various points in the whole project as well as during installation. The radical and/or complexity characteristics of the recommended solution will also affect the amount of time and effort needed for many of these aspects, such as getting approval for the financing and the training.

These other aspects are needed in many projects. Question Forward and PPTR considered implementation in the usual buy-in concept way in present approaches along with the solution design process, starting immediately with People Involvement. That's where the Question Forward Process Worksheet deals with the critical people (contributors, affected people, decision makers) to involve with the subsequent Purposes, Target, and Results questions. So we call this part of Results "installation planning" to distinguish it from many of the factors usually thought to be involved in "implementation"—get buy-in of people who have to change, sell the solution to decision makers. In addition, we consider human enablers (using the systems matrix) for every part of installing the living system. That is, we ask:

**QF: Who will be the human enabler of which part of the solution?**

Further, we consider how (the process element of the systems matrix) the human enablers will support the solution design and implementation.

## QF: What process or set of steps are required for the human enabler (or change agent) to support design and installation of the solution?

A useful way of thinking about installation is as a system itself. That is, every installation effort has purposes, inputs, outputs, a process, an environment, physical enablers, human enablers, and information enablers and their associated dimensions. This is a powerful corrective for a common mistake of thinking of installation as simply a synonym for training. Installation is a much broader consideration of which training is generally only a component. The standards and cost/time tradeoffs noted with the Select questions will often play a critical role in detailing the installation system.

In the case of OTC, the primary installation initiative was to involve a substantial number of change agents, who had some involvement in outsourcing projects, in the process of design and review of the outsourcing guide and tools. This accomplished two key objectives: The guide was richer and more complete because of the experience that the change agents brought to the design task; and the change agents were educated in the process and committed to using the guide even before it was complete. No major training effort was necessary. The change agents who were involved in the development process became coaches for other change agents who were new to the outsourcing process and for those other change agents who had not had the opportunity to be involved in the development process.

## Evaluating Results and Next "Releases"

*"It is less painful to anticipate than react....Expect the unexpected."*
Eberhart Rechtin

In Question Forward we begin with the assumption that any solution we use today will be changed toward the target or at least can always be improved. We live and work in complex systems, which do

194

not lend themselves to understanding and predicting every consequence and impact of implementing a new system or solution. Particularly where human organizations (and all organizations are human) are concerned, we expect to be surprised. As Kurt Lewin, a father of sociology, said, if you want to understand an organization, try to change it.

### QF: How is the solution working and what changes does our evaluation suggest for our next releases?

The process of defining next releases, which occurs with Results questions, is a process of creating a roadmap that we think will take us to our destination, which in Question Forward is our ideal solution or target. We assume that as we learn from the process of installation and use of the new system, we will evaluate what is working well and what isn't and change our roadmap when appropriate. We advocate both a qualitative and quantitative approach to evaluating results. That is: Measures of the system elements and, particularly, measures of purpose accomplishment and feedback from talking with users, customers, and maintainers of systems and solutions—the whole consumer experience.

Because the FIST was selected on the basis of a particular time frame, what is today considered the future target needs to be redone sometime before the end of that time frame.

In our work with clients, we include at a particular point, say in the second year of a three-year time frame, the activity of redoing the whole system using the PPTR questions. We call this the inclusion of a "sunset review," as it is called in government legislation—that is, revisiting the legislation near the end of its designated life existence to determine if it should continue to remain in effect.

Even if one of the releases eventually leads to abandonment of the whole solution concept, treat it as a learning experience rather than a mistake. The group should be open from the PPTR questions to going back to assessing how the whole solution creation process can be improved for future efforts.

## QF: How can we get closer to our target system?

*"Every noble work is at first impossible."* Carlyle

In the case of OTC, after six months, it was clear that the solution was working pretty well. What the evaluations did suggest was that newly outsourced employees wanted more communication with their new leadership team. There were already a number of communication events built into the practice guide, but customers (new outsourced employees) of the practice wanted even more. Further, more change agent coaches were required to support an ever-increasing pipeline of business. So, more change agents were hired and trained to support the outsourcing efforts.

### Results in the Heat of Battle

The key to keeping results-focused in the heat of battle is to use the systems matrix enough, so that the framework becomes second nature and can be called on to take a step back from the action and figure out what questions you need to ask to move the action forward. Even in the series of conversations and meetings that occur for many people in the course of a regular day, the forty-eight Questions Forward in the systems matrix can be a powerful framework to ask:

## QF: What part of the system are we not considering and should explore?

In conversations, ask yourself, "Have we talked about purposes, about outputs and inputs, about the environment, about enablers—people, physical, and information?" This will, we believe, more than any other intervention, help you to become a powerful systems thinker. The good news is that is not rocket science.

Also, keep the questions and ideas from the three foundation questions and already developed in the PPTR process to this point as mental reference points in dealing with the likely obstacles that may be placed in the way of installation of the solution. Almost every comment will have been dealt with in one or more of the PPTR questions. And be wise enough to recognize the rare comment that may not have been adequately addressed in your solution and be ready to ask the Questions Forward you already know: What would be an ideal way of coping with that comment so we can get the solution to work? We can all do this.

## RECAP

**The Results Question Forward: How can we develop a living solution(s) and implementation plans that work within their surrounding environments and systems for achieving the focus and larger purposes and also stay as close as possible to the Target?**

*"Success is never final."* Winston Churchill

Good efforts may be psychologically satisfying, but results are what matter most in business. Good results occur by using the target system as a focus of our design and installation effort. We want to have our first release and subsequent releases be a road map, which leads to our ideal solution, the target system. Good solution design and implementation efforts are achieved by viewing solutions and their installation efforts as systems. The systems framework is the main tool to enable us to work as system thinkers and change agents.

## Reflective Question

How can I start using the systems matrix framework in meetings and conversations?

*Gerald Nadler and William J. Chandon*

# SECTION III. ORGANIZATION QUESTIONS

Section III looks at how asking the right questions leads to the creation of an adaptable organization, one that innovates and achieves continually improving results. Learning from our lives as Question Forward practitioners, as consultants, and as members of organizations has led us to the core theme in this section, which is how we can create an adaptable organization or what we call a "Question Forward Organization (QFO)." A QFO lives with the advantages of change-enabling and creative organizational questions. We argue that in this age of knowledge-working, networked organizations that any successful long-term organizational change effort will have three key organizational questions underlying the approach taken – questions about language, systems perceptiveness, and empowerment.

Similarly, the Question Forward foundation questions, organizational questions, and action questions of PPTR let you and your fellow citizens do better in promoting superior results in professional and societal activities outside of organizations. Chapter 9, the last one, will deal with how Question Forward can improve many specific disciplines, professions, and societal situations, many of which will be the subject of follow-up books with the subtitle of "Ask the Right Questions." It will review societal issues, from local to national to international scopes, to provide actual cases and speculative ones that show how Question Forward can lead to major policy and systems results beyond work and organizations, the focus of this book.

An underlying message of both chapters in this section is that Question Forward provides a basis for releasing the "free" creativity inherent in humans. Many efforts are made in organizations and society to do this – incentives, education, time-off for "doing your own thing," resources to try out ideas, motivational posters and talks. Some people respond to such blandishments, but most do not.

199

Witness the very low rate of suggestions per employee in the United States, even in companies with employee suggestion systems. "Creativity is free" is realistic and prevalent in all situations when the right questions are asked, as illustrated in the following two chapters.

As a reminder, selecting which questions to ask for each of the issues with which you are concerned is aided by considering the following criteria for selecting the "right" question:

- Does it align with foundation, action, and organization Question Forward questions?
- Does it open and expand look-to-the-future responses and possibilities?
- Does it create new Question Forward-type metaphors?
- Does it feel like an interesting or important Question Forward?
- Does it spark creative responses (many options, other Question Forward-type questions)?
- Is it likely to bring people together enthusiastically and with commitment to focus on building a desired future and getting results?

*"Efforts and courage are not enough without purpose and direction."*
John F. Kennedy

# Chapter 8

# BECOMING A
# QUESTION FORWARD ORGANIZATION

**Question Forward : How can we have successful organizations?**

It's one thing for you to be good at using Question Forward yourself. But it takes different skills and knowledge to get others to Question Forward, too.

Our position is that successful organizations in the twenty-first century will be highly proficient in the way they think and take action. Even stronger, we would argue that the one key core competency of all successful organizations is the ability to think together and to take effective action based on that thinking. If you think about it for a second, it is almost as obvious as the nose on our faces and doesn't need much argumentation to support it. As more and more work in organizations becomes knowledge work and networked work (working with groups, teams, other functions, organizations, outsiders, partners, etc.), it makes sense that the most successful organizations will think better, think together, and take the most effective action together.

Our model for the organization of the twenty-first century is what we call a Question Forward Organization (QFO)—one that plans, designs, develops, implements, creates, improves, and solves problems the Question Forward way. How do we get our organizations to adopt more effective ways of thinking together? How do we get our organization to recognize that people are the key to success and greatness, and that technology is an enabler (and not the magic bullet). To become a QFO, an organization's leaders and QF facilitators must incorporate the mental model of foundation questions and PPTR action questions within an organization to create organizational adaptabilty. Powerful practices of thinking and action taking enable organizations to adapt to changing conditions. The good news is that we believe that the single best organizational change intervention that you can use is to implement Question Forward in your organization, to create a QFO.

A management consultant who uses Question Forward joined the board of directors of a $200 million manufacturing company. He found that executives presented recommendations (say, spend $500,000 for a flexible manufacturing cell) in a way that sought a yes or no decision, the either/or dilemma described in Chapter 1. This put the board members into a probing-for-details frame of mind that produced a lot of information about what exists and what happened in the past. If the board decided not to approve the recommendation, the executive most often left the meeting in a dejected mood, assuming that the board did not have confidence in him or her. The new board member proposed that executives should in the future put their recommendations in a Question Forward context:

- What are the purposes of the recommendation?
- What are the relationships of the purposes to the larger organizational and customer purposes?
- What are the scenario options from which the recommendation was selected?
- What justifications besides costs and returns on investment, for the recommendation, relate to the larger purposes?
- What system framework ensures workability and implementation?
- What impact will the recommendation have on future developments and strategy of the company?

When the executives started to do this, the discussion revolved around what could be better for the company and its present and potential customers instead of the facts of the recommendation. In the next fifteen years of the board member's tenure, according to board members and company executives, 50 to 60 percent of the decisions about what to actually implement were better than what was initially proposed. The board members were also much more pleased with the process and felt they obtained a much better perspective about the whole company. A company with clear purposes as guides can act effectively in all its roles.

Furthermore, the examples of actual changes being placed in a Question Forward framework at the board level helped others in the company below the executive ranks to adopt the precepts. A powerful language for innovation and a systems perceptiveness were employed at the board level, and, as a result, a heightened sense of empowerment cascaded through the managers and executives with whom the board worked, and moved the company to become a QFO. Leaders at all levels understood the need to manage people involvement effectively, provide strategic thinking and management to all, and grasp details of operations as well as the big picture.

Another critical point in this case is that concepts, such as Question Forward, are best learned and adopted by being embedded in organizational processes, projects, and experiences. They aren't something "extra" that the organization does. In time, they become "the way things are done." They become part of the organizational culture and thinking processes. They help to overcome the "collective stupidity" that grips organizations with even quite intelligent people who use the question backward approach. What managers *do* (the questions they ask) creates the experiences that are meaningful and empower people to take the right actions.

In addition, a QFO is an illustration of informality—there is no QF department, no QF director, no QF budget (except perhaps for training and some facilitators), no single QF organizational structure, and no QF hierarchy. Bureaucracies were a reasonably effective organizational form in low-technology environments when the pace of change was slow and incremental. Bureaucracies have now become dinosaurs, even in government organizations. Constituencies no longer tolerate change that can be measured by sundials. Becoming a QFO is, we have found, the best way of turning a bureaucracy into an empowered organization, a supporter of the people who want change rather than a reinforcement of rigid lines of authority. Companies are needed to achieve purposes that no single individual could accomplish, and achieving those purposes and their related measures

Gerald Nadler and William J. Chandon

of success in the most effective way requires, we believe, a Question Forward Organization.

> How *you introduce change is often more important*
> *than* what *the change is.*

## A QUESTION FORWARD ORGANIZATION: AN ADAPTABLE ORGANIZATION

To begin the journey to an adaptable organization, there are three key questions that need to be considered. The three key adaptability questions relate to having a rich language of thinking and innovation, a systems perceptiveness, and an empowering culture. These three questions are the core processes upon which any modern organization operates and changes. There are a multitude of other factors or dynamics that affect organizations—workflows, strategies, histories, values, stories, processes, practices, customers, competitors, government, and so on—but we argue that without having an enabling language, a systems perceptiveness, and an empowering culture, the organization is not positioned for long-term success in the twenty-first century.

Consider these comments about the benefits of a QFO made by the superintendent of a school district with 230,000 students in 650 schools: "Our staff thinks of work achievements in terms of end results rather than inputs and efforts, budgets, and manpower. This new way of thinking is changing our culture by focusing it on accountability and measures of success in achieving purposes. Our discussions are very intense, however, always in a positive atmosphere. The level of cooperation within the organization is constantly increasing. Question Forward is indeed a conceptually different thinking approach that has created major change in the way our supervisors, principals, teachers, and even pupils go about planning and solving problems. Our students are now better equipped to give more creative answers to more focused questions they ask."

Now consider an example at the negative end of the spectrum about the factors of a great, living organization. The Enron debacle in

204

the last quarter of 2001 shows a non-Question Forward Organization where throughout most of its history the right questions were *not* asked—using only one performance factor, origination of new business revenues, whether real or mainly speculative; stressing individual as opposed to team work; counting on political contributions to obtain regulations and exemptions favorable to the company; and setting up off-the-books entities to hide debts and concurrently enrich the perpetrators of the schemes. Ultimately, myopic approaches such as this fail.

## A Language for Thinking Together and Innovating

*"A word once spoken can't be caught by rapid horses."* Shigematsu

A project team member kept repeating how his technical expertise was underutilized and that he was being asked to do things he was unskilled for and uncomfortable doing. Yet when the project manager suggested an expanded role that could include some aspects of his technical specialty, he was so cynical and dejected that he wouldn't take the challenge or change. With an introduction to QF and the language or concept of the "ideal solution target," he was able to see that even though his ideal solution was to be more fully engaged in his technical specialty in the future, the current project was an opportunity to do some technical work, but also to try some things he had never tried. Without trying some new things, he had no idea whether they might be compatible with the future he was trying to create. He eventually opened his mind to the fact that there can be many paths to creating his desired future. He adopted more of an attitude of exploration and discovery rather than a rigid, narrow conception of himself and his work. What had been literally inconceivable to him became possible because of a vocabulary that allowed him to consider expanded possibilities. Without the language of an ideal solution and other questions of the QF approach, he was not able to make the connection between the future that he wanted and his current situation. That's the power of a thinking language, it makes impossibilities possible.

**The Language Question Forward: What language of innovation can bring a sense of meaning to and enroll others in bringing creative solutions to life?**

While there is plenty of knowledge that is intuitive (or implicit) and can't be put into words and communicated (the "that's just the way we do it here" sort of thing you have to learn on the job) via language, there is still plenty of explicit knowledge that people use language to communicate to each other, to pass along knowledge. In fact, it's just that sort of knowledge, like history and science, that, passed down through time and generations, makes humans able to progress in general—and specific organizations able to achieve, succeed, and continue to grow through generations of participants or workers.

All organizations have a language. Words they use and words they don't use. Words carry organizational stories (recall the types of information discussed in Chapter 2). To varying degrees, organizations are enabled or disabled by their vocabulary. In our experience, organizations that don't learn very well don't have a very rich vocabulary for thinking together innovatively, don't communicate and cooperate very well. Literally, they cannot conceive of ways of thinking and acting that would be different and more enabled. Bringing in an external consultant or attending a conference or training program can be very useful to help introduce a new vocabulary to an organization. While having a rich vocabulary of Question Forward doesn't ensure an enabled organization, it helps put an organization in a much better position to innovate, learn and grow.

**QF: What shared language can we introduce into our organization that will help enable it?**

Question Forward is agnostic toward the many other languages, philosophies, or tools of the various movements out there (e.g., emotional intelligence, Six Sigma, 360° feedback, total quality). But QF methods can easily help you determine if any particular language will be useful to you or your unique organization, internally and externally with customers, suppliers, the community, and other stakeholders. Remember that one size does not fit all nor does any management fad have your language. For example, the usual performance review conducted in organizations is almost always considered a downer for people because it focuses on what is past. Instead, emphasizing what can be done in the future is the forward-looking attitude engendered by Question Forward.

In fact, the best place to start is to use QF to ask whether the QF language is appropriate for your organization. How you deliver a message can be as important as the content of the message. Surprisingly, our position is that the generalized QF language used in this book is most likely not appropriate for your organization. Any organization already has a complex system of language and symbols (pictures, numbers, stories, metaphors, physical objects that have particular meanings) that are in place.

So, what do you do in your organization? How can you manage conversations of any sort (communication, negotiation, proposal, conflict, facilitation, meetings, interpretation) that should be forward moving, clear, neutral, and temperate, and minimize stress while encouraging creativity and honest expression of differences of opinion and ideas? You have to find, invent, or create a "dialect" of QF that works in your own organization. To converse better with everyone, we need to adopt the practice of asking the right questions and using the right metaphors. The good news is that the underlying fundamental and action questions are valid in any organization. Your task is to create a language and form questions that work in your organization. Question Forward language is essential in establishing a community that has some common set of language "rules" and words that satisfy the criteria for selecting a "right" question (see the Section III introduction).

One organization I was working with could not use the word "target" because it was a highly political organization where employees became "targets" like hunted animals when something went awry. For them, the words "solution possibilities" worked, so they used that language. Another organization had difficulty in using the word "purpose" because it had a religious connotation to its members, so we used the word "objective" for QF's meaning of purpose, and the people felt comfortable using "purpose" as another descriptor of "values and beliefs."

However, we suggest that you at least begin with the language in this book. Then find out what works and what doesn't and begin your creative process of finding your own language of Question Forward.

> *"Nothing shapes our lives so much as the questions we ask."*
> Sam Keen

## Perceptiveness

First off, what do we mean by "perceptiveness"? Simply, we mean the ability to think from a systems perspective (covered in Chapter 3 and in the PPTR action questions) and the ability to work effectively in a modern networked organization.

### The Perceptiveness Question Forward: How can we develop perceptiveness of systems for individuals, customers, suppliers, and society?

The introduction of computer and communications technology has created new organizational forms, which communicate, share knowledge, and work across previously impossible barriers. They function more as a network or spider web of formal and informal relationships across boundaries of geography, time, role, and authority. They are faster, more fluid, and more complex than their industrial era predecessors. To work effectively in a networked organization, several things must happen and certain challenges must be met.

For employees, some of these include the following, elegantly put forward by Robert Kegan, in his book *In Over our Heads: The Mental Demands of Modern Life,* (1994):

- To invent our own work, rather than see it as owned and created by the employer
- To be self-initiating, self-correcting, self-evaluating, rather than dependent on others to frame the problems, initiate

adjustments, or determine whether things are going acceptably well

- To be guided by our own visions at work, rather than be without a vision or be captive of the authority's agenda
- To take responsibility for what happens to us at work externally and internally, rather than see our present internal circumstances and future external possibilities as caused by someone else
- To be accomplished masters of our particular work roles, jobs, or careers, rather than have an apprenticing or imitating relationship to what we do
- To conceive of the organization from the outside in, as a whole; to see our relation to the whole; to see the relation of the part to the whole, rather than see the rest of the organization and its parts only from the perspective of our own part, for the inside out.

To summarize Kegan's points, employees need the ability to think and work in complex systems. According to Kegan's research, less than 50 percent of professionals in the current work environment have adequate intellectual horsepower for the jobs they are responsible to perform.

For organizations, employees with adequate perceptiveness pose certain problems, which they have to adjust to, including:

- Employees who have a perceptiveness of the whole appropriate more power and threaten traditional power structures and compensation programs. If you are going to act like an owner, you don't want to be compensated like an employee.
- Managers are fascinated with simple or objective criteria, (see Chapter 2; long-term growth and environmental responsibility are not easily measured), overemphasize highly visible behaviors (team work and creativity are hard to observe), and/or are hypocrites (do something for the organization as a whole while management is almost the sole beneficiary such as many incentive compensation systems for senior

management). It is often said in management circles that what is rewarded gets done, while what is not rewarded, however important it may be, does not get accomplished if not completely ignored.

So, the question is, What do we do about this? How can we help people to see issues in a big-picture or systems framework? The task sounds daunting, but the good news is that there are some concrete and practical steps that you can take.

### QF: What can we do to increase our organization's level of perceptiveness?

A simple, small-scale illustration shows the benefits to perceptiveness of maintaining a wholeness or even a system matrix consciousness. Everyone has experienced the situation where they are asked to do a simple task that exists in someone else's context—which of three candidates seem best to you for this position in my department, program this model that will fit into the bigger model I designed, buy some potatoes that I need for this recipe. And everyone has experienced the reaction in many of these situations to the proffered answer—but you didn't consider the whole skill level the position needs, you omitted critical variables in the program, those are not the kind of potatoes I need. You missed some obvious (to the person making the assignment) parts of the task, or, in other words, you didn't see the big picture.

Systems consciousness on the part of both of the parties in such situations would significantly help eliminate such outcomes. The perceptive requestor, with a system matrix consciousness, would have explained, for example, the expansion of purposes of the task, some of the output dimensions, and how the requested output fit within the requestor's larger context. The other party, if the requestor doesn't supply the information, should ask questions of the same sort to provide a framework for the task.

A systems consciousness, for instance, in addition to understanding the uniqueness principle would immediately alert everyone to the pitfalls of trying to adopt a "best practice" or copy a solution from somewhere else. Even the recommendation of the authors of an article[34] to "copy the working example *in detail* [sic]" doesn't lead them to conclude that it will work elsewhere all of the time.

**QF: What other tools and programs can we introduce into our organization to enable it with higher levels of perceptiveness?**

Most organizations are too complex and too fluid to be managed well by the formal organizational structures. That is one of the key reasons for the failure of many organizational change efforts, the mistaken belief that all you have to do is draw up a new formal organizational structure by creating a set of PowerPoint charts and you are halfway there to creating or changing an organization.

Successful organizations self-organize, mostly unconsciously across roles and boundaries to get work done. How many times have you heard someone in your or another's organization say something like the following, "The way it is supposed to work is that you fill out the form and submit it to accounting. It should take about three days, but if you really want to get this done quickly and right, give Betty in accounting a call or send her an e-mail and tell her that I told you to contact her. She'll take care of it in ten minutes."

People are, on the whole, smart and resourceful. We figure out what is going to make our life easier to get what we want. In organizations, we recognize quickly that if you want to get things done, you've got to know who to get connected with.

This leads us to suggest that you create cross-organizational and/or cross-functional communities whose purposes are equally both to solve particular business problems and to educate one another. Right there, you'll probably see a rise in perceptiveness.

The main test of whether the perceptiveness level is increasing is whether individuals begin to see the interconnections between systems and also see the possibilities for multiple courses of action, each of which can be described in system matrix scenarios. They increasingly gain access to more choice about what they do. In addition, Question Forward language combines with perceptiveness to minimize negative workplace actions, such as resentment, going it alone and lack of teamwork, and malicious bad-mouthing.

## QF: How could that idea be made effective in the whole system?

Our love affair with technology and its fixes is shown in almost all organizations. A new device, new concept, or new model of a current machine is quickly bought and installed. And the failure rate of such technological imperatives is astoundingly high. Reports[35] say well below 50 percent, and often as low as 20 percent, of change programs are successful. It is not always the fault of the technology; most often it is because the adopters did not consider the systems perspective, let alone the people involvement and organizational uniqueness questions, to determine if it was really needed or how it could be made workable.

Framing the challenge of perceptiveness is also related to the need in organizations of two or more people to communicate issues in a credible way to all in the organization. They must be accessible with an appropriate level of simplicity as well as being complete without being intimidating; the issues must clarify in people's minds what the organization is trying to do. Unfortunately, most organizations assume that sending all kinds of information miscellany to employees is empowerment.

### Empowerment

By "empowerment" we mean the ability to think and design from a systems perceptiveness to taking action that leads to the attainment of desirable results. Empowerment is a word that has been overused in the business literature in the sense of its dictionary definition: "vesting power, authority, or license in some person or group of people to take action." In business, this is interpreted as meaning sharing information with employees, task autonomy, and self-management. Management hopes such "lowering of the levels of decision making" will enrich jobs and improve job satisfaction and morale. Although such empowerment is quite worthwhile, most such

Ask The Right Questions

talk is lip service.[36] Thus many organizations have abandoned its usage.

## The Empowerment Question Forward: How can we empower all people in the organization to be leaders and think of what is currently not possible?

When we use the word "ability," we refer to the positive power that the thinking and questions of an individual can lead to in making changes and in the willingness to take risks in trying something new, not to the formal permission or warrant to exercise decision-making responsibilities. We believe our view of empowerment provides a way to have a sense of meaning and shared purpose, to be a self-leader, to feel significant, to be excited about work, to be part of a community, to have powerful teams. In other words, empowerment as used in the business literature has become a language that is nearly unusable. We have to talk about and rejuvenate it. Empowerment is demonstrated far more by the actions you take and the questions you ask than by a formal program.

There are two main elements of empowerment: capability and intention. Most people recognize the need for capability. If an organization undertakes a major change program, they almost always include some sort of training. But while training is often useful, it is generally not the most critical aspect of capability. Rather, it is the capability to ask the right questions, to get yourself and others unstuck and mobilized around ideas for action, to create as well as acquire enabling knowledge for yourself and others, and to make a commitment without all the data.

The other element of empowerment, intention, is often overlooked. The main mistake organizations make is to assume that people affected by the change, who have not been directly involved in the planning of the change, will see how important or obvious its need is. Not the case. People resent not being included in shaping changes that affect them. This point gets back to Chapter 4 on People Involvement. The best antidote for lack of intention is to include people in the design and implementation of the change. Genuine involvement breeds innovation and commitment.

213

## QF: What capabilities do modern workers need?

What does it mean to be empowered in a knowledge-working, networked organization? There are two components to this answer, one is a technology capability component and the other is a human capability component. That is, in order to think and act powerfully in modern organizations, there is a need for significant technical infrastructure, particularly computers, networks, and telecommunications equipment. We will leave the technical infrastructure part of the discussion for experts in that area. Let's talk about the human component, the social capital of the organization.

Even large scale change can be developed with QF to provide an empowerment perspective for everyone. A 40,000-employee company with many offices in five states decided that its service order system needed a major overhaul to provide much better customer service and reduced costs. The number of people whose work was affected significantly by the service order system was around 16,000. Because all of them could not possibly be involved in the design effort, the People questions of PPTR were carefully planned to involve design team members to represent both functional and geographic areas of the company. Part of their assignment was to regularly explain to their constituencies what was being done in the remaining PTR phases and bring to the once weekly team meetings suggestions and comments.

When the installation plan for implementing the living solution was prepared, it contained a major change in the way the 16,000 people would be trained for their specific roles. Instead of only the usual training going over manuals and simulated practice with the new system, extra time was added to review all parts of what the PPTR actions had been:

- How the design team was selected and their roles
- The broad range of purposes developed, with time taken to ask if the group had others to suggest

- The hierarchy of purposes, and if they might have other versions
- What the focus purposes were and why they were selected and were there others they might have selected
- What possible measures of purpose accomplishment were discussed and why were some selected, and were there others they would suggest
- The range of future ideal system considered, and what others might they suggest
- The FIST and how and why it was selected, and what might they have selected
- The range of ideas considered to stay close to the FIST, and what others might they suggest
- What was selected as the living system now being installed, why, and what might they have selected
- What their specific assignments were in the system and training to do the job
- Encouraging them to continually find improvements in their work and the system as whole leading to using the Target or even changing the FIST
- Presenting the means whereby their ideas and suggestions could be reviewed and implemented as quickly as possible

The extra time beyond usual training efforts allotted for this plan was minimal, in the range of 5-8 percent, but the sense of understanding, belonging, always thinking big, and empowerment was significant.

## QF: What can we do to empower our knowledge organization?

First, recognize that in reality very few if any jobs exist in isolation. Work has really become "cooperative-intellectual-work."

Second, recognize that people seek career growth, learning, and development; exciting work and challenges; meaningful work to make a difference and a contribution; being part of a team; autonomy or sense of control over the job; flexibility, and fun, including some celebrations of success. Do that and you've already gone a major way toward empowering your knowledge organization. After all, thinking, the basis of knowledge work, is the very opposite of rote, mindless work.

Finally, recognize that you have to make it safe for people to embrace empowerment, to minimize or eliminate their anxieties and stress about change. And do what it takes to help them contribute to and accept change, to accept responsibility for doing the best job possible while still opening avenues to creativity.

For example, the leaders of six different large and separate organizations had been given the mandate by the chief information officer (CIO) to combine their information technology services into a shared services model. The shared services model required that they standardize their services across the different groups and that they also manage the services as if they were one organization rather than six.

The task was difficult because they did not immediately have the capability to run a shared services model. They had always worked autonomously and provided very customized and flexible services to their individual clients. So there was no one-size-fits-all fix right away.

That wasn't the worst of it, though: These leaders also had no intention of making the shared model work to begin with. The CIO was new and they neither had confidence in her, nor in the shared model concept. Unfortunately for them, their separate services were too expensive to keep separate any longer, so the shared model had to be implemented.

The initial team meetings were so bad, there was a real chance of a fistfight. So the first thing we did was have the group come up with ground rules that created a safe space and set up policies of twice-weekly meeting attendance, participation in meetings, conduct during meetings, decision making, how to handle disagreements, having an impartial facilitator run all meetings, keeping minutes and action items.

After a few weeks of each manager talking about his or her own service, the managers were relaxed enough to move on to discussions of purposes and ideal solution design. They would go off as individuals between meetings and come back to the group and present ideas for the group to consider. There would be occasional sparks of interest, but the group was in no way gaining alignment on purposes and ideal solutions. However, slowly they were beginning to respect and even appreciate one another. There were increasingly lighter meetings over the next few weeks.

Eventually, to gain some deep alignment, they went off site for a three-day retreat. There were two main objectives: Gain alignment about their purposes as an organization and create a first draft of an ideal solution. Ideas would be conceived in the small group, shared in the large group, and then taken back to small groups to refine. Each of the small groups developed an ideal solution using components of the systems matrix. The final afternoon was devoted to evaluating each of the solution ideas and deciding which one they would recommend to the CIO. They chose an innovative approach based on a franchise model. Each of the units could maintain some autonomy to account for the uniqueness of the units, but there were elements of the shared services model that would be standard.

Eventually, the solution was implemented and was successful. They were able to have a shared services model that still allowed them to maintain satisfied clients with timely and well-delivered service. After a couple months, the new system received higher client satisfaction ratings than the old warlord approach.

The point of this story is that for solutions to work in organizations, for people to be empowered to think and act, they need both the intention and the capability. Additionally, as this example showed, sometimes, with complex situations, it takes a good deal of time to build both—and requires a QF framework to provide the capability to design a complex solution inside of a complex organizational structure. The example also is a case in which there was a need to learn how to function as a networked organization because, even after the implementation of the solution, they remained semi-autonomous organizations.

## QF: What can I do to continually get involvement to help empower people?

The empowerment we describe can be couched in many different ways. For example, one model of a cycle of empowerment[37] is described as learning and growth→increased self-confidence→empowerment of self and others→new experiences and perspectives→redefinition of self and role→new patterns of actions→innovation outcomes→reinforcement→learning and growth. If the innovation outcomes lead to punishment for "stepping out of line," disenchantment occurs and a disempowering cycle starts. The positive perspectives of the model coincide with those we discuss, but omits the critical aspect of *how* does an organization get these outcomes. Merely saying these points in the cycle are good is insufficient. All three of the QFO questions presented in this chapter are what we think demonstrate, the *how* dimension.

*"Learning...requires energy, thought, courage, and support...Learning...is solving our own problems for our own purposes, by questioning, thinking, and testing until the solution is a new part of our lives."* Charles Handy

There are several indicators that could be used to tell how empowerment in a QFO is progressing: Employees volunteer to take part in more uncertain projects, produce many unsolicited new product and service proposals, come up with an abundant number of ideas in all settings that frequently have high returns on investment when they are used, talk often with pride to others about what's new in their organization, and customers compliment you frequently on your ability to anticipate their needs. In many ways, these are also indicators of the release of free creativity in the organization, a form of getting advantages from the value elements of the organization that can't be seen.

## QF: How can a Question Forward language, perceptiveness, and empowerment develop everyone's competencies for continual innovation?

## Adaptability Culture in the Heat of Battle

*"You've achieved success in your field when you don't know whether what you are doing is work or play."* Warren Beatty

In this chapter, you notice that we have not discussed the topic of organizational change. Organizational change is hot these days because people now recognize that organizations are always in a state of change and that has to be dealt with. Plus, technology makes change happen faster, yet all of the technology in the world will not ensure success to an organization. That myth died in the end of the so-called productivity boom of the 1990s (after all, earnings are success, not just productivity!). It is still people that have to embrace technology and use it intelligently to solve business problems.

That said, what is the relationship between organizational change and the three questions that we have discussed? There are many different organizational change models, many of them good. One of the more popular and good ones is John Kotter's model, documented in his book *Leading Change* (1996). He lists eight steps to an organizational change:

1.  Establishing a sense of urgency
2.  Creating the guiding coalition
3.  Developing a vision and strategy
4.  Communicating the change vision
5.  Empowering employees for broad-based action
6.  Generating short-term wins
7.  Consolidating gains and producing more change
8.  Anchoring new approaches in the culture

The only issue of ours Kotter addresses is empowerment. Many other organizational change models don't even include it.

That's OK with us because we think any number of organizational change models can be useful. That said, we do think that what all successful organizational changes have in common, whether it's explicitly stressed or not, is the three Question Forward adaptability culture questions. Ultimately, if any change is going to stick in an

219

organization, it has provided a language for thinking together, it has raised perceptiveness of the big picture, and it has empowered people in the organization to think and act in new ways.

The path that you take to change the existing culture can vary. There are lots of ways of using any organizational change model or combinations of them, and Question Forward and its organizational adaptability questions set out the thinking and action questions to determine what size and timing fits your situation.

The many minute-by-minute, hour-by-hour give-and-take situations that occur in all organizations are the many "battles" that can easily generate disruptive heat. An angry customer calls about a defective product, a financial analyst is checking on a rumor she heard about your company, human resource personnel discuss the merits of candidates for a position, or marketing and product designers review merits of a particular specification—are a mere sample of battles. In a QFO, the possible heat and turbulence of these encounters is greatly diminished by the QF language used, the systems perceptiveness, and the sense of willingness to speak in these terms that empowerment brings. Presenting and defending only one option are highly unlikely, and, if they do occur on the part of one person, the others are able to calmly address whatever is needed— purposes, measures of purpose accomplishment, target and alternatives to it, and the system perspective about the defended option.

The start of any innovative development, the place where a QFO is a must, could also be any of a number of prompts—a recurring delivery shortfall from a supplier, ideas from a dream, how to possibly integrate a new technology, and the latest report on the demographics of possible customers.

An additional point that we need to make about these three questions is that they are interrelated. Having a powerful language and having an expansive perceptiveness are empowering and lead to the many negotiation activities and meetings at all levels to be much more effective. These QF questions provide people with a way of understanding and adopting as needed the many roles of project leader—facilitator, communicator, scout, ambassador, gatekeeper, idea generator, champion, entrepreneur, translator, strategic linkage, and so on. Similarly, having an empowered organization where members can think and act expansively, in effect being leaders in their situations, creates the conditions for evolution and revolution in the organization's language and perceptiveness. It is like being swept up in a tide. It is a way of using experience in a positive way instead of letting it become an anchor to the past where we decide what is possible today and tomorrow by what's occurred before, where we share the knowledge we used to hoard because it made us seem more important.

Finally, in the heat of battle, the best way to start shifting the culture of an organization, we have found, is to use the Question Forward approach, as the board of directors case presented before shows. You can begin slowly by introducing a few of the key questions or you can begin on a large scale by introducing the whole QF approach.

This approach of asking the right questions leads to the development of a QFO of self-leaders and a way of coping with as well as anticipating the external turbulence of today's world. The satisfactions of each person in using language powerfully, having an expanded perceptiveness, and feeling empowered provide a critical way of celebrating, along with parties, monetary rewards, and awards, the results of developing creative and effective living solutions.

*"Question Forward was the missing link I have been in search of for many years. Real solutions to real problems! My congratulations and deepest appreciation for such a meaningful set of questions for creating living solutions."*
A manager who led his business unit to be a QFO

## RECAP

**Question Forward : How can we institutionalize Question Forward as a language of change, a lever to increase perceptiveness, and to develop an empowered culture?**

221

Knowledge work and technology are causing a shift in our organizations. They are becoming more complex, requiring more intellectual horsepower to be effective. In addition, organizations are becoming more connected and networked, less like hierarchies and more like spider webs. These changing organizations are requiring organizations to develop new capabilities in how they operate. We call these capabilities an adaptability organization. Organizations, to keep pace, need to have a powerful language for thinking together, they need to continually raise their level of perceptiveness of themselves and their business as a system within systems, and continually elevate the level of empowerment in their organization.

## Reflective Question

What questions will you ask that are likely to get you and your organization unstuck, committed, and mobilized to shift to the adaptable organization of a QFO and attain better results?

# Chapter 9

# QUESTION FORWARD: A DISCIPLINED
# APPROACH FOR THE POST-RATIONAL WORLD

### Question Forward: How can you think clearly
### in a confused world?

Let's harken back to Machiavelli's question that arguably spawned modern geopolitics: "How can a good man live in an evil world?"

Note the similarity in our question forward; the apparent paradox.

Simply put: What can we do to reach a simple consensus and come up with solutions in a world that has become so damned complicated? You can't even rehab a building without running into near-insurmountable rules and problems!

The reason that it is so difficult is that we live in a very "multi" world. Without belaboring the obvious, the world is indeed different than the days when "rationality, certainty and absolute truth bloomed into an obsession and... clouded and misguided much thinking since."[38] This old thinking accorded highest status to mathematical rationality, just the opposite of the open-minded and informal discipline and reasonableness of Question Forward, where we use mathematical tools only when needed in the overall human-based thinking for creating solutions.

The key part of QF, though, isn't the exposure of the weakness of such mathematical "rationality"; nor is it critical that this sort of thinking is so Eurocentric. It doesn't really matter that it was centered on what is now frequently referred to as "dead white men," in the most politically correct circles. But for a few twists in history, it might have centered around some other group of thinkers. The point is, the cultural globalization of the world, brought about by the astounding strides in transportation and communication technology in the last century, has made every place "here," and everyone part of the supposedly same neighborhood.

In real terms, few places are purely one culture or ethnicity anymore. This means that the Eurocentric perception of what is an obviously rational approach goes right out the window. Beyond that, it means that any collective notion of what makes sense, always culturally biased at its core, won't work anymore. Almost any group, from PTA to workplace to national political party, is made up of people with such varied backgrounds and interests that there is no basic underlying agreement that you can assume.

That's why at its essence, the Question Forward approach is people-centric: It starts with the actual people involved to grow a living solution from the combined ideas, ideals, and aspirations of that particular group.

This people-centric approach is also in step with the generally recognized new reality and needs of a service sector economy…namely that "the most critical resource that companies need to cultivate has shifted, since the 1980s, from capital to people,"[39] and that everything from knowledge management and data collection to customer service is really a person-to-person, individualized experience. That is, one size does not fit all.

As we come full-circle, ironically, and return to a personalized world from the era of mass-market solutions, huge complexities arise. How do we make traveling convenient for each individual? Or education a personalized experience? How do we craft a foreign policy that holds certain truths to be self-evident, when everyone seems at odds about agreeing what these truths might be?

What's the right frame of reference for determining the right problem and for understanding and coping with this new complexity?

This book has laid out a strategy for developing a strategy and process to address business and organizational problems. We know that is only a small part of the whole. Now we take a bigger bite of the apple. We believe Question Forward has applicability in many areas of life. We want to challenge you, the reader, to take QF into the world and do some powerful deeds. In this chapter we look at applying the Question Forward approach to some real-world stinkers of problems.

These stinkers are typified by all residing in the ill-structured arenas of life—for example, in the systems and metasystems of education, politics, health care, regional planning, finance, defense and transportation, and even architecture, negotiation, and career planning.

First some general comments about the approaches taken by various experts in these areas. (And we make no claims to having such topic-specific expertise!)

Op-ed pages of the newspapers are packed with very good questions, and many good answers by countless authorities. But little information, if any, is offered to show which ones to ask, when, and in what order, and in what manner.

The questions and answers put forward by experts may be fine. But only by constructing a conceptual framework within which to evaluate them, can you decide their value and relevance. Even when ninety-four adjectives to the word "thinking" are listed, no guiding framework, other than the assumed questions backward of collect facts, analyze them, find causes, and fix the causes, is provided to indicate what is the right type of thinking to use, when and how its questions are to be posed.[40]

Another far too frequent occurrence in organizations of all types that illustrates why we need to change our mental model for creating solutions is the adoption, one after another, of fad or buzzword programs each of which is supposedly *the* answer to your productivity or morale or quality or team-building or all of the above issues. "Buzzwords are part of the problem, not the solution. Hot techniques dazzle us, then fizzle…why don't we just stop [going from one buzzword to another] and instead start thinking?"[41]

*Dogbert to Dilbert's boss: You've got to implement a Six Sigma program or else you're doomed.*
*Boss: Aren't you the same consultant who sold us the worthless TQM program a few years ago?*
*Dogbert: I assure you that this program has a totally, totally different name.*
*Boss: When can we start?*
Scott Adams, Dilbert cartoon, October 1, 2001

Faddism and analysis paralysis in these situations continue to arise. We suggest they occur because of the questions backward illustrated in Sections I and II. What's more, articles and books continually appear describing the pitfalls and shortfalls of such programs, and suggest ways of overcoming them. But none of the suggestions touch on the fundamental mental model for determining the right questions to ask.[42]

We have had many consulting assignments with hospitals, schools, government agencies, and nonprofit charities that adopted a new fad program and called on us when they found the programs were not producing any results at all. In every case, a primary reason they gave for their difficulties was analysis-paralysis—so much data but no one knew what to do with it all—because their thinking model told them and the fad program said to start with data collection about the critical issues they wanted resolved. And all the data almost assures that the blame game or hunt for scapegoats will take place. Japan's banking crisis, for example, illustrates how question backward and its subsequent impact on human behavior— unwillingness to admit mistakes, placing blame—prevents real action to take care of the bad loans in their portfolios.

## RESULTS TO EXPECT FROM A MENTAL MODEL FOR SOLUTION CREATION: SELECTED SOCIAL AND POLITICAL EXAMPLES

The people-centric Question Forward concept of asking the right questions recognizes and takes advantage of the somehow built-in desire of humans to achieve greater effectiveness and provide a better quality of life. The interesting results of a better quality of life are the enhancement of human dignity and the encouragement of individual betterment. And all of these human drives continue to:

- Produce the most creative (breakthroughs) and effective (benefit/cost ratio, socially responsible) living solution recommendations
- Maximize the likelihood of installing and using the living solution recommendations
- Minimize the use of resources (elapsed time, person-hours, costs) in accomplishing the first two results

Question Forward has produced these kinds of results in social and bureaucratic situations, small to large, personal to governmental, community to social. Some cases are described below to show you, in addition to those already used in previous chapters, how you, as an individual, and your groups can gain benefits with Question Forward outside your work setting or inside quite amorphous non-governmental groups. Then several current issues will be mentioned along with our comments about how Question Forward could be used.

## EDUCATION: A STUDENT-DRIVEN
## LEARNING APPROACH

Mary Patt Kennedy was principal of an elementary school in Florida when she enrolled in the doctoral education program at the University of Central Florida. Her advisor was Prof. William Bozeman, a longtime colleague of ours. Kennedy did her doctoral research on comparing the outcomes of using Question Forward in her school for developing her required plan with the outcomes of thirteen other schools using the conventional approach.[43]

## Table 9-1 SOME RESULTS
## SCHOOL IMPROVEMENT PLANNING*

| | Conventional (13 schools) (e.g., Effective School Planning - 9 schools. Data driven) | | Question Forward (1 school) (People And Purpose Driven) |
|---|---|---|---|
| Quality of plans (independent raters) | 109.83 | ($\sigma$ 15.59) | 135.00 (1st) |
| Number of meetings per school per year | 9.50 | ($\sigma$ 5.47) | 17 (2nd tie) |
| Hours per person | 25.79 | ($\sigma$ 8.20) | 14.69 (2nd) |
| Team Time per school | 1439 | ($\sigma$ 429) | 1300 (4th) |
| Community participation | 3 excellent, 4 good, 7 fair | | Excellent |

*M. P. Kennedy, "An analysis and comparison of school improvement planning models," doctoral dissertation, University of Central Florida, 1994.

Table 9-1 summarizes the main data of her dissertation. Some of the noteworthy interpretations are the following. Based on the ratings of independent evaluators, the quality of the plan of her school was best. Participation was excellent, taking place in the second highest number of meetings. Even though more people were involved, the amount of time each person spent in the meetings was the second lowest and the team time per school was fourth lowest. In other words, the Question Forward mental model for creating solutions (the school improvement plan) produced the most creative and effective recommendation, maximized the likelihood of installing and using it (with a large number of participants being asked the right questions), and minimized the use of resources in achieving these first two outcomes.

In addition, reviewing the research results in terms of human drives leads to an assessment of these implications for the larger social ends. Both the plan and the Question Forward process aligned the work with achieving greater effectiveness, attaining a better quality of life, enhancing human dignity, and encouraging individual betterment for all participants as well the students and teachers.

## Student planned acquisition of required knowledge—SPARK

Margaret Norton learned Question Forward through a program for teaching it to professionals in the education world, from classroom teachers to deans of education schools. Norton was a social studies teacher of sixth- and seventh-grade students. She decided that she could use Question Forward in the instructional design of her study plans to foster individualized learning, and that her students could learn more than at present by using Question Forward in planning the outcomes they wanted as a result of reading required books.[44]

After Norton returned from the Question Forward workshop, she practiced the approach on creating solutions for small issues—plan an office filing system, a one-day's lesson plan, or a one-day conference on composition instruction. Norton decided then to introduce Question Forward to the students so each one could design his or her own study plans for each unit (which she called SPARK ). She introduced some of the concepts (purposes, systems thinking) through the first few weeks of the semester before trying to get the students to use Question Forward for developing their own plans for the first required book.

Norton then used Question Forward to design the unit of instruction where she would introduce the planning process to her class. She prepared notes about how she had used Question Forward to design the unit, passing out forms for each phase of the process. At this time she introduced the structured sheets the students were to use in planning their outcome after reading a required book. As the sheets

*Gerald Nadler and William J. Chandon*

in the following figures show, Norton prepared slightly different sheets for each book assigned in the coming weeks.

*Case Illustration of SPARK*

---

CONTEMPORARY LIFE STUDY UNIT      NAME ...**Ed Hammer**...............

STEP ONE: Decide on the topic for your study this quarter as, for example, Ecology, Generation Gap, Drugs, Crime, Dissent or Conformity, New Morality, The Family, Life Styles, Future Shock, Ethnic Problems, etc.

STEP TWO: List as many possible purposes for studying this topic as you can possibly think of. You may do this as a group even though you plan to do your study by yourself. Sometimes the ideas that other people have will make it easier for you to think about what you are going to do. Work out on *scratch paper* to start with.

1. To read *Dig U.S.A.*

2. To recognize differing viewpoints

3. To learn about alcohol

4. To see how an alcoholic lives

5. To understand how he/she feels being this way

6. To see how his/her family feels about him/her

7. To know if he/she respects himself/herself

8. To know if he/she is losing any friends

9. To know the type of friends he/she is making or already has

10. To learn how many different types of alcoholics there are

11. To learn how the different alcoholics live

12. To know how many other problems they have after they become alcoholics besides their drinking

13. To learn how they became alcoholics

14. To know what they're planning on doing about their problem — if anything

15. To find out what they like about drinking or what they did like about it

16. To know if they started drinking on their own or if someone encouraged them in the beginning

17. To talk to the people on the A.A. plan and ask them different questions about alcoholism to get their opinions

18. To learn how an alcoholic affects his/her family

---

Figure 9-1 lists the purposes Ed Hammer prepared related to the required reading of the book *Dig U.S.A.* The typed material on all of the following figures is what Norton prepared for the students for this book, and the large block printing is what Ed wrote. Notice that Norton stated the first two purposes.

230

## *Case Illustration of SPARK (Continued)*

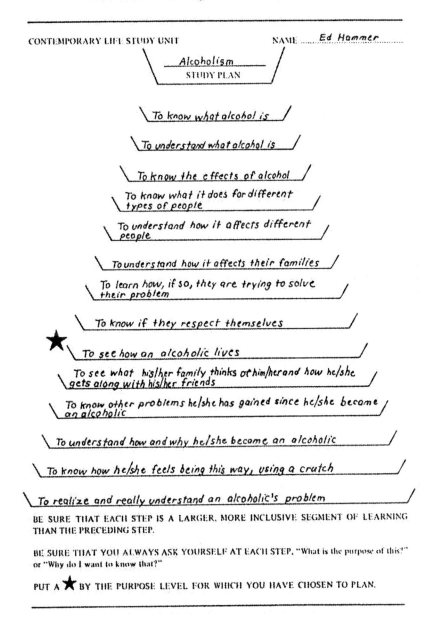

CONTEMPORARY LIFE STUDY UNIT          NAME ...... *Ed Hammer* ........

*Alcoholism*
STUDY PLAN

To know what alcohol is

To understand what alcohol is

To know the effects of alcohol

To know what it does for different types of people

To understand how it affects different people

To understand how it affects their families

To learn how, if so, they are trying to solve their problem

To know if they respect themselves

★ To see how an alcoholic lives

To see what his/her family thinks of him/her and how he/she gets along with his/her friends

To know other problems he/she has gained since he/she become an alcoholic

To understand how and why he/she become an alcoholic

To know how he/she feels being this way, using a crutch

To realize and really understand an alcoholic's problem

BE SURE THAT EACH STEP IS A LARGER, MORE INCLUSIVE SEGMENT OF LEARNING THAN THE PRECEDING STEP.

BE SURE THAT YOU ALWAYS ASK YOURSELF AT EACH STEP, "What is the purpose of this?" or "Why do I want to know that?"

PUT A ★ BY THE PURPOSE LEVEL FOR WHICH YOU HAVE CHOSEN TO PLAN.

Figure 9-2 is the hierarchy of purposes Ed prepared from his initial listing. The star indicates the focus purpose Ed selected.

## Case Illustration of SPARK (Continued)

CONTEMPORARY LIFE STUDY UNIT 1000 ... Alcoholism

| | | RATE | CONTROL |
|---|---|---|---|
| 1. Purpose: To see how an alcoholic lives | | | Self-control |
| 2. Input: Me | | | |
| 3. Outputs: 1. A Report on Alcoholism — Oral<br>2. Me — with knowledge | | 1 Report | |
| 4. Sequence (List steps to be followed in your plan to achieve purpose. List in order and in detail.): | | | |
| 1st week Read a book about alcohol - The effects of it. Will get book Monday - 4/30/73<br>I will take one week to gather material - written material from books, encyclopedias, magazines, etc. Any type of article. Will finish during the weekend. | | 1st week<br><br>1 book, 1 encyclopedia. Look through 2 or 3 magazines. Any type of article about it | Check-Friday- of 1st week For Completion<br><br>I changed from reading a book to seeing filmstrips |
| 2nd week Talk to different people about how alcohol affects them. Whether they are just a social drinker, a heavy drinker, or if they drink once in awhile.<br>Will be entitled - Personal Effects and Feelings Toward Alcohol. | | 2nd week<br><br>Talk to 10 different people who drink heavy or light, including teenagers | Check-Friday - of 2nd week For Completion<br><br>Wasn't completed until 5th week |
| 3rd week Take all of the material I have collected and organize it into different categories. Proofread. Organize for Oral Report. | | 3rd week | Check-Friday- of 3rd week For Completion |
| | | For RATE, tell how many, how much, when items in column 1 will be worked on, learned, finished, etc. | For CONTROL, tell how you are judging progress and success of what you are doing and what changes you make to make your plan work as you want. |

Figure 9-3 is what Ed wrote on the simplified system matrix prepared by Norton and given to the students to detail their planning activities.

## Case Illustration of SPARK (Continued)

CONTEMPORARY LIFE STUDY UNIT TOPIC ......*Alcoholism*......

| | RATE | CONTROL |
|---|---|---|
| **4. Sequence** (continued) | | |
| *4th week* Copy all material over. If happen to find something to add to my work, I will. | *4th week* | Finish and Check for 4th week |
| *5th week* I will catch up on anything that I need to. I decided to do an Oral Report, so I also got a book called *Alcohol and Youth*. | *5th week* Using a book *Alcohol and Youth* – And preparing for my Oral Report on Wednesday | Check – and will be finished Friday of 5th week |
| 5. Environment (What are the physical and psychological surroundings where you carry out plan?) | In my room, in the school library, at school, in class, at home. | |
| 6. Physical Catalysts (What are tools, objects, materials used in plan? They do not change.) | Pen, pencil, paper, people, book, an encyclopedia, a magazine, filmstrips with tapes. | |
| 7. Human Agents (Who will help you carry out your plan? teachers? aides? others?) | Teachers, my mom, other students, and friends. | |
| 8. Information Aids (What must you find out in order to make plan work? a telephone number? speaker's name? an address? whether to get material? certain materials needed are available? etc.) | I have to find out about Alcoholism. I need to find out whether to get material for my report. | |

Figure 9-3 (continued)

---

CONTEMPORARY LIFE STUDY UNIT     NAME ............................
CONTROL DIMENSION REPORT

Circle: Week 1 2 3 4          Date of report ........................

1. What did you say you would get done this week?


2. What did you do this week?


3. What changes do you need to make to keep on target to finish work as planned?

-----------------------------------------------------------------

*SAMPLE STUDENT REPORTS*
(transcribed exactly as written by students)

*Mark, week 1, May 4*
1. Read 2 books, cut out magazine picture to make poster, read paper every week, collect smog level
2. Due to heavy Soc. St and Alg homework only 3/4 of my first book was read, magazine pictures were cut out but lack of poster paper held it up, paper was read every day and smog level checked every day
3. Poster both done next week, faster reading on my books


*Andy, Daryll, & Marcel, week 3, 5/17/73*
1. Interview a conv. hospital's administrator
2. Tried to interview an administrator. When tried to make appointment but found that she wouldn't talk to us. So we went and talked to the head nurse, we found her to be helpful but not what we had really hoped for
3. None

Figure 9-4 is the control dimension report each student had to submit each week. Norton introduced this form to provide her with weekly updates that allowed her to identify students who might fall too far back in the required work as a way of individualizing her work with each student. Submitting a weekly report also motivated the students to try to adhere to their plans.

The results of using SPARK were remarkable for the approximately 250 students Norton had in her classes in just the first year reported here. Learning effectiveness and efficiency were the benefits and advantages to the students. This is demonstrated by many direct and indirect outcomes of the activities (statements in brackets refer to the three dynamics presented in Chapter 8):

- Students did not ask the grouchy question of "why do we have to read this?"—they were too busy finding their own purposes to try this negative approach. [using language powerfully]
- Students produced a wide variety of purposes for each of their plans—to learn (or understand) character development, theme of the book, satire, biography, historical background, author, or secret organizations, to name just a few. [becoming empowered]
- Students quickly grasped the idea that when they finished the sequence (operating steps) they had outlined, they were supposed to know whatever they said their purpose was, even though they gasped the first time this comment was made to them. [understanding perceptiveness]
- Students' end-products were quite varied (well over 50 percent of students) even though they thought primarily about a written report when they started SPARK on their first book. Some of the outcomes were a skit about a book's point of view (which made the two girls involved read another book to prepare the skit), an outside speaker to present details about how a newspaper is printed (printing was pivotal in that book), a student prepared an overhead transparency show for the whole class on historical events behind that book, a system for a one-day teaching unit on poetry, a poem, plans for systems of vocabulary development, and a teaching lesson on folk tales. [becoming empowered]

Norton found many other benefits in using SPARK, some of which are:
- Clears teacher thinking by making sure the teaching material has a definite learning purpose. [using language powerfully]

- Gets students to become responsible in part for their own learning. [becoming empowered]
- Changes teacher-student roles—students view teachers as helpers and resource persons. [understanding perceptiveness]
- Variable rather than either/or outcome—e.g., level of teacher involvement, frequency of use of SPARK, student project types, methodologies to present required content.
- Students realize there is more than one approach to problem-solving; Question Forward for planning, design, improvement, and creating systems; and question backward for determining causes and doing research. [understanding perceptiveness]

The implications of this case are awe-inspiring. What if school districts involved teaching staff, parents, students, and community representatives in strategic planning for the educational process, developed their hierarchy of educational purposes, developed a future ideal system target for their focus purposes, used a systems matrix to determine workability levels, and set up a Release 1.0, Release 2.0, and so on, schedule of betterment?[45]

Have any of us heard this kind of thinking in any of the discussions about educational reform so rampant in the United States? Has any concept of several measures of *student learning*, instead of just multi-response, shallow standardized tests, been considered? Has anyone pointed out that testing, only one way of evaluating educational reform (think values, measures, and control dimensions of a system), is being proposed as the actual reform? Has anyone talked about the way individual student differences in learning styles could be accommodated?

Table 9-1 adds to the SPARK case about how Question Forward would get some of these questions moving toward the living solutions education so desperately needs.

A quick word about technology: note that in both the SPARK and school improvement planning cases, the issue of technology—computers in the classroom, two-way video distance teaching, information gathering from the internet, virtual meetings of committee members—was missing. There is no doubt that technology does and will increasingly impact education, particularly in bringing equality in learning opportunities to remote geographical areas.

The point is not that technology was not used in these cases—it was—but that the Question Forward approach pulls in the technology needed and that all the technology in the world depends on how people—teachers especially in education—are able to determine what needs be to achieved (purposes) and how best to achieve those purposes (future and recommended solutions). The findings in business that executives of leading companies almost always (80 percent) don't "even mention technology as one of the top five factors in their companies' transformation"[46] apply equally well in the rest of society.

## GOVERNMENT: THE GYPSY MOTH
## PEST MANAGEMENT SYSTEM

The gypsy moth pest, imported into the United States in 1869, was denuding primarily oak trees, especially in thirteen states in the northeast, at an alarming rate when Congress appropriated $50 million for a five-year program to resolve the problem before the ungreening of the country became a crisis. Three agencies in the U. S. Department of Agriculture were charged with the assignment. Governments in the thirteen states, industry, and environmental groups also joined the effort. For three and a half years, the groups gathered a lot of data—characteristics, biology, and behavior of the moth, forecasts of its spread and impact; various control methods; environmental impacts; and so on. Consultants submitted reports proposing pest-management systems. But factions developed among all the participants, and each faction objected strongly to one or more proposals. The whole group didn't know how to put together a national gypsy moth pest management system (GMPMS)—analysis-paralysis, defensiveness, and ego had set in.[47]

I was asked by one of the participants who knew about Question Forward what I thought they should do. To start, I suggested the group initially shift its attention from the problem of the gypsy moths to the problem of organizing the group to develop a GMPMS—to use

Question Forward to create the organizational system to put in place to design the GMPMS—planning to plan, in effect *using language powerfully, becoming empowered.* Eighteen key people from the key constituencies and who were in the much larger group met for a day to do this. Most existing biases and differences were set aside by concentrating on the system to set up for planning the GMPMS. By the end of the day, the group had identified a list of people from all stakeholder interests to serve on the GMPMS design task force (twenty-two people, many of whom were not present that day), the purposes of the task force, responsibilities, detailed planning sequence, budget, expected products, and the overall project timeline. The timeline was twice amended later to better-fit real world conditions *understanding perceptiveness.*

The task force met for the first two-day meeting three months later after the needed preparations had been made as the overall timeline spelled out. Purposes were listed, a hierarchy was built, and a focus purpose was selected (to cope with gypsy moths at all levels of their population), measures of purpose accomplishment were set up for this purpose, and many future ideal system suggestions were listed to achieve this and larger purposes *using language powerfully, becoming empowered.* The FIST that was selected called for the establishment of a National Gypsy Moth Pest Management Board (see Figure 9-5) along with a federal pest management coordinator who would integrate all USDA pest programs. Trying to stay as close as possible to the FIST led to developing many details to ensure workability and continual movement toward the target, such as the identification of three levels of activities (field, regional, and national) and the responsibilities of and interactions among the three *understanding perceptiveness.* (An interesting sidelight—at the completion of the project, I asked the participants how much of all the data they had collected in the first three and a half years did they think they used in arriving at the proposal. The consensus was 3 to 5 percent at most.)

The three federal agencies for the first time began, cautiously at first, to coordinate their gypsy moth activities. Antagonisms from the past among the federal, state, industry, and environmental constituencies became minimal. The board started to operate, Question Forward planning sessions to be activated, both for finding ways to move the system closer to the current FIST and for developing a new FIST

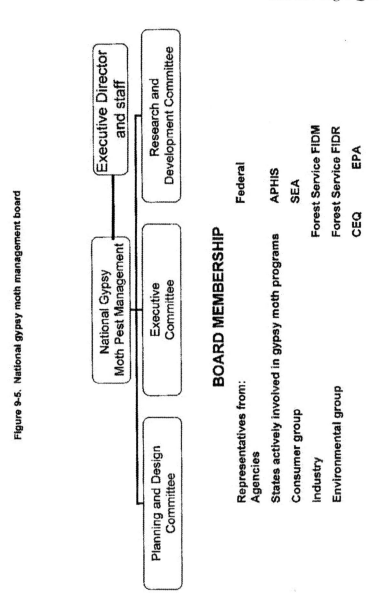

Figure 9-5. National gypsy moth management board

within the two-year time horizon of the first FIST. The latter planning activity is credited by many of the task force people for keeping the board updated and able to continue effective operation over so many years. And, all of these results started to appear fourteen months from the time of the plan-the-planning session.

## SPECULATING ABOUT QUESTION FORWARD BENEFITS RELATED TO CURRENT SOCIETAL ISSUES

*"Reasonableness...has to do with how to put our ideas to work in the service of human welfare."*
Stephen Toulmin

The political and governmental scenes provide a large number of opportunities for Question Forward. A flood of comments describes the need. Just a few are:

- Regulations stifle results (Los Angeles County and most of its eighty-eight cities reduced the total of over 1,000 contractor hindering regulations all the entities had added to the state building codes to just forty-four!).
- Laws and regulations are too specific in telling people *how* to do things instead of dealing with the purposes and outcomes (a New York City regulation requiring an elevator in every renovated multistory building was not waived for Mother Teresa's missionary that wanted to renovate two abandoned buildings into homeless shelters even though the charity's religious beliefs prohibited the use of any modern conveniences, including elevators).
- Ideology dictates solutions rather than purposes and long-term system workability and consequences (diverting part of Social Security taxes to individual investment accounts fails to deal with the purposes and guaranteed retirement benefits of Social Security).
- No one in government can answer my questions about child-care resources (pollution control, mass transit, health insurance, highway improvements, etc.)

In addition, there are many issues that need national and/or international *living* solutions. They are of such magnitude that it is unrealistic to assume that *the* solution exists. Here are a few pressing issues—reducing nuclear testing, dealing with the huge number of land mines in various countries, creating an international criminal court, ensuring corporate transparency and accountability, reducing global climate change, minimizing oil usage per capita in the United States, making health care available for everyone in the United States, reducing availability of chemical and biological weapons, and determining children's rights. If you think these are daunting, consider that the Union of International Associations (http://www.uia.org/data.htm) tracks over 30,000 world problems! Even the generous act of volunteering for a community service needs the receiving agency to consider Question Forward relationships with the volunteers:

- What are our focus and larger purposes?
- What is a coherent and shared vision (FIST) that everyone can understand?
- What role will the volunteer play in enhancing the agency as well as provide the services?
- How can we keep volunteers informed about what's going on and how it affects them?
- What is the appropriate amount of information to share to avoid information overload?

Consider what Question Forward might accomplish with these and many other issues. Not asking these right questions and providing their answers is, in effect, making a profound decision, by default, about the prospects for tomorrow and the future.

- What group or coalition should be organized to plan with Question Forward the political and marketing "campaigns" to be the champions for the change or transformation effort?[48]
- What are the purposes of (higher education, child care, social security, building regulation)?
- Who are the stakeholders' representatives to involve in creating a solution for…?
- What is the hierarchy of purposes for…?
- What factors should be used to select the focus purposes of…?
- What are the values/beliefs we need to associate with the focus purposes?
- What measures should be used to gauge success in focus and larger purpose accomplishment for…?

- What ideal possibilities are there for how the focus and larger purposes could be achieved?
- How can options be built from the ideas into long-term workable system solutions?
- Which option should serve as the future ideal solution target, based on the success measures?
- What can be done for the short term that will eventually lead to the whole target?
- How can we determine the workability (elements and dimensions) of the potential courses of action?
- How will the selected action be incorporated in a full workable system for Release 1.0?
- What should be planned now for changing to the next release?

Laws, regulations, policies, speeches, and decisions that result from this line of reasoning are far more likely to be creative as well as effective; and each of them has to be viewed as a living solution. For example, consider foreign aid to develop chronically impoverished countries. The typical assumption is that we need to install systems there (irrigation, sewage, communications, transportation, etc.) that are common in the United States. However, the success measure of creativity and innovation, essential for improving the economic base of the country, has to be built-in. Another example stems from the emphasis in the new homeland security activities' desire for foolproof systems and technology instead of systems and solutions that fail smartly. "All security systems eventually miscarry in one way or another. Not when this happens to the good [fail smartly] one, they stretch and sag before breaking, each component failure leaving the whole as unaffected as possible."[49]

And the amount of time available to ask the right questions makes no difference in whether or not they should be asked. Even a short amount of time doesn't change the questions—it merely changes the amount of information and/or alternatives developed. But asking the questions makes the people involved to at least consider the import of the actions they do or not take related to each one.

Most of these issues and problems, as noted before, will not have a single solution. Getting started on them with Question Forward is very likely to produce outcomes similar to those obtained in the gypsy moth pest management system—an initial future ideal solution target with the first release including a stipulation that the FIST be redesigned at a specific time. In the meantime progress toward the focus and larger purposes would be made.

What's more, these are the questions to start with even when someone proposes *the* answer, however it was determined. For example, the private investment account proposal for Social Security should be greeted with: What are the purposes of the accounts, and what is the purpose of that, and the purpose of that? What really are the focus purposes? Who are the stakeholders we should get involved in determining this and taking part in answering the remaining questions? What are the long-term measures of purpose accomplishment we want? What are the options to consider, including your proposal? What are the long-term consequences of each option and any unexpected events we should consider? And so on.

The proposal may still be adopted, but it will probably be tempered enough to incorporate political and workability considerations. But the proponents and the legislative bodies need to begin by asking the right questions.

In general, political, and societal settings, the concept discussed in Chapter 8 about creativity is free, making work more meaningful applies equally to all life's work (home, volunteer, study, as well as paid), if you ask the right questions. And a recent report suggests that doing this may well improve mortality![50]

## THE FUTURE OF QUESTION FORWARD

### Question Forward: Where will we be twenty years from now?

Are the "right" questions we present in this book going to be the same in twenty years? Fifty years? We would not be using the thinking concepts of Question Forward if we said yes. Currently,

Question Forward can be thought of as a contrarian way of thinking[51]—only 8 percent of people intuitively think this way. Our goals are to change that and make QF the standard of thinking. Thus, Question Forward is the future target for creating solutions of all types we hope all people will adopt in, say, ten years, and this book is one of the first release actions leading to that target.

At the same time, part of our schedule of additional actions is to continue research into ways of making Question Forward better in preparation for the next FIST for eight to ten years from now. Since we expect changes, we want to be the leaders in developing the new FIST to replace the Question Forward target presented in this book.

To achieve this we've founded an organization designed to support the Question Forward approach in any particular profession or endeavor. Feedback we get from those applying QF will let us further refine its application in all professional realms. The organization will be a repository of data on QF applications and will enable practitioners to pool and share knowledge.

Another project we are starting is to use our research tools to identify who QF change agents are in an organization so that an organizational change program can be built around and with such intuitives rather than around only top management and professional change agents. Once this research is completed and several companies have used the broader range of people in their change programs, the impact on the use of the content knowledge of organizational development and change professionals will be major. It would place in doubt some of the practices that OD people and change agents take for granted.[52]

Another area of development is software to support a Question Forward decision support system. Especially in a geographically dispersed or a virtual organization, it would enable the participants to contribute their responses to the Questions Forward asked, provide a way to build the options with more questions, have links to sources of information the questions and responses need, and maintain records of options selected and identify with system matrix descriptions for later reference those options not used.

One of the benefits of using Question Forward reported to us by facilitators, teams, and managers is the powerful teambuilding they have observed with the approach. Many of these reports say the usual team building exercises, programs, and nature challenges used in their previous groups did not work well at all, whereas the Question Forward approach and dynamics for creating a solution achieved a solid working team without doing something special. Doing productive work as a team was reward enough.

As a final example, the interest in collecting best practices, in addition to its role in the knowledge management buzzword movement, has not produced the expected results of encouraging others to use a best practice (remember the uniqueness principle) because the reports are very difficult to access and use. In addition, almost no benefit is now obtained from the many small parts of a best practice that might be useful in a completely different setting. The research that investigates how both of these hoped-for benefits could be obtained might start with the system matrix to detail the best practices and to form the basis of a computerized database that anyone could access by element/dimension queries when they need that purposeful information (the second Question Forward) about creative results from elsewhere. *Know when you need a wheel.*

## QUESTION FORWARD IN USUAL AREAS OF CONCERN

Individuals and groups face many day-to-day, week-to-week, and year-to-year needs for creating solutions that we did not discuss in the above section about current societal issues. Almost all of these needs have led practitioners and professions with specific content knowledge to assisting others in developing ways of satisfying those needs. Consider these illustrations of needs, in addition to those already mentioned, and recall that each of them has specialists somewhere you could call to help you:

- Career planning
- Communication
- Training and instructional design

- Facilitation
- Change management
- Management consulting
- Negotiation
- Urban and regional planning
- Managing projects
- Executive coaching
- Leadership
- Organizational design
- Psychotherapy
- Conflict management
- Crisis management

As important as the content knowledge is in each of these areas of concern, learning all the answers in that content sets up a virtual end to thought and creativity. You need to ask the right questions about using the content.

Several of our colleagues who are professionals in some of these content areas learned Question Forward and started to use it in their practices. They obtained such good results that they will be joining us as co-authors for the series of books that will use this one as the cornerstone. So, to illustrate, look for books in the future of this type:

*Conflict Management: Ask the Right Questions*
*Strategic Planning: Ask the Right Questions*
*Designing a Home: Ask the Right Questions*
*Negotiation: Ask the Right Questions*
*Facilitation: Ask the Right Questions*
*Customer Service: Ask the Right Questions*
*Team Building: Ask the Right Questions*
*Decision Making: Ask the Right Questions*
*Conversation Management: Ask the Right Questions*
*Curriculum Planning: Ask the Right Questions*
*Coaching: Ask the Right Questions*

So try Question Forward in your own life, and area of professional expertise. And let us know about your results—we are always interested in helping people in their use of the Question Forward ideas.

If you wish to join us for further dialogue about Question Forward and its application in your field or organization, you can find us in cyberspace at www.questionforward.com. We hope this book has sparked some ideas and insights for you.

## RECAP

*POWER is knowing* how *to use knowledge.*

The benefits of Question Forward in usual organizational settings can be obtained in much wider society. The Question Forward discipline of thinking flexibility can be used as an infrastructure that benefits all human endeavors that want to create solutions. Whether professional—architecture, negotiation, career planning, project management, consulting—or societal—education, health care, regional planning, aid to developing countries—the new set of thinking ideas provides a constructive, people-oriented basis for developing the solution breakthroughs so desperately sought by all.

### Reflective Question

What are the issues in your whole life that are not being resolved satisfactorily and how would Question Forward help you and others in developing creative and living solutions for them?

Make life better with Question Forward!
Best Regards, Gerry and Bill

*Gerald Nadler and William J. Chandon*

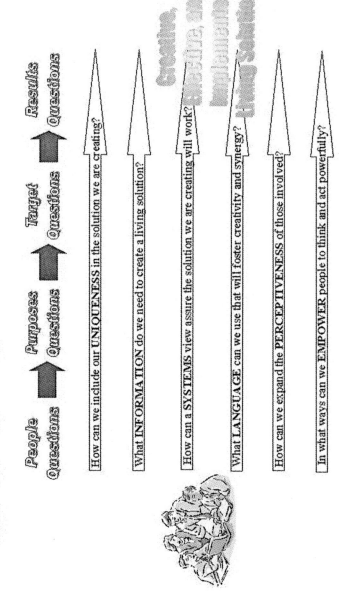

# QUESTION FORWARD Framework

People Questions ➡ Purposes Questions ➡ Target Questions ➡ Results Questions

**Create, Evaluate, and Implement Living Solutions**

How can we include our UNIQUENESS in the solution we are creating?

What INFORMATION do we need to create a living solution?

How can a SYSTEMS view assure the solution we are creating will work?

What LANGUAGE can we use that will foster creativity and synergy?

How can we expand the PERCEPTIVENESS of those involved?

In what ways can we EMPOWER people to think and act powerfully?

248

# About the Authors

Gerald Nadler, Ph.D., is IBM Chair Emeritus in Engineering Management at the University of Southern California. He consults widely for business, charitable and government organizations.

He has received over 25 international and national awards for his work. He is also the author of 13 other books, including *Breakthrough Thinking: The Seven Principles of Creative Problem Solving.*

William Chandon, Ph.D., is a vice-president of The Center for Breakthrough Thinking. He has had many previous consulting and organizational assignments, and now consults in the area of organizational transformation.

Thomas A. Dworetzky is Director of Communications for The Center for Breakthrough Thinking. He is a magazine consultant, writer, publisher and editor, with many years of executive responsibilities in producing national magazines.

*Gerald Nadler and William J. Chandon*

# INDEX

# NOTES

[1] Charles W. McCoy Jr., *Why Didn't I Think of That? Think the Unthinkable and Achieve Creative Greatness*, New York: Prentice Hall Press, 2002.

[2] Steven B. Sample, *The Contrarian's Guide to Leadership*, San Francisco, CA: Jossey-Bass, 2001.

[3] See chapter 3 for an explanation of system elements and dimensions.

[4] James G. Greeno, in "The Science of Learning Math and Science," *Mosaic*, Vol. 23, No. 2, Summer 1992.

[5] Douglas McGray, "The Silicon Archipelago," *Daedalus*, Vol. 128, No. 2, Spring 1999, pp. 147-176.

[6] Manuel Castells, *The Rise of the Network Society*, Oxford: Blackwell Publishers, 1996.

[7] Jane Whitney Gibson and Dana V. Tesone, "Management Fads: Emergence, Evolution, and Implications for Managers," *Academy of Management Executive*, Vol. 15, No. 4 , Nov. 2001.

[8] Malcolm Gladwell, *The Tipping Point: How Little Things Can Make a Big Difference*, New York: Back Bay/Little, Brown, 2000.

[9] R. Fred Bleakly, "Many Companies Try Management Fads, Only to See them Flop," *Wall Street Journal*, 6 July 1993.

[10] "Enhancing Organizational Effectiveness," Committee on Techniques for the Enhancement of Human Performance, Commission on Behavioral and Social Sciences and Education, Washington DC: National Academy Press, 1997.

[11] Paula Phillips Carson, Patricia A. Lanier, Kerry David Carson, and Brandi N. Guidry, "Clearing a Path Through the Management Fashion Jungle: Some Preliminary Trailblazing," *Academy of Management Journal*, Vol. 43, No. 6, December 2000.

[12] John Seely Brown and Paul Duguid, *The Social Life of Information*, Cambridge MA: Harvard Business School Press, 2000.

[13] Robert Finch and John Elder, Eds, *Nature Writing: The Tradition in English*, New York: W. W. Norton, 2001.

[14] John Seely Brown and Paul Duguid, *The Social Side of Information,"* Cambridge, MA: Harvard Business School Press, 2000.

[15] Bruce Lloyd, "The Wisdom of the World: Messages for the New Millennium," *The Futurist*, May-June 2000.

[16] For a sample of what data may mean, see Saul L. Gass, "Model World: When is a Number a Number?" *Interfaces*, Vol. 31, No. 5, Sept.-Oct. 2001.

[17] Oren Harari, *The Leadership Secrets of Colin Powell*, New York: McGraw-Hill, 2002.

[18] Robert Kegan, *In Over Our Heads: The Mental Demands of the Modern Workplace*. Cambridge, MA: Harvard University Press,

[19] C. Locke, R. Levine, D. Searls, & D. Weinberger, *The Cluetrain Manifesto: The End of Business As Usual*, New York: Perseus, 2000

[20] The early use of the principles described in this book were used in middle school classes to let each student learn required material by adapting it to their own interests. See Chapter 9 for more details about Margaret Norton, William Bozeman, and Gerald Nadler, *SPARK: Student Planned Acquisition of Required Knowledge*, Englewood Cliffs, NJ: Educational Technology Publications, 1980.

[21] Paul R., Lawrence and Nitin Nohria, *Driven: How Human Nature Shapes Our Choices*, San Francisco: Jossey-Bass, 2002.

[22] Rob Lebow and William L. Simon, *Lasting Change: The Shared Values That Makes Companies Great*, New York: Wiley, 1999.

[23] Robert Kegan and Lisa Laskow Lahey, "The Real Reason People Won't Change," *Harvard Business Review*, November 2001.

[24] John Heilemann, "The Truth, The Whole Truth, and Nothing but the Truth," *Wired*, Oct 2000.

[25] James C. Collins and Jerry I. Porras, *Built to Last: Successful Habits of of Visionary Companies*, New York: HarperBusiness, 1994.

[26] Steven B. Sample, *The Contrarian's Guide to Leadership*, San Francisco: Jossey-Bass, 2001.

[27] Paul C. Nutt, *Why Decisions Fail: Avoiding the Blunders and Traps That Lead to Debacles*, San Francisco: Berrett-Koehler, 2002.

[28] New techniques are being proposed on a regular basis. In relation to organization charts, see the proposal in Henry Mintzberg and Ludo Van der Heyden, "Organigraphs: Drawing How Companies Really Work," *Harvard Business Review*, Sept.-Oct. 1999.

[29] To review an assessment of different software packages, see, as an example of twenty-seven software products, Daniel T. Maxwell, "Decision Analysis: Aiding Insight VI," *OR/MS Today*, June 2002, pp. 44-51.

[30] There are many prioject management techniques that could be used when the number of tasks becomes large, as in designing a new or changed product, developing a new or changed process, working out a health-care protocol for a new surgery method, or redesigning an educational curriculum. Because a project is itself a system, it can be developed with the Question Forward principles. Many of the project management tools use what they call systems views. One that was derived in 1981 from the system matrix is the "design structure matrix" (Donald V. Steward, "The Design Structure System: A Method for Managing the Design of Complex Systems," *IEEE Transactions on Engineering Management*, Vol. 28, No. 1, February 1981). For later developments, see Tyson R. Browning, "Applying the Design Structure Matrix to System Decomposition and Integration Problems: A Review and New Directions," *IEEE Transactions on Engineering Management*, Vol. 48, No. 3, August 2001.

[31] Techniques are always being proposed that presumably give you more details and insights into alternatives than those already available. See, for example, Henry Mintzberg and Ludo Van der Heyden, "Organigraphs: Drawing How Companies Really Work," *Harvard Business Review*, September 1999.

[32] See endnote in Chapter 6 about the Daniel T. Maxwell article.

[33] Niall Ferguson, *The Cash Nexus: Money and Power in the Modern World*, New York: Basic Books, 2001.

[34] Gabriel Szulanski and Sidney Winter, "Getting it Right the Second Time," *Harvard Business Review*, January 2002.

[35] Paul Strebel, "Why Do Employees Resist Change?" *Harvard Business Review*, May-June 1996. Also see Paul C. Nutt, "Surprising but True: Half the Decisions in Organizations Fail," *Academy of Management Executive*, Vol.13, No. 4, 1999.

[36] Chris Argyris, "Empowerment: The Emperor's New Clothes," *Harvard Business Review*, May-June 1998.

[37] Robert Quinn and Gretchen M. Spreitzer, "The Road to Empowerment: Seven Questions Every Leader Should Consider," *Organizational Dynamics*, Autumn 1997.

[38] Stephen Toulmin, *Return to Reason*, Cambridge MA: Harvard University Press, 2001.

[39] Arie de Geus, *The Living Company*, Cambridge MA: Harvard Business School Press, 1997.

[40] James L. Adams, *The Care and Feeding of Ideas: A Guide to Encouraging Creativity*, Reading MA: Addison-Wesley Publ. Co., 1986. The ninety-four are listed in five broad categories—strategic (e.g., critical, analytical, rational, narrow, judgmental, objective), personality related (e.g., optimistic, compulsive, warped, introverted), disciplinary (e.g., scientific, legal, sociological, historical, market-oriented), overall quality (e.g., quick, fuzzy, plodding, mercurial, muddled), and miscellaneous (e.g., visual, literal, exaggerated, aesthetic, efficient, random).

[41] Henry Mintzberg, *The Rise and Fall of Strategic Planning*, New York: The Free Press. 1994

[42] Margaret C. Brindle and Peter N. Stearns, *Facing Up to Management Faddism: A New Look at an Old Force*, Bridgeport CN: Quorum Books, 2001; also see an article one reviewer (in *Academy of Management Executive*, Vol. 15, No. 3, August 2001) labeled "Are popular management techniques a waste of time?" B. M. Staw and L. D. Epstein, "What Bandwagons Bring: Effects of Popular Management Techniques on Corporate Performance, Reputation, and CEO Pay," *Administrative Science Quarterly*, Vol. 45, 2000. Another article acknowledges that getting "all" the data about a best practice will still "never" provide a perfect replication but does not question the thinking model that led the authors to propose getting all the data; Gabriel Szulanski and Sidney Winter, "Getting it Right the Second Time," *Harvard Business Review*, January 2002.

[43] Mary Patt Kennedy, "An analysis and comparison of school improvement planning models," doctoral dissertation, University of Central Florida, 1994. (At the time of her research, the Question Forward concepts were called Breakthrough Thinking.)

[44] Margaret Norton, William Bozeman, and Gerald Nadler, *Student Planned Acquisition of Required Knowledge*, Englewood Cliffs NJ: Educational Technology Publications, 1980. The concepts now called Question Forward are called PTR in

this book, and we use the former in this description of the ideas to avoid confusing the reader. SPARK is the acronym for this application.

[45] One countywide strategic plan we know about was developed this way. Contact Prof. William Bozeman, College of Education, University of Central Florida, Orlando FL.

[46] Jim Collins, "How Great Companies Tame Technology," *Newsweek*, 29 April 2002.

[47] A more detailed description of this case is Case History B1 in Gerald Nadler, *The Planning and Design Approach*, New York: John Wiley, 1981. (PDA is the acronym used in the detailed case history)

[48] Larry Hirschhorn, "Campaigning for Change," *Harvard Business Review*, July 2002.

[49] Charles C. Mann, "Homeland Insecurity," *Atlantic Monthly*, September 2002.

[50] "Boring, passive work may hasten death: Study," a Reuters article as reported by Rob Walker in "Work Daze," *New York Times Magazine*," 23 June 2002.

[51] For a another perspective on "different" ways of thinking, see Steven B. Sample, *The Contrarian's Guide to Leadership*, San Francisco: Jossey-Bass, 2001.

[52] For an example of how Question Forward can improve the typical change or organizational development profession, see Chapter 4 and Appendix D in the report on *Recapitalizing the Navy: A Strategy for Managing the Infrastructure*, Washington DC: National Academy Press, 1998.

Printed in the United States
1498000004B/197